THE BEDFORD SERIES IN HISTORY AND CULTURE

The New York Conspiracy Trials of 1741

Daniel Horsmanden's *Journal of the Proceedings*

WITH RELATED DOCUMENTS

Related Titles in

THE BEDFORD SERIES IN HISTORY AND CULTURE

Advisory Editors: Lynn Hunt, *University of California, Los Angeles*
David W. Blight, *Yale University*
Bonnie G. Smith, *Rutgers University*
Natalie Zemon Davis, *Princeton University*
Ernest R. May, *Harvard University*

THE INTERESTING NARRATIVE OF THE LIFE OF OLAUDAH EQUIANO, WRITTEN BY HIMSELF
Edited with an Introduction by Robert J. Allison, *Suffolk University*

NOTES ON THE STATE OF VIRGINIA *by Thomas Jefferson with Related Documents*
Edited with an Introduction by David Waldstreicher, *University of Notre Dame*

Defending Slavery: Proslavery Thought in the Old South: A Brief History with Documents
Paul Finkelman, *University of Tulsa College of Law*

THE CONFESSIONS OF NAT TURNER *and Related Documents*
Edited with an Introduction by Kenneth S. Greenberg, *Suffolk University*

NARRATIVE OF THE LIFE OF FREDERICK DOUGLASS, AN AMERICAN SLAVE, WRITTEN BY HIMSELF *with Related Documents, Second Edition*
Edited with an Introduction by David W. Blight, *Yale University*

William Lloyd Garrison and the Fight against Slavery: Selections from THE LIBERATOR
Edited with an Introduction by William E. Cain, *Wellesley College*

DRED SCOTT V. SANDFORD: *A Brief History with Documents*
Paul Finkelman, *University of Tulsa College of Law*

SOUTHERN HORRORS *and Other Writings: The Anti-Lynching Campaign of Ida B. Wells, 1892–1900*
Edited with an Introduction by Jacqueline Jones Royster, *Ohio State University*

UP FROM SLAVERY *by Booker T. Washington with Related Documents*
Edited with an Introduction by W. Fitzhugh Brundage, *University of North Carolina at Chapel Hill*

PLESSY V. FERGUSON: *A Brief History with Documents*
Edited with an Introduction by Brook Thomas, *University of California, Irvine*

BROWN V. BOARD OF EDUCATION: *A Brief History with Documents*
Waldo E. Martin Jr., *University of California, Berkeley*

THE BEDFORD SERIES IN HISTORY AND CULTURE

The New York Conspiracy Trials of 1741

Daniel Horsmanden's *Journal of the Proceedings*

WITH RELATED DOCUMENTS

Edited with an Introduction by

Serena R. Zabin

Carleton College

BEDFORD/ST. MARTIN'S Boston ♦ New York

For Bedford/St. Martin's

Publisher for History: Patricia A. Rossi
Director of Development for History: Jane Knetzger
Developmental Editors: Jessica Angell, Jane Knetzger
Editorial Assistant: Carina Schoenberger
Assistant Editor, Publishing Services: Maria Burwell
Production Supervisor: Jennifer Wetzel
Marketing Manager: Jenna Bookin Barry
Project Management: Books By Design, Inc.
Text Design: Claire Seng-Niemoeller
Indexer: Books By Design, Inc.
Cover Design: Donna Lee Dennison
Cover Photo: Title Page of Journal Outlining Conspiracy, 1744 © Bettmann/CORBIS
Composition: Stratford Publishing Services
Printing and Binding: Haddon Craftsmen, an RR Donnelley & Sons Company

President: Joan E. Feinberg
Editorial Director: Denise B. Wydra
Director of Marketing: Karen Melton Soeltz
Director of Editing, Design, and Production: Marcia Cohen
Manager, Publishing Services: Emily Berleth

Library of Congress Control Number: 2003108787

Manufactured in the United States of America.

9 8 7 6
f e d

For information, write: Bedford / St. Martin's, 75 Arlington Street, Boston, MA 02116 (617-399-4000)

ISBN-10: 0-312-40216-3
ISBN-13: 978-0-312-40216-7

Foreword

The Bedford Series in History and Culture is designed so that readers can study the past as historians do.

The historian's first task is finding the evidence. Documents, letters, memoirs, interviews, pictures, movies, novels, or poems can provide facts and clues. Then the historian questions and compares the sources. There is more to do than in a courtroom, for hearsay evidence is welcome, and the historian is usually looking for answers beyond act and motive. Different views of an event may be as important as a single verdict. How a story is told may yield as much information as what it says.

Along the way the historian seeks help from other historians and perhaps from specialists in other disciplines. Finally, it is time to write, to decide on an interpretation and how to arrange the evidence for readers.

Each book in this series contains an important historical document or group of documents, each document a witness from the past and open to interpretation in different ways. The documents are combined with some element of historical narrative—an introduction or a biographical essay, for example—that provides students with an analysis of the primary source material and important background information about the world in which it was produced.

Each book in the series focuses on a specific topic within a specific historical period. Each provides a basis for lively thought and discussion about several aspects of the topic and the historian's role. Each is short enough (and inexpensive enough) to be a reasonable one-week assignment in a college course. Whether as classroom or personal reading, each book in the series provides firsthand experience of the challenge—and fun—of discovering, recreating, and interpreting the past.

Lynn Hunt
David W. Blight
Bonnie G. Smith
Natalie Zemon Davis
Ernest R. May

Preface

In 1741, the New York Supreme Court held a series of trials to investigate rumors of a conspiracy to burn down the city of New York, murder most of its white inhabitants, and turn the city over to Britain's Catholic foes. The trials implicated a wide range of New Yorkers, black and white, male and female, slave and free. When the trials finally drew to a close after six months, the court had overseen the execution of thirty slaves and four whites by burning and hanging, and the expulsion from New York of more than seventy other people. In all, nearly two hundred people were arrested and interrogated.

This volume features the most important source for the trials of 1741, written by one of the participants. Three years after the trials, one of the Supreme Court justices, Justice Daniel Horsmanden, gathered the court documents that remained and published them, together with an introduction and other editorial comments. Horsmanden's *Journal of the Proceedings in the Detection of the Conspiracy* remains the most extensive contemporary account of the trials and their deadly aftermath.

Horsmanden collected, shaped, and published his account for one reason: to prove that there had indeed been a conspiracy and that the courts had rescued the city from a threat that even after three years had not fully subsided. His *Journal* is strongly opinionated and laden with detail. Carefully used, however, it reveals far more than the judge's own prejudices. Indeed, the evidence for the trials opens a window onto a number of worlds: a community, a city, a port, an empire. The document exposes, on both individual and societal levels, the relationships between blacks and whites, elites and laborers, women and men, the local and the global. Along with related documents in this volume, the *Journal* reveals the richly multicultural society of colonial New York, as well as its intimate connections with a larger Atlantic world, and raises vital questions about liberty and empire in the years leading up to the American Revolution. Moreover, like so many courtroom dramas, the trials tell an incredible story, suspenseful, complex, and full of vivid characters. These trials force us to pay attention to the ways in which justice and judicial systems are culturally and historically specific; they change over time.

This collection of documents, along with the introduction, puts the trials of 1741 into the contexts of slave conspiracies, early American port cities, and the world of the eighteenth-century Atlantic. It allows students to read the central text, Horsmanden's *Journal,* as both a valuable document for social history and a cultural artifact produced by a specific historical time and place. Historians have recently begun to pay renewed attention to slavery and slave uprisings in early America; this volume also makes it possible for students to add their own interpretations to historians' debates.

The introduction to the volume sets the trials in the historical framework in which the participants lived, the trials occurred, and the *Journal* was written. The essay presents the social, racial, legal, political, and military aspects of 1741. It also situates these trials in the current lively historiographical debates over slave conspiracies and slave conspiracy trials in general. Most important, the introduction guides the reader into the complicated and dangerous world of New York in the spring and summer of 1741.

In its original form, Daniel Horsmanden's *Journal* is unwieldy and repetitive. This edition makes his text more accessible to students by abridgment and division into chronological, thematic chapters. It also provides headnotes to the chapters and the related documents, and glosses for unfamiliar eighteenth-century words. The Note about the Text (p. 37) further describes the abridgment process.

The six additional documents in this collection provide a wider perspective on the trials of 1741. The first is a New York newspaper report, which describes a suspected uprising on the West Indian island of Antigua in 1736. The account shows a striking number of similarities with the slightly later New York trials. Two other documents are particularly useful in evaluating the *Journal* as a historical record. They present alternative reports of slave confessions, sent in the summer of 1741 by the lieutenant-governor of New York to his London supervisors at the Board of Trade. Since one confession matches Horsmanden's version almost exactly while the other is notably different, together they allow the reader to judge the extent to which Horsmanden deliberately altered testimony. The other three documents included, all letters written while the trials were still in progress, reveal individuals' attempts to make sense of the proceedings. The governor of New York wrote the first to his supervisors at the Board of Trade to explain the machinations of the conspirators. The second, from an anonymous New Englander, castigates the New York court for its willingness to believe that there was any conspiracy at all. The final letter is from Horsmanden himself, in which he explains to a friend the fascination that the investigation holds for him.

The volume concludes with several additional tools. The chronology of the conspiracy trials of 1741 and related events allows students to follow the rapid pace of the trials while keeping in mind other relevant social, military, and political trends, both in New York and around the British Empire. The questions for consideration help readers to pull together the most important themes of these documents; they work well as either discussion or writing assignments. Finally, the selected bibliography provides a guide for those who want to follow up questions about early New York, colonial slavery and slave revolts, and the eighteenth-century British Empire.

ACKNOWLEDGMENTS

I may safely say that without John Murrin this project would never have come to be. He first proposed the idea to me, and he set the process in motion. At least equal thanks go to Jan Lewis, who for six years has inspired and encouraged my explorations of Horsmanden's *Journal* and the New York of 1741. Many people read early and late drafts of this manuscript and offered substantive and thoughtful feedback. I would especially like to thank Thomas J. Davis, Arizona State University; Michael P. Johnson, Johns Hopkins University; Susan E. Klepp, Temple University; Philip Morgan, Johns Hopkins University; Billy G. Smith, Montana State University, Bozeman; and two other readers for their careful criticisms. The result is a greatly improved volume. The early American workshop at the University of Minnesota and my colleagues Parna Sengupta and Javier Morillo-Alicea contributed fresh perspectives on the introduction. Nikki Lamberty was tireless in tracking down permissions and illustrations, and at the last minute she found me some much-needed research assistance. Kate Haulman gave generously and frequently of her time and thought.

Students at Carleton College generously allowed me to test different versions of this edition with them. I would like in particular to thank the students in my 2000 and 2002 first-year seminars on trials in early America; their questions and discussions had a greater and better impact on the final version than they may realize. Amanda Hane's close reading of the full manuscript from a student's perspective was indispensable. At Bedford/St. Martin's, Elizabeth Wallace, Jessica Angell, Patricia Rossi, Joan Feinberg, and David Blight were invaluable in bringing this book from idea to reality. Jane Knetzger not only guided it through the development process, but she also gave the text one of the most meticulous and engaged readings I could ever hope to receive.

Finally, my deepest thanks to Christopher Brunelle, whose support, intelligence, and perfect pitch for all things verbal make so many parts of my life possible and joyous.

Serena R. Zabin

Contents

PART TWO
The Document 41

PART THREE
Related Documents 161

APPENDIXES

Illustrations

PART ONE

Introduction: Fear, Race, and Society in British New York

On a cold night in February 1741, three slaves robbed Rebecca Hogg's small shop near the East River docks in New York City. A white sailor from a warship docked in the harbor had told the slaves that the shop was well stocked, and it was. The men stole money, cloth, and such luxury goods as snuffboxes and jewelry, and even managed to grab the silver knee buckles belonging to Hogg's husband. Two of the slaves, Prince and Cuffee, took their booty home, but the third, a man known to his owner as Caesar but who also used the name John Gwin, brought his loot to a dockside tavern. The tavernkeepers, John and Sarah Hughson, had a reputation for flouting the law by receiving stolen goods and by selling alcohol to slaves, and they were willing to help Gwin dispose of the goods. Neither the Hughsons nor anyone else could have imagined how quickly this ordinary theft would lead to the most extensive slave conspiracy trials in the history of New York.

With the sailor's help, city constables tracked the goods as far as the Hughsons' tavern the next day and arrested Gwin. The following day, authorities picked up Prince. Both men denied any involvement. Although the constables strongly suspected that the Hughsons were accessories to the robbery, and despite several searches of the tavern and a rigorous interrogation of John Hughson, they found no evidence. A break in the case came a few days later when the Hughsons' indentured servant, Mary Burton, hinted to the wife of one of the constables that she knew something about the Hughsons' lawbreaking behavior. At the same time, the constables arrested a lodger in the tavern, a young Irish woman named Peggy Kerry, who was rumored to be Gwin's kept mistress and the mother of his child.

A little more than two weeks after the theft, Fort George, the garrison at the southern tip of Manhattan that contained the governor's mansion, caught fire. The house, the chapel, the barracks, and the governor's offices within the garrison's walls were all destroyed. A spark from a plumber soldering a pipe on the roof was first blamed for the fire. Then a rash of other fires throughout the city followed. Fires were common in eighteenth-century cities, and at first there seemed to be little cause for alarm. Then the pace of the fires accelerated, with four fires on April 6 alone. The rumor, moreover, that a slave had been seen sprinting away from a burning building made some wonder if these fires were due to arson rather than accident. The colony's highest court, the New York Supreme Court, wasted no time in launching an investigation. Although a thorough investigation of New York's households revealed nothing, a hint from an informant led the third Supreme Court justice, Daniel Horsmanden, who was to hear the trials of the Hogg robbery, to surmise that there was a connection between the fires and the theft. He and other white New Yorkers suspected a citywide conspiracy. The destruction of the city's fort immediately conjured possibilities of a foreign attack. In 1741, Britain was at war with Spain, and New York had just sent five hundred volunteers to help Britain recover Puerto Bello in Cuba from the Spanish. If this was a conspiracy, was it a domestic rebellion or an enemy invasion?

The trials for the Hogg robbery opened in this atmosphere of anxiety and suspicion. When Mary Burton implied that she knew that her master's illegal activities were more far reaching than just the theft, the court was eager to learn more. Her testimony, as well as that from some of the defendants, helped to create the notion of an elaborate biracial plot to burn the city of New York and hand it over to Britain's Catholic foes. As the trials continued, Mary Burton became the prosecution's chief witness. Without her evidence there would have been no trials, and as she repeatedly embellished her story the investigation deepened. As the trials escalated, white soldiers as well as black slaves confessed their involvement in the plot. Eventually, Burton declared that the ringleader was an itinerant Latin teacher named John Ury, whom the courts accused of being a papist priest and a Spanish spy.

A seedy tavern burglary and an international papist plot to all intents and purposes seem entirely unrelated, yet it took the courts only a few months to move from investigating common theft and arson to investigating an enormous conspiracy. At the time, not everyone was convinced that there was a real conspiracy, and this debate has continued to the present day. This Introduction, however, seeks to answer another and equally intriguing question: How did a relatively ordinary theft escalate into such an extraordinary trial? To find the answer, we need to investigate the atmosphere of instability, fear, and suspicion of 1740s New York City in which the thefts occurred. The city of New York and the British Empire of which it was a part were both in flux. Although both sought order, neither could ultimately control the continual flow of people, goods, and ideas that characterized them. Slavery in New York was a similarly contradictory combination of rigid prescriptions and more flexible practices. Both white and black New Yorkers were familiar with successful, thwarted, and suspected slave revolts around the British Empire; nearly constant reports of large and small acts of resistance from around the Atlantic rim gave all New Yorkers a context and a language with which to understand an unstable world that included human bondage. Finally, the seamy interracial tavern in which the investigation began and the racially divided courtroom in which it ended provided specific contexts that were necessary for the investigation and trials to take the forms that they did. These pieces all came together in an explosive mix that created the conspiracy trials of 1741.

The most extensive source for studying these trials is Supreme Court Justice Daniel Horsmanden's own account of the case. Even as the trials were winding down, the judge collected his own notes and those of the other two judges of the court, the attorney general, and the lawyers who had helped in the prosecution. In 1744, three years after the initial fires, Horsmanden edited, collated, and published these notes as *A Journal of the Proceedings in The Detection of the Conspiracy Formed by Some* White *People, in Conjunction with* Negro *and other* Slaves, *for Burning the City of New-York in America, and Murdering the Inhabitants* (see Figure 1). The judge had a very particular reason for publishing his account. Many colonists, possibly distressed at the loss of their human property or at the extent and length of the trials, later

A
JOURNAL
OF THE
PROCEEDINGS
IN
The Detection of the Conſpiracy
FORMED BY
Some *White* People, in Conjunction with *Negro* and other *Slaves*,
FOR
Burning the City of *NEW-YORK* in AMERICA,
And Murdering the Inhabitants.

Which Conſpiracy was partly put in Execution, by Burning His Majeſty's Houſe in Fort GEORGE, within the ſaid City, on Wedneſday the Eighteenth of *March*, 1741. and ſetting Fire to ſeveral Dwelling and other Houſes there, within a few Days ſucceeding. And by another Attempt made in Proſecution of the ſame infernal Scheme, by putting Fire between two other Dwelling-Houſes within the ſaid City, on the Fifteenth Day of *February*, 1742; which was accidentally and timely diſcovered and extinguiſhed.

CONTAINING,

I. A NARRATIVE of the Trials, Condemnations, Executions, and Behaviour of the ſeveral Criminals, at the Gallows and Stake, with their *Speeches* and *Confeſſions*; with Notes, Obſervations and Reflections occaſionally interſperſed throughout the Whole.

II. AN APPENDIX, wherein is ſet forth ſome additional Evidence concerning the ſaid Conſpiracy and Conſpirators, which has come to Light ſince their Trials and Executions.

III. LISTS of the ſeveral Perſons (Whites and Blacks) committed on Account of the Conſpiracy; and of the ſeveral Criminals executed; and of thoſe tranſported, with the Places whereto.

By the Recorder of the City of NEW-YORK.

Quid facient Domini, audent cum talia Fures? Virg. Ecl.

NEW-YORK:
Printed by *James Parker*, at the New Printing-Office, 1744.

Figure 1. *Journal of the Proceedings,* 1744, Title Page of Original Edition. The very complete title of the eighteenth-century edition emphasizes the solution of the mystery of the city's fires.

Collection of The New-York Historical Society.

wondered if there really had been any threat from slaves. Horsmanden, however, was positive that there had been a slave conspiracy and that New Yorkers were willfully closing their eyes to the evidence of their narrow escape from danger. He published his *Journal,* he said, so that people would stop trying to convince themselves that there had been no conspiracy at all.

Because of its avowedly partisan intent, Horsmanden's *Journal* has been nearly as controversial as the events it describes. The *Journal* is undoubtedly intended as the prosecution's argument, not an unbiased and objective recounting of evidence. Until lately, many historians believed that Horsmanden's text was too unreliable to use as a source document. More recently, however, historians have begun to explore ways to read the *Journal* with an eye to two important questions. One deals with the conspiracy itself. Was there a conspiracy at all, or did Horsmanden invent it in order to justify the court's actions? If there had been a conspiracy, moreover, what was its goal and who were the participants? The other deals with the *Journal* as text. With its extensive depositions, interrogations, and editorial interventions, what can this *Journal* tell us about life, culture, and race in eighteenth-century New York City?

Therefore, as with any piece of historical evidence, one must read the *Journal* on two levels: first for what it reveals about the course of the trials, and second for how and why both Horsmanden and the culture in which he lived produced this particular account of the trials of 1741. Horsmanden's *Journal* is not a transparent window onto the 1741 trials. It is, however, a rich and complex source for exploring the thoroughly multicultural society of colonial New York, its intimate connections with a larger Atlantic world, and the vital and complex questions of liberty and slavery in the years before the American Revolution, all within the fascinating and disturbing story of the trials of 1741.

NEW YORK CITY ON THE EVE OF THE TRIALS

Events and activities like the robbery at the Hoggs', fencing the stolen goods at the Hughsons', and using a tavern generally as a place for blacks and whites to socialize together were particularly urban phenomena.[1] They could happen only in communities whose fluid populations were large enough so that not everyone knew everyone else by

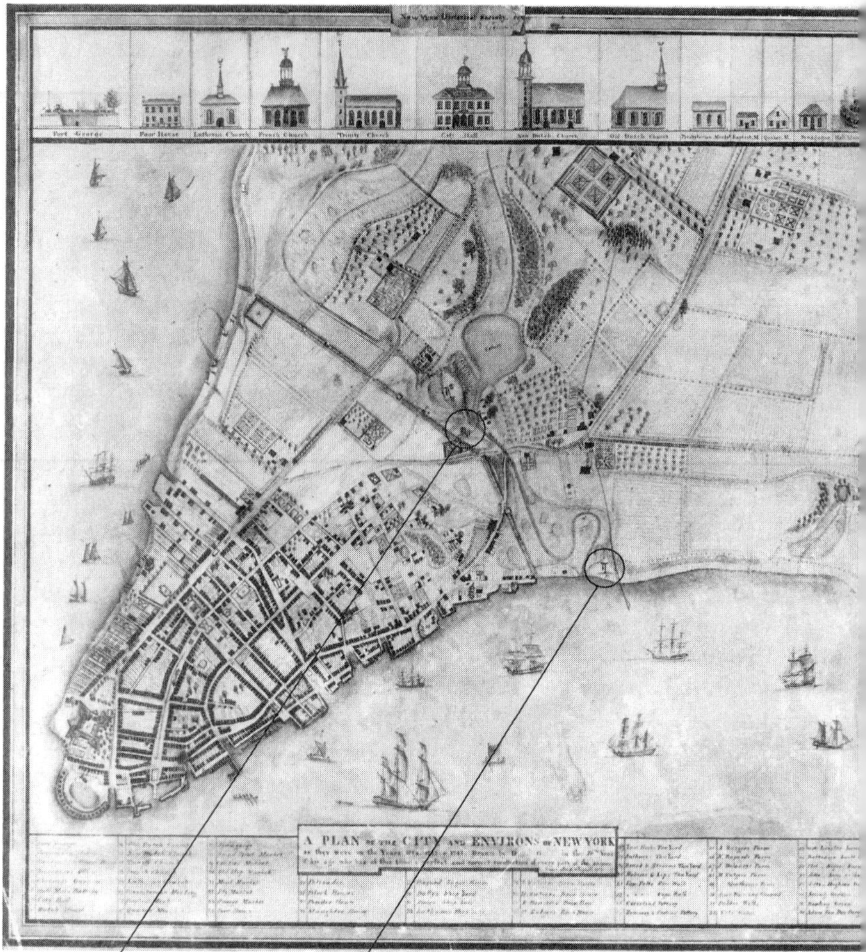

Figure 2. *A Plan of the City and Environs of New York as They Were in the Years 1742, 1743, and 1744,* by David Grim, 1813. This map, drawn from memory when Grim was seventy-six years old, is our only piece of visual evidence for the executions that resulted from the 1741 trials. Note the gallows and the bodies burning at the stake.

Collection of The New-York Historical Society.

sight, and whose goods were plentiful enough that they could pass through a secondhand economy without being immediately recognizable to their previous owners.

In 1741, New York was one of the four largest port cities in British North America. Like those of its rivals, Boston, Philadelphia, and Charleston, New York's economy and culture rested heavily on its Atlantic trade with the West Indies and Europe. The Dutch had first founded New York in 1624 as a trading post named New Amsterdam, and under Dutch rule the settlement had huddled close to the two waterways that made trade possible, the East River and the Hudson (or North) River. The first slaves were brought to Manhattan only two years later, in 1626. After the English conquered the city in 1664, settlement expanded slowly northward, but the east side of the city, alongside the wharves and shipyards, remained far more populated and developed.[2] (See Figure 2.)

The city's layout lent weight to the court's fears that the conspiracy to destroy it had begun in a dockside tavern. These docks were the commercial and economic center of the city, and they kept shipbuilders, coopers, longshoremen, and other dockworkers busy. Merchants built their storehouses close to the docks. On the southern tip of the island of Manhattan stood Fort George, containing the garrison, the city's battery of cannon, the governor's house, and the city archives (see Figure 3). The fort represented both the city's military strength and its connection to Great Britain, and to torch it would have been a symbolic as well as destructive act of defiance against British officials.

When the city began to expand, the elites moved their homes (and those of their slaves) farther away from the water. As a result, the wharves became increasingly inhabited by soldiers from the fort and sailors from the ships that filled the harbor. Hughson's tavern, located conveniently close to the Hudson River on Stone Street, catered to these transient residents as well as to slaves.[3] Although slaves and working whites maintained separate living quarters, they often mingled in taverns.

The threat of an uprising was particularly unnerving to elite New Yorkers because although the edges of the city along the wharves tended to be inhabited by poor whites, slaveowning elites had not created homogeneous wealthy neighborhoods in the center of the island. Rather, slaves lived with their owners scattered throughout the city, so neither British troops nor local authorities could cordon off an uprising within any one specific area of Manhattan. If all the slaves accused

A View of FORT GEORGE with the CITY of NEW YORK from the SW.

in the conspiracy were to set their owners' houses on fire, the entire city would be in danger.

Fires were not an idle fear on the part of New Yorkers. In a city filled with closely built wooden houses, fires could easily demolish entire neighborhoods. The city had two inefficient hand-pumped fire engines, but it was the human bucket brigade who did most of the work. And although fires were a constant concern in early modern cities, the sheer number of fires in the spring of 1741—ten in the space of one month—was highly unusual.

The fear of fires and a deeper-seated, more pervasive unease were both exacerbated in March 1741 by the extraordinarily hard winter that still had not yet ended. That December, one newspaper editor commented "the Cold is so excessive, that while I am Writing in a Warm Room by a good Fire Side the Ink Freezes in the Pen." At the end of the century, William Smith recorded in his *History of New York,* "The winter which ushered in this year (ever since called the hard winter,) was distinguished by the sharpest frost, and the greatest quantity of snow, within the memory of the oldest inhabitant. The weather was intensely severe from the middle of November to the latter end of March."[4] On the one hand, as chimneys filled with soot from unusually heavy use, the likelihood of fires increased. But it was food and fuel shortages that made this a particularly difficult winter for the poor, as newspapers reported and officials realized.[5] Even after the snow melted, the hard times continued. The city, which regulated the price of bread, had held the prices down so low that the bakers went on strike. Indigent New Yorkers rioted in the streets.[6]

In the midst of all this deprivation, Burton and other witnesses described great feasts in the Hughsons' tavern that winter. Whether or not these feasts actually occurred, such testimony reflects New Yorkers' concerns about food during a harsh winter. One enslaved man, Jack, told the judges that on a Sunday afternoon early in January, he sat down at a table loaded with "a goose, a quarter of mutton, a fowl, and two loaves of bread."[7] The amount of meat in particular made this

Figure 3. *View of Fort George with the City of New York from the Southwest* (the Carwitham View of New York), 1731–1736, engraved by John Carwitham. Notice the prominence of the British flags and fort.

Courtesy of the Library of Congress, Prints and Photographs Division, LC-USZ62-19360.

a notable meal. Apart from the trials, however, no independent evidence indicates whether the Hughsons proffered such bounty. Did John Hughson have a secret supply of provisions to feed his followers? Or were the tales of the feasts created in the imagination of those who did not have enough to eat?[8]

COLONIAL NEW YORK SOCIETY

Testimony from defendants, both black and white, shows how bitterly they resented their place at the bottom of the social hierarchy. One slave was reported to have declared that "a great many people had too much [money] and others had too little," while another witness recounted a white tavern keeper advising slaves to "burn the houses of them that have the most money." Yet according to these witnesses, the aim of the conspiracy was not so much to eradicate status altogether as to *reverse* the status of the city's highest and lowest. In the aftermath of the uprising, John Hughson was to become king, John Gwin (Caesar) would be the governor, and the white spouses of the city's elite gentlemen would become the conspirators' wives.[9]

This testimony demonstrates that all New Yorkers understood the hierarchies of status, race, and gender, even as they imagined inverting some of them. In this world turned upside down, an indigent tavern keeper could become a king and a slave a governor, but a white man would still have a more powerful position than a black one. Likewise, even as black men imagined taking the power of life and death over white men, they envisioned white women as passive bodies to be handed over from one man to another, bestowing their own elite gentlewoman status on their new husbands.

Economic status was therefore only one of the social measures by which New Yorkers distinguished themselves from one another. Ethnicity, race, family, age, and gender combined with wealth to create social divisions known in the eighteenth century as "rank." In the settled, small villages of Old and New England where neighbors knew one another, rank was relatively easy to determine. In larger seaport cities, however, ascertaining status was far more difficult. With a population of roughly 11,000 people, many of whom were itinerant sailors, soldiers, and recent immigrants, New York was an excellent place for confidence tricksters, failed merchants, and runaway servants to try to create a new identity. In this fluid context, rank was often less self-evident than elites in particular might have hoped. The possibility for social confusion in New York at times drove authorities to try all the harder to strengthen the boundaries of traditional ranks and privileges.[10]

When judges, witnesses, jurors, and defendants faced each other in the city's courtroom, a carefully calibrated system of social rank conditioned the authority and credibility of speeches and interactions. Unlike waterfront taverns like the Hughsons', one of the few public places in which blacks and whites could mingle socially, the courtroom was a place where social distinctions were reinforced. The participants of the 1741 trials represented a wide range of ranks; they spanned every gradation of status from free to enslaved, although almost everyone fell somewhere between the two extremes. Gender, race, and economic status were important elements of rank, but no one element worked independently of the others. As witnesses gave testimony in the trials about the radical reordering of society that the conspiracy sought, judges and lawyers used their speeches in the trials to harshly condemn any infraction of status boundaries. White defendants came under particular reproach for racial mixing.

Through its verdicts, the court hoped to fashion a society with clear social distinctions between slaves, elite whites, indentured servants, free blacks, and free whites, as well as between men and women in all of these categories. These distinctions were set and enforced by legal and social limitations. For example, slaves could not by law own property. Married white women similarly could not legally own property, since nearly all their legal rights were "covered" by their husbands in a legal fiction known as *coverture*. Indentured servants like Mary Burton, whose labor was "bound" to a master for a set period of time, were completely dependent on their masters for food, shelter, and clothing. Poorer whites, most often those who could not afford to pay court fines, were just as likely as convicted slaves to be whipped by the public hangman at the whipping post. In fact, only a limited number of elite white men were truly "free." Almost all white women, young people, and poor laborers were dependent on, respectively, their husbands, their parents, and their masters. For some, like indentured servants, this status was temporary, but for others it was permanent.

Yet the fixed rules of hierarchy rarely existed in practice, particularly in eighteenth-century New York City. Slaves had marriages that were openly acknowledged, if not legally supported, by their owners. In one of the most unusual reversals revealed in the 1741 trials, the slave John Gwin paid for the room and board of a free, unmarried white woman, Peggy Kerry. Likewise, the store that was robbed belonged to a married woman, Rebecca Hogg, who by law could not openly own property.[11]

Two of the most important figures in the trials are Supreme Court Justice Daniel Horsmanden (see Figure 4) and the prosecution's star witness, the indentured servant Mary Burton. A closer look at them reveals some of the ways that the lives of both elite and laborers do not always perfectly conform to legal boundaries. Horsmanden and Burton, a middle-aged male elite and teenaged female servant, come from opposite ends of the white social scale, but their lives share surprising similarities that show how the fluidity of New York's social structure undercut categorical hierarchies.

Third Justice Daniel Horsmanden came from the top echelons of the city's social structure, as did his two colleagues on the Supreme Court bench, Chief Justice James DeLancey and Second Justice Frederick Philipse. Throughout colonial North America, white men of elite status tended to have the greatest physical and personal autonomy. From this rank came the city's lawyers and grand jury members. Political theories of the time held that only wealthy men, who were free of the demands of owners, employers, and family members, had the independent judgment and self-discipline needed to be a public official. Such men often came from the wealthiest stratum, but even at the very top, rank was precarious and jealously guarded. The three judges of the Supreme Court, for example, had their assigned places as Chief (or First), Second, and Third Justice. Moreover, few people were completely independent; even wealthy Chief Justice DeLancey's family depended on patronage from their supporters in England.[12]

Horsmanden's place on the bench gave him extensive powers of life and death over the defendants who came before him, yet his own elite status was also relatively insecure. Horsmanden had arrived in New York only ten years earlier to seek his new fortune after he lost his inheritance—and had to flee his English creditors—in the wake of Britain's first major stock market failure in 1720.[13] He was thirty-six years old on his arrival, and he had little private means that would support him in the manner of a gentleman. Although he was related to the Byrds, one of the richest families in Virginia, he had no access to their wealth. He had been trained as a lawyer in England, but the fees he could charge for practicing law would never be large enough to help him accumulate an independent fortune. For that sort of money he needed a political appointment that would give him both prestige and access to lucrative land grants. Horsmanden did have elite con-

Figure 4. *Portrait of Justice Daniel Horsmanden,* 1770s, Painted by Matthew Pratt. Horsmanden, the author of the *Journal,* was chief justice of the New York Supreme Court from 1763 until his death in 1778.

Special Collections Department, Harvard Law School Library.

nections in England, and he used them to get a recommendation for a place on the governor's advisory council in New York. After obtaining his place in this select circle of political appointees, he immediately began to look for ways to build his fortune.

Eighteenth-century New York was famous for its political infighting, and Horsmanden did not escape criticism. Within six months of his appointment, others on the council attacked him for being a man "who has no visible estate in this Government and [is] in necessitous circumstances."[14] His opponents had evidence from his creditors to prove his poverty, and the lack of a "visible Estate" advertised Horsmanden's dependence on others for his money and status. Horsmanden therefore was forced to spend a considerable amount of time currying favor with New York's governor, and at last his efforts began to pay off. He was granted some land for development and resale, a permanent position as the Secretary (or "Recorder") of the Council, and, in 1737, a judgeship on the Supreme Court. His political appointments provided him with increased prestige, but they did not pay well enough for him to have an independent fortune. Although many New York lawyers and politicians turned to trade for their income, Horsmanden pinned his hopes on land speculation. As he wrote to another friend on the governor's council, "Lands are at Present the best View I have of making money."[15] He never managed to get as much land as he wanted, however, and never shed his reputation as a gentleman who was just scraping by.

In April 1741, when the trials for the conspiracy began, Horsmanden was the third and most junior member of the Supreme Court. For the next few months, he dedicated his energies to the conspiracy trials. In November 1741, nearly three months after the last of the convicted conspirators had been executed, he agreed to arrange, index, and annotate an edition of the colony's laws. In return, the assembly offered to pay him £250.[16] Although Horsmanden was desperately in need of the money, he was far more concerned about the conspiracy. He spent the money, but Horsmanden never quite got around to preparing New York's laws for publication; bringing the *Journal* into print took all his time.[17]

At the time, Horsmanden complained to his friend Cadwallader Colden that his political enemies "took indefatigable pains in Traducing and Villifying my Character in marking me out as a Person unsafe to Converse with, as if I were a Spy & Betrayer of Confidence. . . ."[18] When his friendship with Governor Clinton fell apart in 1747, one of the reasons the governor gave the Board of Trade for ejecting Horsmanden from the Council was that he was too dependent on the government for his income.[19] Economic instability and personal mobility could be almost as dangerous for a Supreme Court justice as they could be for the man who was eventually convicted of masterminding the conspiracy. A year after he lost his place on the Council, Horsmanden married Mary Reade Vesey, a wealthy widow much older than he. Even his contemporaries drew the obvious inference that he had married for money.[20] Whatever the circumstances of his marriage, it is clear that once he had joined a family in New York and at last had a "visible estate," his financial and political problems were over.

The contrast between Mary Burton's legal status and her standing in the 1741 trials is even more marked than Horsmanden's. It was primarily on the basis of her testimony that the court executed over thirty people. And yet Burton was not a person of standing in New York City. She was a sixteen-year-old indentured servant: young, dependent, poor, female, and apparently without living family. Given the traditional hierarchies of the eighteenth century, any of these characteristics might have prevented judges from taking her testimony seriously. Why was she believed?

The fact that so many people did listen to Burton reminds us that class and gender were not inevitable and unchanging markers of power. Some people did, at times, mistrust Burton's testimony because she was a servant. When Chief Justice James DeLancey first heard Burton's testimony at the beginning of July, he was clearly suspicious and lectured her on the dangers of perjury. Most of the time, however, her status as Hughson's servant gave her credibility as an eyewitness. No one could have been better placed to know what happened in a dockside tavern. Although many people suggested that Burton was making up false testimony, no one claimed that she was unbelievable because she was a woman. No one ever suggested that her physiology affected her rationality. Although the court marked her status in their condescending characterizations of her, they did not dismiss her testimony on those grounds.

Of course, Burton told some people exactly what they wanted to hear. Her expansion of the circle of people involved in the conspiracy helped to justify the pace of executions. Her demeanor, particularly her initial hesitation to name names, helped convince authorities that she was trustworthy. As Horsmanden later explained in a letter to a friend (see *Letter to Cadwallader Colden,* Document 4), the court reasoned that if she was afraid, there was some reason for it beyond a servant's fear of her master.

In fact, far from finding that the legal climate restricted her, Mary Burton managed to turn it to her advantage. By the end of the trials, her master and mistress were dead, and she had acquired a tidy sum of money. The lieutenant governor had earlier promised a reward of £100 to any white person who implicated a member of the conspiracy, and Mary Burton successfully claimed the reward. The city bought out the rest of her indenture and then paid her the remainder of the money, £81. This sum, worth over $25,000 in twenty-first-century U.S. dollars, would have allowed her to begin a life of far greater independence and comfort than most indentured servants could ever have imagined.

SLAVERY IN COLONIAL NEW YORK

Difficult as it is to recreate the life and world of a wealthy Supreme Court judge or even a white indentured servant, it is even more difficult to do so for an enslaved African or African American in New York. Pre-Revolutionary New York slaves left few financial records and no written reflections of their lives. The official regulations of slavery found in the colony's slave code must be balanced with the hints of lived experience that emerge from demographic data, chance mentions in the letters and travel accounts of whites, and, most especially, court records such as the 1741 trials.[21]

The testimony given by witnesses throughout the trials clearly shows the closely intertwined lives of whites and blacks. Nonetheless, the courts and newspapers consistently feared that the underlying aim of the conspiracy was to reject the racial hierarchy of white over black and overthrow slavery. Colonial officials had long worried that New York's slaves were not fully under white control. Throughout the eighteenth century, the black population in New York hovered around 15 percent of the total, making New York the largest black community north of the Chesapeake.[22] There were few free blacks. Urban slavery tended to distribute blacks widely across the city; both women and men performed a large variety of jobs, including domestic, skilled, and marine work. As opposed to the agricultural communities of the South, no one segment of the economy relied entirely on slave labor. Thus, despite the high numbers of slaves in New York, the city remained, in historian Philip Morgan's useful formulation, a "society with slaves" rather than a slave society.[23]

The slave population in New York was a diverse mixture of native-born New Yorkers and more recent arrivals. Most newly imported slaves came from the West Indies, but nearly 40 percent came directly from the west coast of Africa.[24] Large numbers of these had names that reflected their Akan-Asante culture's practice of commemorating the day on which they were born: Quashee or Quash for Sunday,

Quaco or Quack for Wednesday, Cuffee or Cuff for Friday, for example. The names of those arrested in the trials show a thorough mix of these West African names, ordinary English names (e.g., Tom), and classical names often given as jokes by masters (Pompey). Slaves like John Gwin, whose owner named him Caesar, often renamed themselves.

Slaves worked in elite homes and dingy stores, on the waterfront and in artisan shops, laboring for and with their masters. Because city slaves rarely worked on plantations and never in gangs, all of their work environments were biracial. These mixed-race workplaces were not necessarily amicable—some artisans complained that the use of slaves undercut paid white labor—but they continually brought blacks and whites together in work as well as leisure.

In comparison to slaves elsewhere, black women and men in New York City had at least a limited freedom to move throughout the city as they worked. The kind of work that slaves did there contributed to their ease of movement. Unlike slaves in southern plantation economies, most urban slaves performed either domestic or artisanal chores, as well as unskilled heavy labor. A considerable number of men and boys sailed on merchant ships. New York suffered from periodic labor shortages, so hiring out slaves was common practice. Slaves were occasionally able to hire themselves out, choosing their new master and pocketing some of the wages. Although slave labor was essential to the economic life of the city, day-to-day control of slaves was rarely as complete as it was on plantations.[25]

New York officials worried constantly about their lack of control over the city's slaves. To allay their anxieties, they passed increasingly draconian laws, although they rarely enforced them. When the English first took New Netherland from the Dutch in 1664, they passed few slave regulations, although they did affirm the legality of inheritable lifelong slavery.[26] In 1702, the New York General Assembly passed its first "Act for Regulating Slaves," which they significantly expanded after a 1712 slave revolt raised fears of slave uprisings. In 1730, the assembly, claiming that "many Mischiefs have been Occasioned by the too great Liberty allowed to Negro and other Slaves," passed a still more extensive slave code that served as the foundation for slave regulation for the rest of the century. Slaves were forbidden to gather in groups of more than three, to drink in taverns without the permission of their owners, or to travel at night without a lantern. Nighttime burials, a West African tradition, were forbidden. The underlying rationale behind these laws was an attempt to separate slaves from each other. Based on the premise that slaves met primarily to plan revolts, these laws tried to ensure that slaves would always be under the supervision of whites.[27]

Like the laws that governed white social status, however, these laws were difficult or impossible to enforce. Slaves met frequently at the African Burial Ground, at pumps and wells where they drew drinking water for tea, and, of course, at taverns. Owners did not supervise their slaves day and night, and struggling tavern keepers would rather take their chances in breaking the law than lose business. As the evidence from the 1741 trials makes clear, card playing, cockfighting, and other sorts of entertainments were available at taverns. Officers searching for Gwin in the Hughsons' tavern walked right by him; they clearly saw nothing odd in a black man sitting in a tavern on a Sunday morning. In 1724, the high sheriff complained in writing that no one was enforcing the law "for regulating Negro and Indian Slaves in the Night time."[28]

Although social events like slave funerals were usually attended only by blacks, interracial socializing was at least as common as single-race gatherings among slaves and working whites. Peggy and Gwin's affair was only the best documented of these relationships. At taverns and in markets, white servants, apprentices, and laborers danced and drank with blacks.

It would be a mistake, however, to imagine that slavery in New York was not oppressive. For example, family life was nearly impossible. Although slaves could marry in some churches, the law did not recognize such unions, nor did it prevent masters from selling children apart from their parents. Even slave spouses who lived in the same city were constrained by their condition. One defendant in these trials, Quack, had a wife who was the governor's cook; he was frequently turned away from visiting her by the governor's military guard.

Violence was also an intrinsic part of slavery in colonial New York, as the outcome of the trials of 1741 shows. As was true for whites also, insolence or theft could be punished with public whippings, in which the offender was tied to a cart and dragged around the city; the cart stopped at busy intersections so that the lashes would be administered as publicly as possible. Slaves could also suffer extensive private beatings without recourse. When one white New Yorker's slave died in 1735 after a beating, a coroner's jury declared that the cause of death was "the Visitation of God."[29]

Finally, the possibility of freedom for most slaves in New York was slim. New York slave codes made it increasingly difficult for owners to manumit their slaves by including provisions that insisted that the owner ensure the freed man or woman would not become a drain on public assistance. Most owners preferred to pass their slaves on to their heirs when they died rather than to free them. The few free blacks in the area tended to live on the outskirts of the city. Although daily life was less restricted for slaves in New York than for rural or plantation slaves, their hopes of freedom were not notably greater.[30]

FEAR OF SLAVE REVOLTS

For nearly thirty years preceding the 1741 trials, many white New Yorkers had lived in a slave society permeated by fears of slave revolts. In 1712, roughly two dozen slaves, most of them Africans who had recently arrived in New York, set fire to a building and ambushed the whites who came to put it out. They killed at least nine whites before the governor managed to call out the soldiers stationed in the garrison. The rebels escaped to the woods that night, but soldiers and militia hunted down most of them soon thereafter. Six killed themselves before they could be captured. The courts interrogated seventy slaves within the next two weeks and eventually found twenty-five guilty of murder or attempted murder. Those who confessed or implicated others were freed, but slaves who refused were punished brutally. Twenty were simply hanged, but the last five were executed in ways that would serve as a model for judicial sentences thirty years later. Three were burned at the stake, one of them "with a slow fire that he may continue in torment for eight or ten hours." Another was hanged in chains and starved to death, a torture known as gibbeting, and a third was tied, spread-eagled, to a wheel while he was slowly beaten to death, a punishment known as "breaking on the wheel." The corpse of the gibbeted man was left to decompose in public.

These public punishments and the public display of corpses ensured that New Yorkers, white and black, would remember the attempted uprising, although not everyone learned the same lessons. White New Yorkers would recall the association of fire, revolt, and murder. Black New Yorkers, as one slave indicated when the court first called him to testify, remembered not only the executions but who escaped punishment and how.[31] Those who confessed or implicated others had all been pardoned in 1712; in 1741, slaves may have used the same tactics to escape punishments.

These same public punishments and spectacles of dead corpses continued in the trials of 1741, as captured in a map of the city drawn from memory many years after the trials, which still indicated the location of gallows where bodies were hanged and the stake at which they were burned (see Figure 2, p. 6). Such places of execution had become designated urban sites that reminded all New Yorkers of the punishments that awaited transgressors.

The years between the 1712 revolt and the trials of 1741 saw continued unrest. In New York in 1720, then in New Jersey in 1734, 1738, and 1739, slaves threatened revolt, burned barns, and attacked their masters.[32] None resulted in widespread investigations, however.

Other events, more recent but farther away, also put the city on edge. In 1736, authorities in the Caribbean island of Antigua uncovered a plot to blow up the island's gentry while they were at a ball. Some Antiguans asserted that every slave on the island was somehow involved. Authorities moved quickly to crush the planned revolt. Within four months they had executed eighty-eight slaves. Seventy-seven were burnt at the stake; the others were either gibbeted or broken on the wheel.[33] New Yorkers got a full account of the conspiracy when the *New-York Weekly Journal* ran a lengthy five-part report (see Document 1). As with the 1712 New York conspiracy, the punishments would have seemed familiar, but white New Yorkers might have seen other resemblances to their own community. The reports of black conspirators drinking and plotting in taverns heightened their own concerns about the presence of disorderly houses and unlicensed taverns in New York.

The Stono Rebellion added a new twist to the fear of slave conspiracies: foreign influences. Slaves and free whites alike knew that Spain had offered freedom to any British slave who could escape to Florida, and Spanish officials refused to return runaway slaves to British claimants. In September 1739, a group of slaves began a revolt near the Stono River in South Carolina. Their numbers steadily increased as they made their way toward the Spanish city of St. Augustine in Florida. They sacked and burned buildings on their route and killed about twenty whites before the militia caught up with them. Most were killed in a number of battles with the white militia, but a number of the rebels escaped. It seems likely that they were trying to reach Gracia Real de Santa Teresa de Mose, a community in Spanish Florida that consisted almost entirely of escaped slaves to whom the Spanish government had given sanctuary. Soon thereafter, New York slaves learned they too could find freedom in Spanish territories when local papers carried Georgia governor James Oglethorpe's declaration of war against Spanish Florida because the Spanish governor continued to "foment and countenance slaves in rebellion."[34]

It seemed clear now that slave revolts could be both instigated and supported by foreign governments trying to drive the British from their colonies in North America. King Charles II of Spain explicitly proclaimed that he would offer freedom to any runaway slaves, and his governors consistently upheld and announced this policy. Further, the fact that the Stono Rebellion coincided with the start of Britain's official declaration of war against Spain (King George's War) gave weight to the theory that slave revolts were more than domestic uprisings. The specter of war was always present in New York even as constables focused on domestic crimes such as theft and unlicensed taverns.

NEW YORK IN THE EMPIRE

When Rebecca Hogg first discovered the robbery of her shop, she questioned the white sailor who had been in her shop the day before and who had passed the word on to his enslaved friends that it was well-stocked for a raid. The sailor immediately implicated John Gwin. He told the constables that he had seen Gwin passing the money in the Hughsons' tavern. Because the sailor had come from a warship, the authorities assumed that Gwin was a free man also associated with the military, and they rushed off to the Hughsons' looking for a soldier.

The constables' assumption that Gwin was a soldier was wrong, but not surprising. There were plenty of soldiers in New York, and not just in the taverns.[35] New York was home to the only permanent garrison in British North America, housed in Fort George.[36] The British Crown kept a permanent force in New York because of its easy access to the Indian and Canadian interior via the Hudson, and to the other parts of the British Empire in the Atlantic from its harbor. The widespread presence of soldiers, sailors, and other guardians of imperial power in New York indicated the city's close ties to the British Empire.

When Justice Horsmanden opened the trials in 1741, New York was already involved in the second of the three great eighteenth-century imperial wars between Britain and its Catholic rivals, France and Spain. From 1702 to 1713 (Queen Anne's War), 1739 to 1748 (King George's War), and 1754 to 1763 (the French and Indian War), Britain

1702-13 Queen Anne's War
1739-48 King George
1754-63 Fr & Indian

Figure 5. *Map of the British Empire in 1741.* British New York had to prepare for attack on their northern borders from the French and on their ports from the Spanish. Most of the city's garrison was fighting in the Spanish colony of Puerto Rico.

was at war with its foreign enemies. As the map of the British Empire indicates (Figure 5), the three empires struggled for political and economic dominance in Europe, North America, and the West Indies. New Yorkers fought both on land and at sea.[37]

In New York and elsewhere in North America, however, the fight was also against the fearful power of the Catholic papacy. Anti-Catholicism permeated the British Empire, often exacerbated by rumors of "Popish plots" to overthrow a reigning Protestant king and replace him with a Catholic.[38] New York's intimate connection with its first English ruler, the Catholic Duke of York (later James I), provoked several generations of religious tension between the staunchly Protestant Dutch and James's Catholic governors, beginning with Leisler's Rebellion against James's absolutist government in 1689.[39] After the Glorious Revolution secured the Protestant succession for the monarchy, the New York government codified its restrictions against Catholics. In August 1700, the New York General Assembly passed a law against "Jesuits and popish priests" that mandated life imprisonment for anyone who confessed to being a Catholic priest or anyone who might "otherwise appear to be such by preaching & teaching of others to say any popish prayers by Celebrating masses granting of absolutions or using any other of the Romish Ceremonies & Rites of worship."[40] The appearance of being a Catholic priest was as illegal in New York as being one. The law was intended to prosecute French Catholic missionaries who were working with native Americans near the Canadian border. It seems, however, that the law was never invoked until the trial of John Ury, the putative ringleader of the 1741 conspiracy.[41] Finding the "hand of popery" in a slave conspiracy made the uprising seem both more terrifying and more deplorable. Ury's refusal to acknowledge King George II as the head of the Anglican church, and his teaching of Latin, the language most closely associated with Catholicism, immediately marked him for suspicion among conformist New Yorkers. In his letter to the Lords of Trade (see Document 3), Lieutenant-Governor George Clarke expressed his doubts about Ury on precisely these grounds.

Fighting during King George's War was particularly fierce in the wealthy West Indies, of which Britain, France, and Spain all claimed possession. The summer before the trials began, the garrison in New York had sent six hundred men in an attempt to capture Cuba.[42] Some of these New Yorkers fought alongside Admiral Vernon, who took Puerto Bello in Cuba from the Spanish in November 1739, a naval success that aroused great public enthusiasm for the war throughout the British Empire.[43]

British naval ships were not the only vessels that Britons sent out against their Catholic foes. British privateers—state-sponsored pirates—intercepted French and Spanish ships laden with sugar, cocoa, indigo, and gold. Privateers brought back the cargoes and the black crews to British ports for sale. New York was at the forefront of this particularly lucrative form of profiteering.

Privateering captains not only sold the captured cargoes at auction, they also tried to have any captured black sailors sold as slaves. Since Spain and France used both free and enslaved black and mixed-race men as sailors, New York often had a considerable number of foreign black sailors in its taverns and households. These sailors often protested to the courts that they were free subjects of a foreign king, and frequently, especially when they could find the support of a Spanish governor or British official, they won their freedom suits in the courts. These men could be exchanged for white prisoners of war and sent home to the Spanish West Indies. Not all foreign black sailors managed to free themselves, however, and many died in slavery.

By 1741, at least 150 foreign black sailors had been condemned to slavery in New York by the local vice-admiralty court.[44] A few of these Spanish sailors were among the first to be arrested when the roundup of slaves began after the four fires on April 6. It was their presence in New York that first gave rise to the suspicion that this was an international and Catholic conspiracy.

Some New York slaves apparently took equal notice of the black Spanish sailors' cosmopolitan knowledge. New Yorkers testified that Spanish sailors were considered braver and more violent than "York Negroes." The Spaniards' reputations quickly brought them to the attention of the court but do not seem to have overly prejudiced their trials. Of the six Spanish sailors who came to trial, however, only one was executed, and this is approximately the same ratio as the execution of native New York slaves.

Although several of the men spoke no English, their experience in foreign ports had made them adept at learning local customs quickly. It took them little time to uncover the principles of New York slave law, including the decree that only slaves could be convicted on the basis of slave testimony alone. They therefore argued that they were not really slaves, but instead illegally held prisoners of war. As a result, they insisted, the court could not convict them with slave testimony. They lost the argument, and their attempt to make it heightened authorities' concern that the conspiracy might have international implications.

New Yorkers both rich and poor were linked to the British Empire in other ways besides war. One of the most important connections was through an influx of consumer goods: china, tea, sugar, and, most of all, cloth. The silver knee buckles, snuffboxes, and even the speckled linen that Gwin and Prince stole all represent the expansion of what some historians have called "the consumer revolution" of the eighteenth century. Beginning in the 1720s, North Americans imported ever-larger amounts of goods from elsewhere in the British Empire and around the Atlantic. Moreover, the variety and nature of these items shifted dramatically from those imported in the seventeenth century. That earlier period emphasized imports that provided more comfort. The elaborate tea sets that appeared in the early eighteenth century hardly changed the physical effects of drinking tea, but they entirely re-created the social value of performing that activity. In the eighteenth century, the nature of imports changed from comfort to status. These later goods often had meaning for early Americans far beyond their practical value. In fact, the truly revolutionary part of the consumer revolution was not the rise in the amount of goods that North American colonists were importing; rather, the shift came because colonists gave meaning to certain kinds of goods. Using items such as tea trays and wearing stylish clothing indicated politeness and gentility.[45] Expensive fabrics such as silk or cotton were no longer restricted to the wealthy. The middling sort and the poor could join the international consumer market, sometimes through trade in a secondhand market. Even slaves could participate. When the investigation into the conspiracy began, two slaves were discovered to have trunks of goods that, as Horsmanden later wrote, "the aldermen thought improper for, and unbecoming the condition of slaves. . . ."[46] Everyone had a stake in the commercial British Empire.

TAVERNS AND CRIME

Taverns were ordinary and necessary elements of every port city. Drinking establishments could be anything from ornate two-story houses, offering drink in silver tankards to such esteemed customers as the governor and his advisers, to grimy, dark shacks by the docks in which poor laborers and slaves might share a drink. Both sorts of taverns served beer, ale, and rum, although more elite establishments might also serve wine. Taverns were an essential part of daily life for almost all New Yorkers, white and black. They were the primary place people gathered for warmth, community, and conversation.[47]

But taverns could also have a much less savory reputation. Those in rougher parts of town or with poorer clienteles were often labeled "disorderly houses." This term had no specific legal definition, although it was a general rubric for places that encouraged specifically forbidden behavior, most often excessive drinking or gambling, suspicious economic transactions, or interracial socializing. Thus, when New York officials first suspected John and Sarah Hughson of illegal trading, it was the Hughsons' profession more than any previous knowledge of their character that implicated them. It was usually the neighbors, rather than a constable or other official, who charged a local tavern with being a disorderly house. When the Hughsons went to trial, for example, their next-door neighbor, Francis Silvester, testified that "he often reproached Hughson with keeping such a disorderly house, which very much offended his neighbors."[48] A tavern keeper could be fined, whipped, or even banished for running a disorderly house. It was in these disorderly houses that authorities and respectable New Yorkers feared that plots of theft and rebellion would be hatched.[49]

Nor was it unusual that city constables found Rebecca Hogg's stolen goods in a tavern. Poorer taverns often acted as unregistered pawn shops, in which the proprietor exchanged drink or cash for goods, particularly clothing. The women who ran the taverns, either singly or with their husbands, usually were in charge of this side of the business. Often these pawned goods belonged legally to the customer, but occasionally they were stolen. Many tavern keepers did not concern themselves too closely with the origin of the goods, and a few actually served as fences for stolen goods, reselling them in an underground economy. All taverns offered credit to their customers, although those with a poorer clientele often settled debts with goods or services rather than cash. The extension of credit to slaves or apprentices was illegal but widespread, since it allowed slaves and others with limited discretionary income to enjoy the social world of the tavern. Such taverns, however, seemed to elite New Yorkers simply dens of iniquity.[50]

To judge from the number of proprietors accused of illegally entertaining slaves in their taverns, mixed-race socializing was widespread in working-class establishments. These interactions had an economic basis when slaves brought to white tavern keepers goods to pawn or fence. At times, these social encounters could be as simple as two men having a drink together. But interracial socializing could also be sexual. When John Gwin arrived at the Hughsons' tavern on the night of the robbery, he went straight to the room of his Irish lover, Peggy Kerry. The fact that New York, like other port cities, in the 1740s had more white women than white men and more black men than black women contributed to the likelihood of interracial sexual relationships between black men and white women.[51] Their prevalence did nothing, however, to assuage many white New Yorkers' fears about the degeneracy that they thought such relationships represented. The affair between Gwin and Kerry simply confirmed to many that New York's slaves were not remaining within their prescribed roles, and their interracial relationship inspired some of the angriest rhetoric heard during the trials.

Although prostitution was as common in New York taverns as elsewhere, taverns were rarely brought to court on charges of procuring prostitutes or otherwise acting as brothels. It is true that taverns run by single women—with no man to police their sexual habits—were more likely to be brought up on charges of being a disorderly house, since the courts often assumed that single working women were prostitutes or sexually promiscuous. An occasional woman faced charges for running a "bawdy house" of prostitution.[52] Overall, however, the complaints against the Hughsons' tavern were typical in their concerns about whites and blacks drinking together. Most prosecutions of disorderly houses were based on an accusation of serving alcohol to black slaves and thus providing opportunities for interracial mixing.[53]

When Rebecca Hogg first urged the city constables to look into the robbery, neither she nor the perpetrators had any idea that the investigation might yield anything out of the ordinary. Theft was a common problem in colonial cities; it accounted for nearly one quarter of all criminal prosecutions in British New York, and its incidence was on the rise through the 1740s.[54] This was not the first time Gwin and Prince had both been caught stealing; five years earlier, they had been convicted for stealing gin from a warehouse. The usual penalty for both white and black New Yorkers who had been convicted of larceny was a public whipping.[55] However, the trial led to Gwin and Prince's being not simply whipped but hanged—the reason for their deaths lay in the involvement of whites in the crime. The discovery of both John Gwin and Rebecca Hogg's goods in the Hughsons' tavern uncovered for white officials a widespread interracial criminal underworld.

LEGAL CONTEXT OF THE TRIALS

Judge Horsmanden's edition of the transcripts from the 1741 trials reveals the hybrid of legal forms that made up slave trials in eighteenth-century New York. The officials who conducted many of the slave trials in colonial America did not adhere strictly to one set of procedures; instead, they drew from both British common law and from local slave codes. This conflation makes the transcripts a confusing guide to a history of legal procedure, but it nevertheless reveals British colonial attitudes about what constituted credible evidence, sources, testimony, and justice.

The 1741 trials occurred in an unusual legal context. In the slave code passed after the 1712 uprising, the New York General Assembly declared that most serious crimes committed by slaves, including murder, arson, rape, and conspiracy, would be tried in a special court consisting of three judges and five other male officials. Only owners willing to pay an extra sum could obtain a jury trial for their slaves. These special courts bypassed the usual common law proceedings of arrest warrants, rules of evidence, cross-examination, and juries.[56]

The trials of 1741, however, were not held in the special slave court. Because the case was inherently biracial and the investigation involved large numbers of whites as well as blacks, the judges and lawyers of the city decided that, in spite of the provincial act that had created these special slave courts, whites and blacks would be tried together in the New York Supreme Court. As a result, all the accused, slave and free, had grand jury indictments, jury trials (including the right of the accused to challenge jurors, which both the Hughsons and some slaves used), and other standard safeguards of the British common law system.

Consequently, a grand jury, consisting of seventeen of the wealthiest and most elite men in the city, heard the initial evidence of arson, theft, and disorderly houses. They then interviewed Mary Burton and other witnesses, and from their testimony declared that there was enough evidence for the cases to go to trial before a regular, or petit, jury (technically speaking, the grand jury "indicted" or "found bills of indictment against" the defendants). The members of the grand jury served throughout the first three months of the trials, but the members of the petit jury, who sat on individual cases and determined whether the defendants were guilty or not guilty, were chosen for each trial. Members of the petit jury, while also white and male, tended to be less wealthy and elite than members of the grand jury.

They might be artisans, shopkeepers, or merchants. Some served on multiple juries, and others on only one. Since nearly half the households in New York City had slaves, many of the petit jury members probably owned slaves themselves.

Familiar as some of these procedures may seem to modern readers, two elements of the trials in particular are unusual by today's standards: the absence of defense lawyers and the standards for the admission of evidence. Defense lawyers were actually forbidden in criminal cases in English courts. The early modern British legal system acted on the premise that lawyers were necessary only to explicate points of law rather than to make a case. Thus, it was assumed that the judge could clarify any important legal questions for the defendant. Moreover, English courts argued that since the defendant knew the facts better than anyone else, he or she was the best person to explain what had really happened. Defense lawyers began to appear in English courts in the 1730s, but their emergence came too late to North America for those accused in 1741.[57] Throughout the trials, the defendants spoke in their own defense and cross-examined their own witnesses. With no advocate for the defense to check their actions, judges correspondingly had great power in directing the course of a trial.

The judge's authority was particularly extensive in deciding whose evidence could be used to convict a defendant. The biracial trials of 1741 made the question of admissible testimony still more complicated. Under New York's revised slave code of 1730, one slave's testimony was enough to convict another slave of conspiracy, although it was not sufficient to convict free blacks. Whites could be convicted only by evidence from other reputable whites. The testimony of convicted criminals was not admissible in white trials, nor was slave testimony. Thus, the evidence of both Mary Burton and of the Hughsons' daughter Sarah, both white, was especially crucial for the conviction of the accused priest John Ury. Slave testimony could be used, however, against other slaves. All the defendants, both white and black, were aware of these rules of evidence and often tried to use them as best they could.[58]

The evidence itself for these trials rested heavily on depositions (referred to also as "examinations" or "informations") and confessions. Physical evidence was essentially absent, and there is no evidence of direct physical compulsion or torture during the examinations. The psychological pressures to confess and implicate others, as some of the accused testify, was immense, however. The promise of a pardon or reduced punishment was a powerful inducement to confess. Confessions at executions, particularly at the stake, were treated as especially valuable, based on the widespread belief that one would not die with a lie on one's lips.

THE *JOURNAL* AS A DOCUMENT

No complete interpretation of the trials ends with the establishment of their context, however. We also must scrutinize the question of the conspiracy itself, and especially the text on which study of the trials must rely. Daniel Horsmanden's *Journal* raises a host of questions about its purpose, its intended audience, and the circumstances of its writing and publication. The larger meaning of the trials can be defined only in relation to the nature of the text.

The reliability of both Horsmanden and his text has been fundamental to the question of whether there was a conspiracy, and what sort of conspiracy it may have been. Horsmanden certainly believed that there had been a slave conspiracy, and he wrote the *Journal* in order to convince those who doubted it was so to agree with him, as his letter to his friend Cadwallader Colden demonstrates (see Document 5). The text, therefore, is the argument for the prosecution. Horsmanden's hopes that the *Journal* would "awaken us from that supine security, which again too generally prevails" implicitly defines the attitudes that he is attacking, namely, the disbelief and complacency of white New Yorkers.

It is impossible to remove Daniel Horsmanden from his text. The *Journal*'s selection, order, emphases, and editorial insertions are Horsmanden's, and he shaped the account carefully; authorial bias makes the *Journal* a difficult source to use. But it is part of the task of a historian to analyze the biases of contemporary observers in order to create a narrative about the past. Moreover, the *Journal*'s importance increases with the paucity of independent evidence for these trials. The original records of the Supreme Court in which the trials were held have not been preserved. A 1911 fire at the New York State Library in Albany destroyed many of the legal papers that could have either corroborated or contradicted Horsmanden's account.

And yet the independent sources that we do have tend to resemble the testimony that Horsmanden reprints. An analysis of some of the slave examinations that the governor sent to the Board of Trade in London, now preserved in the Public Record Office in London, makes it clear that Horsmanden neither invented nor embellished the slaves' testimony (see Document 2). Although the texts from London are not verbatim copies from the courtroom, there is little significant factual difference between the governor's and the justice's versions. If anything, as these examinations show, Horsmanden occasionally cut back evidence in the interests of economy and clarity.

Furthermore, Horsmanden's *Journal* was a product of its historical moment. Horsmanden published his account just when printers and preachers were discovering the power of the press for advertising.[59] Like many who tried to create a market for their wares, Horsmanden advertised his *Journal* in the local newspapers (see Figure 6). Similar to popular commonplace books of its day, in which one recorded passages or quotations for future reference or education, the *Journal* is a hybrid document, a compilation of trial notes, interpretation, and letters and speeches written by many different people. The sources for many of the biases are equally mixed. Much of Horsmanden's and other lawyers' animus against Catholics, for example, is borrowed from traditional sixteenth- and seventeenth-century anti-popery declamations. At the same time, however, when pointing to the due process that the defendants received, Horsmanden frequently lays claim to the Enlightenment ideal that Justice is blind. It is often under the cover of these claims of fairness that the worst of the legal manipulations appeared, as the inducements to confess make clear.

The polemical nature of the *Journal* makes it clear that even from the beginning there has been little consensus on what really happened in the spring and summer of 1741. Lately, several historians have argued that there had been an uprising planned in New York that was part of a wave of slave uprisings across the early modern Atlantic.[60] Others agree that there was some sort of conspiracy, but nothing so ambitious as an attempt to burn down the city of New York and take its inhabitants as prisoners. This was the conclusion of the editors of the first reprint of the *Journal,* who asserted in 1810 that "no doubt can be had of the actual existence of a plot; but its extent could never have been so great as the terror of those times depicted."[61] It has likewise been argued that the conspirators planned only to commit thefts and simple arson (possibly in tandem), or that it was the very upswell of rebellious talk in taverns itself that constituted a revolt.[62] Another interpretation sees the trials as an attempt by an insecure British governor and his supporters (foremost of whom was Horsmanden) to bring together white New Yorkers by clearly delineating those who were dangerously deviant because of their color, religion, or class.[63] Finally,

ON *Saturday next will be publiſhed,* A Journal of the Proceedings againſt the Conſpirators at *New-York,* in 1741, and 1742. *Thoſe Gentlemen that live in Town, who have ſubſcribed for this Journal, are deſired to ſend for their Books to the Printer hereof, and to pay the Reſidue of their Subſcription Money to him. As there are but few more printed than what are engaged for, any Perſon that intends to purchaſe them, muſt apply ſpeedily,* Price 10 s.

The Printer hereof having by him a Number of the *Journals of the Proceedings againſt the Negroes,* who lately plotted the Deſtruction of this City; and as he has been a conſiderable Loſer by printing that Book, he propoſes to ſell 'em very cheap, viz. 3 ſ. a Piece, ſticht, which is not quite one third of what they were at firſt ſold for :---And as it may be a neceſſary Memento in all Families in this Colony; ſo 'tis probable they will never have ſuch another Opportunity of getting them ſo cheap again; and thoſe who are inclined to purchaſe, are deſired to be expeditious, leſt they be diſappointed.

Figure 6. *Newspaper Advertisements for Horsmanden's Text.* These notices appeared in the *New York Weekly Post-Boy,* May 14, 1744 (top), and October 10, 1748 (bottom). Most eighteenth-century books were sold by subscription, so the publisher printed only as many as had been ordered. After a cheaper, pirated edition appeared in London in 1747, demand for the originals plummeted, and the printer had to sell them off at bargain prices.

Collection of The New-York Historical Society.

still other historians have dismissed the entire episode as a moment of mass hysteria, brought on either by fear of slaves or fear of Catholics.[64]

The 1741 trials have most recently seen a resurgence of interest as other suspected slave conspiracies have undergone reexamination. A recent fierce debate among historians over Vesey's Rebellion, an alleged 1822 slave revolt in Charleston, South Carolina, that produced a controversial set of trials and an even more controversial account of them, has reignited interest in the larger methodological and historical questions that Horsmanden's text raises. As one historian has asked, "Is it possible ever to determine the truth behind charges of slave plots when the evidence has been gathered by powerful whites who controlled the circumstance and set the terms by which the enslaved are allowed to speak, at the peril of their lives?"[65] Interpretive positions can sometimes also speak to the politics of the present. On one hand, arguing for the existence of a conspiracy affirms the ability of slaves to recognize and protest their oppression. Yet one historian has argued that to believe that there was a conspiracy is to align oneself with the racism of a court that executed so many black men on so little evidence. It may be that the "the truth, the whole truth and nothing but the truth" behind the trials of 1741 can never be absolutely known. Nonetheless, Horsmanden's text encompasses all of these possibilities of interpretation, and, perhaps more important, it reveals the attitudes and circumstances of those living in a crowded and fascinating city on the outposts of the British Empire.

When viewed in these multiple settings of uncertainty and fear, the trials of 1741 are an unparalleled source for uncovering eighteenth-century American port culture. They are a snapshot of the most important issues historians face when trying to understand colonial America: the relationship of a city to the British Empire and to the Empire's political and military struggles; slave life and resistance, including the close and often tense relationships between whites and blacks; and the use of two of the most important public spaces in early modern cities, the taverns and the courts. Just as the trials need these contexts in order for historians to make sense of them, so the settings themselves come to life in the pages of the *Journal.*

NOTES

[1]Douglas Greenberg, *Crime and Law Enforcement in the Colony of New York, 1691–1776* (Ithaca and London: Cornell University Press, 1974), 57–59. Also see Sharon V. Salinger, *Taverns and Drinking in Early America* (Baltimore and London: Johns Hopkins University Press, 2002), 128.

[2]For the development of New York City's neighborhoods, see Carl Abbott, "The Neighborhoods of New York, 1760–1775," *New York History,* 55 (January 1974): 35–54; Bruce Wilkenfield, "New York City Neighborhoods, 1730," *New York History,* 57 (April 1976), 165–82; and Nan Rothschild, *New York City Neighborhoods: The Eighteenth Century* (San Diego: Academic Press, 1990).

[3]See, for example, the evidence of Eleanor Ryan, who boarded there with her husband, a soldier at the fort, chap. 4.

[4]*New York Weekly Journal,* December 22, 1740. William Smith, *History of the Province of New York,* ed. Michael Kammen (Cambridge: Belknap Press of Harvard University Press, 1972), 2:49.

[5]T. J. Davis, *A Rumor of Revolt: The "Great Negro Plot" in Colonial New York* (New York: The Free Press, 1985), 27–30.

[6]*New York Weekly Journal,* May 18, 1741.

[7]Jack's confession, Monday June 8, 1741.

[8]Robert Darnton, *The Great Cat Massacre and Other Episodes in French Cultural History* (New York: Basic Books, 1984), 31–35.

[9]Mary Burton's testimony, April 22; Peggy Kerry's testimony, May 9.

[10]Serena Zabin, "Places of Exchange: New York City, 1700–1763" (Ph.D. diss., Rutgers University, 2000), chap. 1. The famous trickster Tom Bell tried some of his first swindles in New York City in the 1730s and 1740s. Steven C. Bullock, "A Mumper among the Gentle: Tom Bell, Colonial Confidence Man," *William and Mary Quarterly,* 3rd ser., 55 (April 1998): 231–58; and Carl Bridenbaugh, "'The Famous Infamous Vagrant' Tom Bell," in *Early Americans* (New York and Oxford: Oxford University Press, 1981).

[11]For women and trade, see Jean P. Jordan, "Women Merchants in Colonial New York," *New York History,* 43 (1977): 412–39; Patricia Cleary, "'She Will Be in the Shop': Women's Sphere of Trade in Eighteenth-Century Philadelphia and New York," *The Pennsylvania Magazine of History & Biography,* 119 (1995): 181–202; and Deborah Rosen, *Courts and Commerce: Gender, Law, and the Market Economy in Colonial New York* (Columbus: Ohio State University Press, 1997).

[12]Jessica Kross, "Power Most Ardently Sought: The New York Council, 1675–1775," in *Power and Status: Officeholding in Early America,* ed. Bruce C. Daniels (Middletown: Wesleyan University Press, 1986); and Stanley N. Katz, *Newcastle's New York: Anglo-American Politics, 1732–1753* (Cambridge: Belknap Press of Harvard University Press, 1968).

[13]Daniel Horsmanden to Charles Cotton, New York, July 2, 1756, Horsmanden Papers, Addenda, No. 31, NYHS, cited in Mary Paula McManus, "Daniel Horsmanden: An Eighteenth-Century New Yorker" (Ph.D. diss., Fordham University, 1960), 4, fn. 4.

[14]*New York Colonial Documents,* V:976.

[15]For lawyers in trade, see James Alexander, Horsmanden to Colden, New York, July 23, 1736, *NYHS Collections,* 51 (1918): 153.

[16]Charles Z. Lincoln, William H. Johnson, and A. Judd Northrup, eds., *The Colonial Laws of New York from the Year 1664 to the Revolution* (Albany: J. B. Lyon, State Printer, 1894), 3:719, November 27, 1741.

[17]In July 1745, the assembly established a committee to investigate why Horsmanden had not yet prepared the laws. I. N. Phelps Stokes, comp., *The Iconography of Manhattan Island, 1498–1909* (New York: Robert H. Dodd, 1915; reprint, New York: Arno Press, 1967), IV:590. William Smith Jr. and William Livingston agreed to take over the project in 1750, and the laws appeared in 1752. *Colonial Laws,* 3:907, November 24, 1750.

[18]Daniel Horsmanden to Cadwallader Colden, November 11, 1734, New-York Historical Society, *Collections,* 51 (1918): 117

[19]Clinton to the President of the Board of Trade, October 30, 1748, *Acts of the Privy Council of England, Colonial Series* (6 vol.; Hereford: for his Majesty's Stationery Office, 1908–1912), VI:271. Cited in McManus, "Daniel Horsmanden," 130.

[20]Smith, *History of New York,* 2:100. McManus, "Daniel Horsmanden," 130–31.

[21]Some very interesting findings are emerging slowly from the study of the African burial ground, but little of that work has been published.

[22]Edwin G. Burrows and Mike Wallace, *Gotham: A History of New York City to 1898* (New York and Oxford: Oxford University Press, 1999), 127; Thelma Willis Foote, "Black Life in Colonial Manhattan, 1664–1796" (Ph.D. diss., Harvard University, 1991), 78, table 4.

[23]Philip D. Morgan, "British Encounters with Africans and African-Americans, circa 1600–1780," in *Strangers within the Realm: Cultural Margins of the First British Empire,* ed. Bernard Bailyn and Philip D. Morgan (Chapel Hill and London: University of North Carolina Press for the Institute of Early American History and Culture, 1991), 157–219. For slavery in New York, see Foote, "Black Life"; Graham Russell Hodges, *Root and Branch: African Americans in New York and East Jersey, 1613–1863* (Chapel Hill and London: University of North Carolina Press, 1999); and Edgar J. McManus, *A History of Negro Slavery in New York* (Syracuse: Syracuse University Press, 1966).

[24]Burrows and Wallace, *Gotham,* 128–29; Foote, "Black Life," 31, table 1, and 58, table 3.

[25]For labor, see Thomas J. Davis, "These Enemies of Their Own Household: Slaves in 18th Century New York," in *A Beautiful and Fruitful Place: Selected Rensselaerswijck Seminar Papers,* ed. Nancy Anne McClure Zeller (Albany: New Netherland Publishers, 1991), 171–79. For sailors, see W. Jeffrey Bolster, *Black Jacks: African American Seamen in the Age of Sail* (Cambridge and London: Harvard University Press, 1997). For hiring out, see Hodges, *Root and Branch,* 83, 107–14.

[26]*Colonial Laws,* I:18, October 24, 1684.

[27]*Colonial Laws,* II:560, October 29, 1730.

[28]Remonstrance of February 2, 1724. Misc. Mss. Dugdale, William, NYHS.

[29]*New York Weekly Journal,* January 5, 1735.

[30]Hodges, *Root and Branch,* 70–74.

[31]Horsmanden, Friday, May 22, 1741.

[32]Hodges, *Root and Branch,* 89–91.

[33]David Barry Gaspar, *Bondmen & Rebels: A Study of Master-Slave Relations in Antigua, with Implications for Colonial British America* (Baltimore and London: Johns Hopkins University Press, 1985), chap. 1.

[34]*The New York Weekly Journal,* May 22, 1740; Peter Wood, *Black Majority: Negroes in Colonial South Carolina from 1670 through the Stono Rebellion* (New York: Knopf, 1974), chaps. 11 and 12; Jane Landers, *Black Society in Spanish Florida* (Urbana and Chicago: University of Illinois Press, 1999), 19–60; Landers, "Gracia Real de Santa Teresa de Mose: A Free Black Town in Spanish Colonial Florida," *American Historical Review,* 95 (February 1990): 9–30.

[35]There were 110 in the garrison in 1734 (see letter of M. de Beauharnois to the Marquis of Maurepas, October 10, 1734, E. B. O'Callaghan, ed. *Documents Relative to the Colonial History of the State of New York* (hereafter, DRCHNY) (Albany: Weed, Parsons, Printers, 1853–87).

[36]Gov. George Clarke to Lords of Trade, August 21, 1741, *DRCHNY.*

[37]For New York at war, see John Shy, "The American Colonies in War and Revolution, 1748–1783," in *The Oxford History of the British Empire II: The Eighteenth Century,* ed. P. J. Marshall (Oxford and New York: Oxford University Press, 1998); also Richard Pares, *Colonial Blockade and Neutral Rights* (New York and Oxford: Oxford University Press, 1938).

[38]Linda Colley, *Britons: Forging the Nation, 1707–1837* (New Haven: Yale University Press, 1992).

[39]Adrian Howe, "The Bayard Treason Trial: Dramatizing Anglo-Dutch Politics in Early Eighteenth-Century New York City," *William and Mary Quarterly,* 3rd ser., 47, no. 1 (1990): 57–89.

[40]*Colonial Laws,* I:84, August 9, 1700.

[41]John Gilmary Shea, paper read before the New-York Historical Society, May 6, 1862, included in *The trial of John Ury for being an ecclesiastical person, made by authority pretended from the See of Rome, and coming into and abiding in the province of New York, and with being one of the conspirators in the Negro plot to burn the city of New York, 1741: Abridged from The New York conspiracy, or, A history of the Negro plot, with the Journal of the Proceedings against the conspirators, at New York, in the years 1741-2. By Daniel Horsmanden. 2d ed. 1810* (Philadelphia: Martin I. J. Griffin, 1899), 54–56.

[42]Five hundred of these were volunteers; see Lt. Gov. Clarke to the Duke of Newcastle, September 22, 1740, *DRCHNY.*

[43]Kathleen Wilson, "Empire, Trade and Popular Politics in Mid-Hanoverian Britain: The Case of Admiral Vernon," *Past & Present,* 121 (1988): 74–109.

[44]James G. Lydon, "New York and the Slave Trade, 1700–1774," *William and Mary Quarterly,* 3rd ser., 35 (1978): 375–94, 386.

[45]Among much recent work on consumerism, see T. H. Breen, "The Meaning of

Things," in *Consumption and the World of Goods,* ed. John Brewer and Roy Porter (New York: Routledge, 1994), 249–60.

[46]April 13, 1742.

[47]For class distinctions in eighteenth-century taverns, see Salinger, *Taverns and Drinking in Early America;* and Peter Thompson, *Rum Punch and Revolution: Taverngoing and Public Life in Eighteenth-Century Philadelphia* (Philadelphia: University of Pennsylvania Press, 1999). For the governor's drinking habits, see Carl Bridenbaugh, ed., *Gentleman's Progress: The Itinerarium of Dr. Alexander Hamilton, 1744* (Chapel Hill: University of North Carolina Press, 1948), 41–49, 173–85.

[48]June 4, 1741.

[49]Greenberg, *Crime and Law Enforcement,* 52–53 and 97–98. For the disorderly house as a "catch-all for disorderly conduct generally," see Julius Goebel Jr. and T. Raymond Naughton, *Law Enforcement in Colonial New York: A Study in Criminal Procedure (1664–1776)* (New York: The Commonwealth Fund, 1944; reprint, 1970), 100–101.

[50]Zabin, "Places of Exchange," chap. 4; Salinger, *Taverns and Drinking,* especially 133. For laws against the extension of credit, see *Colonial Laws,* II:651, December 16, 1737.

[51]Burrows and Wallace, *Gotham,* 165, and David Narratt, *Inheritance and Family Life in Colonial New York City* (Ithaca: Cornell University Press, 1992), 238.

[52]Zabin, "Places of Exchange," chap. 4; e.g., Sarah Crosby was indicted for keeping a "Common Bawdy House." Manuscript minutes of the Court of General Sessions, New York Municipal Archives, August 5, 1730.

[53]Salinger, *Taverns and Drinking,* 129–30.

[54]Greenberg, *Crime and Law Enforcement,* 140.

[55]Goebel and Naughton, *Law Enforcement,* 704–6.

[56]*Colonial Laws,* I:250, December 10, 1712.

[57]John H. Langbein, "The Criminal Trial before the Lawyers," *The University of Chicago Law Review,* 45 (Winter 1978): 263–316; Goebel and Naughton, *Law Enforcement,* 574.

[58]*Colonial Laws,* II:684, November 29, 1730.

[59]Frank Lambert, "'Pedlar in Divinity': George Whitefield and the Great Awakening, 1737–1745," *Journal of American History,* 77, no. 3 (1990): 812–37.

[60]Peter Linebaugh and Marcus Rediker, *The Many-Headed Hydra: Sailors, Slaves, Commoners, and the Hidden History of the Revolutionary Atlantic* (Boston: Beacon Press, 2000), 174–210; and Hodges, *Root and Branch,* 91–99.

[61]Burrows and Wallace, *Gotham,* 159–64; Preface to *The New York Conspiracy, or a History of the Negro Plot, with the Journal of the Proceedings against the Conspirators at New-York in the Years 1741–2* (New York: Southwick & Pelsue, 1810; reprint, New York: Negro Universities Press, 1969).

[62]For arson and theft, see Zabin, "Places of Exchange"; Ferenc M. Szasz, "The New York Slave Revolt of 1741: A Re-Examination," *New York History,* 48 (1967): 215–30; William Smith, *A History of New York: A Continuation, 1732–1762,* ed. Michael Kammen (Cambridge: Belknap Press of Harvard University Press, 1972), 2:53. For "loose talk" see Davis, *Rumor of Revolt.*

[63]Foote, "Black Life in Colonial Manhattan, 1664–1796," chap. 5.

[64]Winthrop D. Jordan, *White over Black: American Attitudes toward the Negro, 1550–1812* (Chapel Hill: University of North Carolina Press for the Institute of Early American History and Culture, 1968; Penguin Books, 1969), 116–22; Herbert Aptheker, *American Negro Slave Revolts* (New York: International Publishers, 1963), 192.

[65]Robert A. Gross, "*Forum:* The Making of a Slave Conspiracy, Part 2," *William and Mary Quarterly,* 3rd ser., 59 (January 2002): 135–36. See also Michael P. Johnson, "Denmark Vesey and His Co-Conspirators," *William and Mary Quarterly,* 3rd ser., 58 (October 2001): 917–76 and responses, "*Forum:* The Making of a Slave Conspiracy, Part 2," *William and Mary Quarterly,* 3rd ser., 59 (January 2002): 137–202.

A Note about the Text

In 1747, three years after Horsmanden's New York publisher printed the *Journal,* a publisher in London printed a pirated copy. The cheaper London editions flooded the market and, within the year, the New York publisher sold the rest of his copies at a steep discount. Few of these eighteenth-century copies remain.

In 1810, an anonymous editor republished the 1744 text in its entirety, updating the spelling, punctuation, and use of italics. Although, with minor exceptions, the text itself is identical to the earlier edition, the 1810 editors made one major alteration: the title.

Daniel Horsmanden had called his text *A Journal of the Proceedings in The Detection of the Conspiracy Formed by Some* White *People, in Conjunction with* Negro *and other* Slaves. . . . His title explicitly points to the biracial nature of the conspiracy and at the same time points to whites as the ringleaders of the conspiracy. As part of Horsmanden's belief that the trials would speak for themselves, he put his emphasis on the court evidence itself, "the proceedings," rather than on his shaping of the testimony. Likewise, in an attempt to deflect attention from his role in the compilation of the text, Horsmanden's name does not appear on the title page or in the text itself.

The title that the nineteenth-century editors chose reflects a very different purpose from Horsmanden's. The 1810 edition is called *The New-York Conspiracy or a History of the Negro Plot.* The title removes whites from center stage and reformulates the "conspiracy" as a "Negro plot." It also turns the "Journal" of Horsmanden's title to a "History," which implies a much more active authorial role. The title page in turn announces that the text is "by Daniel Horsmanden, Esq." As the 1810 introduction (not reproduced here) asserts, the point of this edition is not to prove to New Yorkers that there had been a slave conspiracy. Instead, the editors wrote, "we look back with astonishment on the panic occasioned by the Negro plot, and the rancorous hatred that prevailed against the Roman catholics."[1] New York's gradual emancipation law had passed in 1799, and New Yorkers were clearly concerned with establishing their moral superiority over both the South and their slaveholding ancestors.[2] As a result, they offered their readers Horsmanden's text as a sign of the previous century's unenlightened state rather than a document advocating any belief in a widespread interracial uprising.

The original *Journal* in its entirety runs to approximately four hundred pages. Such a wealth of evidence is far too unwieldy for the classroom, where the mass of detail can overwhelm all but the most determined reader. This abridgment makes accessible a text and a historical event that for the most part has been known only to early American or African American specialists.

Some elements of the original are lost in the cutting of the text. The details in some of the testimony—in particular, the names, places, and owners of individual slaves—are a useful source for a social history of New York. Likewise, the legal questions of venues, adjournments, and enlargements of the courts are of great value to legal scholars. For these details, please refer to an unabridged edition.[3] In this edition, I have tried to reproduce Horsmanden's own emphases of evidence and speeches while exposing the narrative threads of the text that lie hidden in the unexpurgated version. I have done so in part by dividing the *Journal* into seven chapters while maintaining the chronological order of events and evidence. All previous editions presented the material in a continuous stream, divided only by dates.

This text is based on the 1810 edition of Horsmanden's *Journal,* because of its relative availability as well as its more modern orthography. For the most part, I have cut the text silently, using ellipses only when excising part of a speech. Footnotes preceded by a number were written by me; the rest are Horsmanden's original footnotes. I have also completed the abbreviations in the related documents.

[1]Preface to *The New-York Conspiracy.*

[2]Shane White, *Somewhat More Independent: The End of Slavery in New York City, 1770–1810* (Athens, Ga., and London: University of Georgia Press, 1991), 80–88.

[3]There are two modern reprints of the 1810 edition; neither is in print. In 1969, Negro Universities Press reprinted the 1810 edition, and in 1971, Thomas J. Davis completely reset and indexed the 1810 edition (Boston: Beacon Press).

Major Figures in the 1741 Trials

Throughout the course of the trial, hundreds of people passed through the Supreme Court. There is no need to remember most of their names. The most important players are listed here.

The Court

Daniel Horsmanden: Third Supreme Court justice and recorder of the city of New York.
Frederick Philipse: Second Supreme Court justice.
James DeLancey: Chief justice of the Supreme Court.
Richard Bradley: Attorney general for New York.

The Defendants

Names in parentheses are the slave's owner's.

Caesar (Vaark): Also known as John Gwin or John Quin. A slave convicted of stealing goods from the Hoggs and Abraham Meyers Cohen; suspected of leadership in the conspiracy; probably fathered a child with Peggy.
Prince (Auboyneau): A slave convicted with Caesar of stealing goods from the Hoggs and Abraham Meyers Cohen; suspected of deep involvement in the conspiracy.
Cuffee (Adolph Philipse): Also known as Cuff. A slave convicted of burning his master's storehouse as part of the conspiracy.
Quack (Roosevelt): Also known as Quaco. A slave convicted of burning the governor's house in Fort George as part of the conspiracy.
John Hughson: A tavern keeper convicted of receiving stolen goods, aiding and abetting arson. The court believed him to be one of the leaders in the conspiracy.
Sarah Hughson, the elder: The wife of John Hughson; also convicted of receiving stolen goods and aiding and abetting arson.

Sarah Hughson, the younger: The daughter of John and Sarah Hughson; convicted with her parents of supporting arson; eventually gave evidence for the court against John Ury.

Peggy Kerry: Also known as Margaret Carey, Margaret Keary, Margaret Kerry, Margaret Salinburgh, Margaret Sarinbirr; and Margaret Sorubiero. A single woman who lived at the Hughsons'; Caesar was probably the father of her child; convicted of receiving stolen goods and supporting arson.

John Ury: Also known as John Jury and John Doyle. An itinerant Latin teacher, Ury was accused of being a Catholic priest and Spanish spy. He was convicted on charges of masterminding the conspiracy.

Witnesses

Mary Burton: The Hughsons' sixteen-year-old indentured servant; the most important witness for the prosecution.

Sandy (Niblet): Also known as Sawney; a slave who was another essential witness for the prosecution, especially for evidence against the Spanish prisoners and other slaves.

William Kane: An Irish soldier stationed in New York, Kane was implicated in the conspiracy; also gave extensive testimony about Ury's activities as a priest and as the leader of the conspiracy.

Rebecca Hogg: The owner of the shop robbed by John Gwin, Prince, and Cuffee, Hogg first led the authorities to take a close look at the Hughsons.

PART TWO

The Document

DANIEL HORSMANDEN

A Journal of the Proceedings in The Detection of the Conspiracy

Formed by Some White *People, in Conjunction with* Negro *and other* Slaves, *for Burning the City of* New-York *in America, and Murdering the Inhabitants*

PREFACE

Justice Daniel Horsmanden's original preface is the clearest exposition of his rationale for publishing the transcripts of these trials as well as his own biases and hopes. His book is intended, he argues, to demonstrate to his readers that New York had barely escaped total destruction. Horsmanden is sure that the facts will speak for themselves. Although he admits that he has emphasized particular trials by setting them out almost in their entirety, while others he only excerpted, he explains that the great part of the text is simply unmediated primary evidence. The justice also describes the process by which the lawyers and judges took down the depositions and the grounds on which he found—and expects the reader to find—the evidence persuasive.

Note: For the most part, cuts to Horsmanden's text are silent; ellipses are used when excising part of a speech or numbered list.

The preface explains that there was no official court reporter who took down the evidence verbatim, so some of the testimony was reconstructed from the notes of the judges and lawyers. Horsmanden admits that the Journal *may seem a bit long and dense, but he defends the bulk of the entire book on the grounds that he did not want to summarize much of the evidence in his own words. Rather, he felt that the depositions themselves would be the best possible evidence for convincing skeptics of both the justice of the proceedings and of the grave danger New York faced. The judge elucidated the method by which depositions were taken from slaves: The court interrogated the accused as soon as they could, often before the defendants were committed to the jail.*

It is in this section that Horsmanden addresses one of the most controversial elements of the trials: the multiplication of accusations and the expansion of the plot from a simple case of theft to an international plan to overthrow the city. The judge admits that it may seem, as the trial continued, that the witnesses were inventing ever bigger and wilder stories, but, he argues, if one reads the depositions carefully, one can find hints of the new revelations in previous examinations. He defends the validity of slave testimony by explaining that the depositions were taken immediately, usually before slaves could be committed to jail and have a chance to compare and fit together their stories. Likewise, Horsmanden explains the process by which the defendants were given the chance to face their accusers. Conversely, Horsmanden admits that these depositions are not entirely straightforward, for which he gives two reasons: one, that slaves and examiners experienced a language barrier, and two, his belief that slaves had an intrinsic propensity to lie and obfuscate the truth. It is worth noting the extent to which other evidence throughout the Journal *supports or undermines Horsmanden's claims about slave testimony.*

Original Preface

The reader must not expect in the following sheets, a particular and minute relation of every formality, question and answer, that passed upon the trials; it may suffice, if he be assured he has the substance; for indeed more cannot be expected, when it is considered, that we have no one here, as in our mother country, who make it a business to take notes upon such occasions, or any others, that we know of, who are so dexterous at short-hand, as to be sufficiently qualified for such a purpose; but he will be sure to have all that could be collected from the notes that were taken by the court, and gentlemen at the bar; with all which the compiler has been furnished.

Upon a review of the proceedings, in order for this undertaking, the bulk of them, which was the product of about *six months inquiry,* seemed somewhat discouraging: No doubt they might have been contracted, if this work had been proceeded upon in the method of an historical relation only, wherein the compiler would have been more at liberty to abstract the several originals; but it was concluded, a *journal* would give more satisfaction, inasmuch as in such a kind of process, the depositions and examinations themselves, which were the groundwork of the proceedings, would appear at large; which most probably would afford conviction, to such as have a disposition to be convinced, and have *in reality* doubted whether any particular convicts had justice done them or not, notwithstanding they had the opportunity of *seeing* and *hearing* a great deal concerning them; and others, who had no such opportunities, who were prejudiced at a distance in their disfavour, by frivolous reports, might the readier be undeceived: for as the proceedings are set forth in the order of time they were produced, the reader will thereby be furnished with the most natural view of the whole, and be better enabled to conceive the design and dangerous depth of this *hellish project,* as well as the justice of the several prosecutions.

The parties accused of the conspiracy were numerous, and business by degrees multiplied so fast upon the grand jury, *which bore the burthen of this inquiry,* that there would have been an immediate necessity for others to have lent a helping hand in taking examinations *from the beginning,* if the judges had not found it expedient to examine the persons accused, upon their first taking into custody, whereby it seemed most likely the truth would bolt out, before they had time to cool, or opportunity of discoursing in the jail with their confederates, who were before committed.

The examinations thus taken by the judges, were soon after laid before the grand jury, who interrogated the parties there from in such manner, as generally produced from them the substance of the same matter, and often something more, by which means there accrued no small advantage; for though where the last examination brought to light new discovery, yet it will be seldom found, there is any thing in such further examinations contradictory to the former, but generally a confirmation of them; and in such case, the setting forth the same at large, may not be thought a useless tautology; not that this will happen often, and where it does, it will be chiefly found in the examinations and confessions of negroes, who, in ordinary cases, are seldom found to hold twice in the same story; which, for its rarity therefore, if it carried not with it the additional weight of the greater appearance of truth, may make this particular the more excusable; and further, this is a *diary* of the proceedings, that is to be exhibited, therefore, in conformity to that plan, nothing should be omitted, which may be of any use.

All proper precautions were taken by the judges, that the criminals should be kept separate; and they were so, as much as the scanty room in the jail would admit it of; and new apartments were fitted up for their reception: but more particular care was taken, that such negroes as had made confession and discovery, and were to be made use of as witnesses, should be kept apart from the rest, and as much from each other, as the accommodations would allow of, in order to prevent their caballing[1] from each other first, as well upon the trials, as otherwise, and then generally confronted with the persons they accused, who were usually sent for and taken into custody upon such examinations, if they were to be met with; which was the means of bringing many others to a confession, as well as were newly taken up, as those who had long before been committed, perhaps upon slighter grounds, and had insisted upon their innocence; for they had generally the cunning not to own their guilt, till they knew their accusers. But notwithstanding this was the ordinary method taken, both by the judges and grand jury, to send for the parties as soon as impeached, (which however might sometimes through hurry be omitted) yet several who happened then to be out of the way, were afterwards forgot, and slipped through our fingers, from the multiplicity of business in hand, as will hereafter appear; which *therefore* is particularly recommended to the notice of their owners.

The trouble of examining criminals in general, may be easily guessed at; but the fatigue in that of negroes, is not to be conceived, but by those that have undergone the drudgery. The difficulty of bringing and holding them to the truth, if by chance it starts through them, is not to be surmounted, but by the closest attention; many of them have a great deal of craft; their unintelligible jargon stands them in great stead, to conceal their meaning; so that an examiner must expect to encounter with much perplexity, grope through a maze of obscurity, be obliged to lay hold of broken hints, lay them carefully

[1] *caballing:* The forming of secret and harmful intrigues.

together, and thoroughly weigh and compare them with each other, before he can be able to see the light, or fix those creatures to any certain determinate meaning.

[Horsmanden here explains that the slaves' depositions were reconstructed from notes taken at the time, and that although there were no verbatim records, the evidence that the accused gave to the court was always in essence identical to the depositions given beforehand. Horsmanden goes on to explain the necessity of publishing the Journal.*]*

There were reasons indeed, for making these matters public, which could not be withstood.

There had been some wanton, wrong-headed persons amongst us, who took the liberty to arraign the justice of the proceedings, and set up their private opinions in superiority to the court and grand jury; though God knows (and all men of sense know) they could not be judges of such matters; but nevertheless, they declared with no small assurance (notwithstanding what we saw with our eyes, and *heard* with our ears, and every one might have judged of by his intellects, that had any) *that there was no plot at all!* The inference *such* would have drawn from thence, is too obvious to need mentioning; however this moved very little: It was not to *convince* (for that would have been a vain undertaking; *the Ethiopian might as soon change his skin*) much less was it to gratify *such.*

But there were two motives which weighed much; the *one,* that those who had not the opportunity of *seeing* and *hearing,* might judge of the justice of the proceedings, from the state of the case being laid before them; the *other,* that from thence, the people in general, might be persuaded of the necessity there is, for every one that has negroes, to keep a very watchful eye over them, and not to indulge them with too great liberties, which we find they make use of to the worst purposes, caballing and confederating together in mischief, in great numbers, when they may, from the accounts in the ensuing sheets, from what they *see* has happened, *feel* the consequence of giving them so great a latitude, as has been customary in this city and province, and thereby be warned to keep themselves upon a strict guard against *these enemies of their own household,* since we know what they are capable of; for it was notorious, that those among them, who had the kindest masters, who fared best, and had the most liberty, nay, that those in whom their masters placed the greatest confidence, insomuch, that they would even have put their own swords into their hands, in expectation of being defended by them against their own colour, did nevertheless turn out the greatest villains. It even appeared that these *head fellows* boasted of *their superiority* over the more harmless and inoffensive; that they held them in an inferiority and dependence, a kind of subjection, as if they had got such dominion over them, *that they durst not,*[2] *at any time, or upon any occasion, but do as they would have them;* from whence it may be guessed, how likely the defection was to be general.

The principal inducement, therefore, to this undertaking was, *the public benefit;* that those who have property in slaves, might have a lasting memento concerning the nature of them; that they may be thence warned to keep a constant guard over them; since what they have done, they may one time or other act over again, especially if there should in future times, appear *such monsters in nature,* as the *Hughsons, Ury the priest, and such like,* who dare be so wicked as to attempt the seducing them to such execrable purposes: and if any should think it not worth their while to learn from the ensuing sheets (what by others perhaps may be esteemed) *a useful lesson,* the fault will be their own; and really it was thought *necessary,* for these and other reasons needless here to mention, that there should be a standing memorial of so unprecedented a scheme of villainy.

Perhaps it may not come forth *unseasonably* at this *juncture,* if the distractions occasioned by this *mystery of iniquity,* may be thereby so revived in our memories, as to awaken us from that supine security, which again too generally prevails, and put us upon our guard, lest the enemy should be yet within our doors.

City of New-York, 12th April, 1744

INTRODUCTION

The introduction, which sets out the events in the six weeks that preceded the first trial, primarily addresses the thefts and fires that awakened the initial suspicions. The city officials responded by announcing a reward for information and by ordering a search of all the houses in the city for stolen goods. In this section, Horsmanden introduces most of the major figures in the investigation: John and Sarah Hughson, Peggy Kerry (Margaret Sorubiero or Salingburgh), Mary Burton, John Gwin (Caesar), and Cuffee. Although this is not Horsmanden's intent, this section is rich

[2] *durst not:* Dare not.

with details about the social and economic (including shopping) lives of ordinary sailors, servants, slaves, and other working men and women.

Introduction

As a robbery committed at Mr. Hogg's, paved the way to the discovery of the conspiracy, it may not be improper to introduce the ensuing journal and narrative, with an account of that felony, as well as the many fires which alarmed this city, close upon the heels of each other, within less than three weeks, occasioned by this infernal scheme, till they both came under the inquiry and examination of the grand jury, at the Supreme Court: and indeed there is such a close connexion between this felony and the conspiracy, as will appear by the several steps and examinations taken by occasion of the former, that the narrative of the robbery could not well be omitted; for the inquiry concerning that, was the means of drawing out the first hint concerning the other; nay, this felony and such like, were actually ingredients of the conspiracy, as will appear by the sequel.

On Saturday night the 28th February, 1740-1,[3] a robbery was committed at the house of Mr. Robert Hogg, in the city of New-York, merchant, from whence were taken divers[4] pieces of linen and other goods, and several silver coins, chiefly Spanish, and medals, and wrought silver, etc. to the value in the whole, of sixty pounds and upwards.

The occasion of this robbery, as was discovered, and will appear more fully hereafter, was one Wilson, a lad of about seventeen or eighteen years of age, belonging to the Flamborough man of war, on this station, who having acquaintance with two white servants belonging to gentlemen who lodged at Mr. Hogg's house, Wilson used frequently to come thither on that pretence, which gained him easy admittance: but Wilson, it seems, had a more familiar acquaintance with some negroes of very suspicious characters, particularly Caesar, belonging to John Vaarck, baker; Prince, to Mr. John Auboyneau, merchant; and Cuffee, to Adolph Philipse, Esq*[uire]*.

[3] *1740-1:* Until 1752, Britain and the British colonies used an older Julian calendar, while the rest of western Europe had moved to the Gregorian calendar (the calendar that is in use today). According to the Julian ("Old-Style") calendar, the first of the year is on March 25. Thus, most British newspapers and documents until the adoption of the New Style calendar in 1752 labeled dates from January 1 to March 24 with two years (e.g., 1740–41).

[4] *divers:* Several, many.

The Thursday before this robbery was committed, Wilson came to Mr. Hogg's shop, with one of the man of war's people, to buy some check linen, and having bargained for some, part of the money offered in payment, was of Spanish coin, and Mrs. Hogg opening her bureau to change the money, pulled out a drawer in the view of Wilson, wherein were a considerable quantity of milled Spanish pieces of eight;[5] she soon reflected that she had done wrong in exposing her money to an idle boy in that manner, who came so frequently to her house, and immediately shut up the bureau again, and made a pretence of sending the money out to a neighbour's to be weighed.[6]

Mrs. Hogg's apprehensions happened to be right; for this boy having a sight of the money, was charmed with it, and, as it seems, wanted to be fingering of it. He told his comrades of the black guard, the beforenamed Caesar, Prince and Cuffee, where they might have a fine booty, if they could manage cleverly to come at it; he said it was at Hogg's house in the Broad street; his wife kept a shop of goods, and sold candles, rum, molasses, etc.

The negroes catched at the proposal, and the scheme was communicated by them to John Hughson, who kept a public house by the North River, in this city, a place where numbers of negroes used to resort, and be entertained privately (in defiance of the laws) at all hours, as appeared afterwards, and will be shewn at large in the ensuing sheets. Thither they used to bring such goods as they stole from their masters or others, and Hughson, his wife and family, received them: there they held a consultation with Hughson and his family, how they should act, in order to compass the attainment of this booty.

The boy (Wilson) told them the situation of the house and shop; that the front was towards Broad-street, and there was a side door out of the shop into an alley, commonly called the Jews-Alley,[7] and if they

[5]*Spanish pieces of eight:* A Spanish coin, also known as a Spanish dollar. Foreign coins were common in New York, since the colonies were always short of specie (hard currency). Coins from all over Europe as well as the Spanish Empire were always accepted as legal tender throughout the colonies.

[6]Because metal coins were so rare in the colonies, people often clipped metal off the edges of coins, saving the gold or silver filings to melt down. This, in turn, devalued the coinage. Coins had to be weighed to determine if they were heavy enough to be given their full value.

[7]*Jews-Alley* was the colloquial name for Mill Street, on which the Jewish synagogue stood. The synagogue Shearith Israel had opened in 1730. Jews constituted between 1 and 2 percent of the city's population in the 1730s and 1740s. See Leo Hershkowitz and Isidore S. Meyer, introduction to *Letters of the Franks Family (1733–1748)* (Waltham: American Jewish Historical Society, 1968), xix–xx.

could make an errand thither to buy rum, they might get an opportunity to shove back the bolt of the door facing the alley, for there was no lock on it, and they could come in the night afterwards, and accomplish their designs.*

At Hughson's lodged one Margaret Sorubiero, alias Salingburgh, alias Kerry, commonly called Peggy, or the Newfoundland Irish beauty, a young woman about one or two and twenty; she pretended to be married, but no husband appeared; she was a person of infamous character, a notorious prostitute, and also of the worst sort, a prostitute to negroes; she was here lodged and supported by Caesar (Vaarck's) before mentioned, and took share (in common with Hughson's family) of the spoils and plunder, the effects of Caesar's thefts, which he brought to Hughson's; and she may be supposed to have been in most of their wicked secrets; for she had lodged there the summer before: thither also Caesar used frequently to resort, with many other negroes; thither he also conveyed stolen goods, and some part of Hogg's goods.

With this Peggy, as she will be hereafter commonly called, Caesar used frequently to sleep at Hughson's, with the knowledge and permission of the family; and Caesar bargained with and paid Hughson for her board; she came there to lodge a second time in the fall, not long before Christmas, 1740, big with child by Caesar, as was supposed, and brought to bed there not many days before the robbery at Hogg's, of a babe largely partaking of a dark complexion.

Here is laid the foundation of the characters of Hughson and his family, which will afford frequent occasion of enlarging upon; and from such a hopeful earnest[8] the reader may well expect a plentiful harvest.

Wilson coming to Mrs. Hogg's on Sunday morning, to see his acquaintance as usual, she complained to him, that she had been robbed the night before, that she had lost all the goods out of the shop, a great deal of silver Spanish coins, medals and other silver things, little suspecting that he had been the occasion of it, notwithstanding what she apprehended upon pulling out the drawer of money before him, as above; but as she knew he belonged to the man of war, and that several of those sailors frequented idle houses in the Jews-Alley, it happened that her suspicions inclined towards them; she imagined he

*At nights they usually let people in at the front door, in another street, and went through the parlour into the kitchen, which Wilson well knew.

[8]*earnest:* Foretaste; first installment of something to be received later in greater abundance.

might be able to give her some intelligence about it, and therefore described to him some things that she had missed, viz. snuff-boxes, silver medals, one a remarkable eight square piece, etc. Whereupon Wilson said, he had been the morning at Hughson's house, and there saw one John Gwin, who pulled out of his pocket a worsted cap full of pieces of coined silver; and that Mr. Philipse's Cuffee, who was there, seeing John Gwin have this money, he asked him to give him some, and John Gwin counted him out half a crown in pennies, and asked him if he would have any more; and then pulled out a handful of silver coin, amongst which, Wilson said, he saw the eight square piece described by Mrs. Hogg.

SUNDAY, MARCH 1

This morning search was made for John Gwin at Hughson's, supposing him to have been a soldier of that name, a fellow of suspicious character, as Mrs. Hogg conceived; and the officers making inquiry accordingly for a soldier, they were answered, there was no such soldier used that house; but it fell out, that Caesar, the real person wanted, was at the same time before their faces in the Chimney corner: the officer returned without suspecting him to be the person meant, but the mistake being discovered by the boy (Wilson) that the negro Caesar before mentioned went by that name, he was apprehended in the afternoon, and being brought before Wilson, he declared that he was the person he meant by John Gwin.

Caesar was committed to prison.

MONDAY, MARCH 2

Caesar (Vaarck's negro) was examined by the justices, and denied every thing laid to his charge concerning Hogg's robbery, but was remanded.

Prince (Mr. Auboyneau's negro) was this day also apprehended upon account of the same felony: upon examination he denied knowing any thing of it. He was also committed.

Upon information that Caesar had shewn a great deal of silver at Hughson's, it was much suspected that Hughson knew something of the matter, and therefore search was made several times at his house, yesterday and this day, but none of the goods or silver were discovered.

Hughson and his wife were sent for, and were present while the negroes were examined by the justices, and were also examined themselves, touching the things stolen, but discovered[9] nothing; and they were dismissed.

TUESDAY, MARCH 3

Hughson's house having been searched several times over by Mr. Mills, the under-sheriff, and several constables, in quest of Hogg's goods, without effect, it happened this evening, that Mary Burton* came to the house of James Kannady, one of the searching constables, to fetch a pound of candles for her master; Kannady's wife knew the girl by sight, and who she belonged to living in the neighbourhood near them, and having heard of the robbery, and the several searches at Hughson's, she took upon her to examine Mary, "whether she knew any thing of those goods, and admonished her to discover if she did, lest she herself should be brought into trouble, and gave her motherly good advice, and said if she knew any thing of it, and would tell, she would get her freed from her master." Whereupon at parting, the girl said, "she could not tell her then, she would tell her tomorrow; but that her husband was not cute[10] enough, for that he had trod upon them," and so went away. This alarmed Kannady and his wife, and the same evening Ann Kannady went to Mr. Mills, the under-sheriff, and told him what had passed between her and Mary Burton. "Whereupon Mills and his wife, Mr. Hogg and his wife, and several constables, went with Ann Kannady and her husband, down to Hughson's house; and Ann Kannady desired the under-sheriff to go in first, and bring Mary Burton out to her; but he staying a long time, Ann Kannady went into Hughson's house; and found the under-sheriff and his wife, and Mary Burton, in the parlour, and she then denied what she had before said to Ann Kannady, as above; then Ann Kannady charged her home with it; till at length, Mary Burton said she could not tell them any thing there, she was afraid of her life; that they would kill her. Whereupon they took the girl out of the house, and when they had got a little way from thence, she put her hand in her pocket, and pulled out a piece of silver money, which she said was part of Hogg's money, which the negro had given her. They all went to Alderman Bancker's with her, and Ann Kannady informing the alderman, that she had promised Mary Burton to get her freed from her master; he directed

[9] *discover:* To divulge or reveal a secret.
*An indentured servant to John Hughson, came to him about mid-summer, 1740.
[10] *cute:* Acute, or sharp.

that she should lodge that night with the under-sheriff at the City-Hall for safety; and she was left there accordingly." For Mary Burton declared also, before the alderman, her apprehensions and fears, that she should be murdered or poisoned by the Hughsons and the negroes, for what she should discover.

The alderman sent for John Hughson, and examined him closely, whether he knew any thing of the matter? but he denied that he did at first, until the alderman pressed him very home[11] and admonished him (if it was in his power) to discover those who had committed this piece of villainy; little suspecting him to have been previously concerned; he was at last prevailed with to acknowledge he knew where some of the things were hid, and he went home, fetched and delivered them.

WEDNESDAY, MARCH 4

This day the mayor having summoned the justices to meet at the City-Hall, several aldermen met him accordingly, and sent for Mary Burton and John Hughson and his wife; and Mary Burton, after examination, made the following deposition before them.

"Mary Burton, of the city of New-York, Spinster,[12] aged about sixteen years, being sworn, deposed,

1. "That about two o'clock on Sunday morning last, a negro man who goes by the name of John Gwin (or Quin) came to the house of John Hughson, the deponent's [Mary Burton's] master, and went in at the window where one Peggy lodges, where he lay all night.

2. "That in the morning she saw some speckled linen in the said Peggy's room; that the said negro then gave the deponent two pieces of silver, and bid Peggy cut off an apron of the linen and give to the deponent, which she did accordingly.

3. "That at the same time the said negro bought a pair of white stockings from her master, for which he was to give six shillings; that the said negro had two mugs of punch, for which, and the stockings, he gave her master a lump of silver.

4. "That her master and mistress saw the linen the same morning.

5. "That soon after Mr. Mills came to inquire for one John Quin, a soldier, who he said, had robbed Mr. Hogg of some speckled linen, silver, and other things.

[11] *home:* Closely, thoroughly, directly.
[12] *Spinster:* Here, any unmarried woman.

6. "That after Mr. Mills was gone, her mistress hid the linen in the garret; and soon after some officers came and searched the house; and when they were gone and found nothing, her mistress took the linen from the place she had before hid it in, and hid it under the stairs.

7. "That the night before last, her master and mistress gave the said linen to her mistress's mother,* who carried it away. . . .

9. "That the said negro usually slept with the said Peggy, which her master and mistress knew of."

Upon this occasion, it seems, Hughson and his wife, finding that Mary Burton was inclinable to discover them in their villainy, touching this robbery, thought proper to say something to blacken her character, in order to take off from the credit of her testimony, and declared that she was a vile, good-for-nothing girl, or words to that purpose; that she had been got with child by her former master, etc. the truth whereof, however, was never made out. But at length Hughson finding that he was near going to jail, and as fearing the consequence of provoking her, changed his note, and said she was a very good girl, and had been a trusty servant to them: that in the hard weather last winter, she used to dress herself in man's clothes, put on boots, and went with him in his sleigh, in the deep snows into the commons, to help him fetch firewood for his family, etc.

The deputy town clerk, when Mary Burton was under examination, as he was taking her deposition, exhorted her to speak the truth, and all she knew of the matter; she answered him, that she hardly dared to speak, she was so much afraid she should be murdered by them; or words to that purpose. Whereupon the clerk moved the justices, that she might be taken care, not knowing that she had been removed from her master's the night before, by order of a magistrate.

After Mary Burton, John Hughson and his wife, and Peggy, were examined: Peggy denied every thing, and spoke in favour of Hughson and his wife: Peggy was committed, and John Hughson confessed as followeth:

Examination.—1. John Hughson said, "That on Monday evening last, after Mr. Mills had been to search his house for goods which had been stolen from Mr. Hogg, one Peggy, who lodged at his house, told him that John Quin had left some checked linen and other things with her; that she delivered to the examinant the said checked linen, which he delivered to the mother-in-law Elizabeth Luckstead, with directions

*Elizabeth Luckstead.

to hide them: that soon after the said Peggy delivered him sundry silver things in a little bag; which he carried into the cellar, and put behind a barrel, and put a broad stone upon them, where they remained till last night about ten or eleven o'clock, when he delivered them to alderman Johnson and alderman Bancker.[13]

2. "That while the said silver things lay concealed in his cellar, the constables came and searched his house for the said stolen goods, but did not find them.

3. "That this morning the said Peggy gave him a little bundle with several silver pieces in it; which he soon afterwards brought into court, and delivered it to the justices then present."

Hughson absolutely refused to sign the examination, after it was read over to him; and thereupon the deputy town clerk asked him if it was not true as he had penned it; he answered, yes, it was, but he thought there was no occasion for him to sign it. He was admitted to bail, and his wife Sarah likewise; and recognizances[14] were entered into with two sureties each, for their appearance in the Supreme Court on the first day of the next term.

Caesar and Prince were likewise again examined, but would confess nothing concerning the robbery; Caesar was remanded, and Prince admitted to bail upon his master's entering into recognizance in ten pounds penalty, for his appearance at the next Supreme Court.

But Caesar acknowledged, that what Mary Burton had deposed concerning him and Peggy, as to his sleeping with her, was true.

Deposition.—John Vaarck, of the city of New-York, baker, being duly sworn and examined, saith,

1. "That about two o'clock this afternoon, his negro boy told him, there were some things hid under the floor of his kitchen: that thereupon he went to look, and found the linen and plates, now shewn him, which he took out, and carried to the mayor. . . .

WEDNESDAY, MARCH 18

[Early in the afternoon, the roof of the governor's house inside the fort caught fire. The chapel next to it quickly caught as well, and despite a

[13]Aldermen were elected officials, one from each of the seven wards, who served on the city's Common Council.

[14]*recognizance:* A legal bond to return when called by the court.

bucket brigade and fire engines, both buildings, along with the governor's offices and stables, were totally destroyed. The fire did not spread outside the fort, but it was hot enough to burn for a full thirty-six hours.]

Mr. Cornelius Van Horne, a captain of one of the companies of the militia, very providentially beat to arms in the evening, and drew out his men with all expedition; had seventy odd of them under arms all night, and parties of them continually going the rounds of the city until day light. This incident, from what will appear hereafter, may be thought to have been a very fortunate one, and deserving of a more particular remark, though at that time *some people were so infatuated,*[15] *as to reproach that gentleman for it, as a madman.*

The only way of accounting for this misfortune at this time was, the lieutenant governor[16] had ordered a plummer[17] that morning to mend a leak in the gutter between the house and the chapel which joined upon one another, and the man carrying his fire-pot with coals to keep his soddering-iron hot, to perform his work; and the wind setting into the gutter, it was thought some sparks had been blown out upon the shingles of the house; but some people having observed, that upon the first alarm, as before, near half the roof, as they guessed, was covered with smoke, and that no spark of fire appeared without, nor could any be seen, but within; it was by them concluded, that the reason assigned was not likely to be the right one, especially when it was considered, that at length the fire broke out in several places of the roof, distant from each other, but no one imagined it was done on purpose.

FRIDAY, MARCH 20

Prince, the negro of Mr. Auboyneau, who was bailed out of prison, as before mentioned, was recommitted by the mayor, and alderman Bancker.

WEDNESDAY, MARCH 25

[Exactly one week later, Captain Peter Warren's house caught fire. There was little damage, and people initially assumed it was a chimney fire.]

[15]*infatuated:* Foolish.

[16]The lieutenant governor was the highest-ranking British official in New York in 1741; the appointed governor remained in England and never came to New York to take up his position.

[17]*plummer:* Plumber.

Philipse → Cuff

Auboyneau → Prince

Vaarck → Caesar / John Gwin

Walter → Quaco

WEDNESDAY, APRIL 1

[Precisely one week later, Winant Van Zant's warehouse near the docks by the East River caught fire. This fire, too, was caught before it spread beyond incinerating the warehouse and its contents. This time, a man smoking a pipe on the haystacks stored inside was blamed for the fire.]

SATURDAY, APRIL 4

[In the evening, there were reports of two fires. One was in a stable owned by a Mr. Quick in Maiden Lane, near the East River, the other a few smoldering coals near the straw bed of a slave in Ben Thomas's house, which stood next door to the house of a privateering captain.]

SUNDAY, APRIL 5

[The next day someone found coals in the bottom of a haystack near attorney Joseph Murray's stable, on the south end of Broadway, but the embers were extinguished before the fire caught. Some people claimed that there was a path of coals leading to the neighboring house, an aspersion that cast some suspicion on the slave that lived there.]

The *five* several fires, viz. at the fort, captain Warren's house, Van Zant's store-house, Quick's stable, and Ben Thomas's kitchen, having happened in so short a time succeeding each other; and the attempt made of a sixth on Mr. Murray's haystack; it was natural for people of any reflection, to conclude that the fire was set on purpose by a combination of villains, and therefore occasioned great uneasiness to every one that had thought; but upon this supposition nobody imagined there could be any further design; than for some wicked wretches to have the opportunity of making a prey of their neighbour's goods, under pretence of assistance in removing them for security from the danger of flames; for upon these late instances, many of the sufferers had complained of great losses of their goods, and furniture, which had been removed from their houses upon these occasions.

This Sunday as three negroes were walking up the Broadway towards the English church, about service time, Mrs. Earle looking out of her window, overheard one of them saying to his companions, with a vaporing[18] sort of an air, "Fire, Fire, Scorch, Scorch, A LITTLE, damn it, BY-AND-BY," and then threw up his hands and laughed; the woman

[18] *vaporing:* Boasting or grandiloquent.

conceived great jealousy[19] at these words, and thought it very odd behaviour at that juncture, considering what had so lately happened; and she putting the natural construction upon them her apprehensions made her uneasy, and she immediately spoke of it to her next neighbour Mrs. George, but said she did not know any of the negroes.

About an hour after, when church was out, Mrs. Earle saw the same negroes coming down the Broadway again, and pointed out to Mrs. George the person who had spoke the words, and Mrs. George knew him, and said that it is Mr. Walter's Quaco.

These words, and the airs and graces given them by Quaco when he uttered them, were made known to a neighbouring alderman, who informed the rest of the justices thereof at their meeting the next day.

MONDAY, APRIL 6

[On this day four different fires broke out. The first was near the fort. The second was at the house of Mrs. Hilton, which stood next to Captain Jacob Sarly's house on the other side.]

But there was a cry among the people, the Spanish negroes; *the Spanish negroes; take up the Spanish negroes.* The occasion of this was the two fires (Thomas's and Hilton's) happening so closely together, only one day intervening, on each side of captain Sarly's house; and it being known that Sarly had purchased a Spanish negro, some time before brought into this port, among several others, in a prize taken by captain Lush;[20] all which negroes were condemned as slaves, in the court of Admiralty, and sold accordingly at vendue;[21] and that they afterwards pretending to have been free men in their own country, began to grumble at their hard usage, of being sold as slaves. This probably gave rise to the suspicion, that this negro, out of revenge, had been the instrument of these two fires; and he behaving himself insolently upon some people's asking him questions concerning them, which signified their distrust; it was told to a magistrate who was near, and he ordered him to gaol,[22] and also gave direction to constables to commit all the rest of that cargo, in order for their safe custody and examination.

[19]*jealousy:* Suspicion, mistrust.

[20]John Lush was one of New York's most successful privateers. The five Spaniards accused in the conspiracy were among the twenty sailors he had brought into New York as part of his prizes in 1739 and 1740 (*New-York Weekly Journal,* May 5, 1740).

[21]*vendue:* Auction.

[22]*gaol:* Jail.

[That afternoon, as the magistrates were examining Captain Sarly's slave Juan, Adolph Philipse's storehouse caught fire in the third conflagration of the day; soon thereafter an alarm for a fourth fire rang out.]

While the people were extinguishing the fire at this storehouse, and had almost mastered it, there was another cry of fire, which diverted the people attending the storehouse, to the new alarm, very few remaining behind; but a man who had been on the top of the house, assisting in extinguishing the fire, saw a negro leap out at the end window of one of them, from thence making over several garden fences in great haste; which occasioned him to cry out, *a negro; a negro;* and that was soon improved into an alarm, *that the negroes were rising:* The negro made very good speed home to his master's; he was generally known, and the swiftness of his flight occasioned his being remarked, though scarce any knew the reason, but a few which remained at the storehouse, why the word was given, *a negro, a negro;* it was immediately changed into *Cuff Philipse, Cuff Philipse:* The people ran to Mr. Philipse's house in quest of him; he was got in at the back door; and being found, was dragged out of the house, and carried to jail, borne upon the people's shoulders. He was a fellow of general ill character; his master being a single man, and little at home, Cuff had a great deal of idle time, which, it seems, he employed to very ill purposes, and had acquired a general bad fame.

Many people had such terrible apprehensions upon this occasion, and indeed there was cause sufficient, that several negroes (and many had been assisting at the fire at the storehouse, and many perhaps that only seemed to be so) who were met in the streets, after the alarm of their rising, were hurried away to jail; and when they were there, they were continued some time in confinement, before the magistrates could spare time to examine into their several cases, how and for what they came there, many others first coming under consideration before them, against whom there seemed to be more direct cause of suspicion; but in a few days, those against whom nothing in particular was alleged, were discharged.

Quack (Walter's) was sent for and committed; he remained in confinement some days without examination, from the hurry the magistrates were in; but at length, Mrs. Earle and Mrs. George being sent for by the justices, they declared concerning him to the effect before

*Sunday, 5th April.

mentioned:* and Quack being brought before them, and examined, by his excuse admitted he had spoken the words he was charged with; but it being soon after we had the news of admiral Vernon's taking Porto Bello, he had contrived a cunning excuse, or some abler heads for him, to account for the occasion of them, and brought two of his own complexion to give their words for it also, that they were talking of admiral Vernon's taking Porto Bello; and that he thereupon signified to his companions, that he thought that was but a small feat to what this brave officer would do by-and-by, to annoy the Spaniards, or words tantamount; so that it happened Quack was enlarged from his confinement for some time.

Others considering that it was but eighteen days after the fort was laid in ashes, that these words were uttered; and that several other fires had intervened, as before related, and but the next day after Quick's stable and Ben Thomas's house were on fire; and the attempt upon Mr. Murray's haystack discovered that very morning; they were apt to put a different construction upon Quack's words and behaviour; that he thereby meant, "that the fires which we had seen already, were nothing to what we should have by-and-by, for that then we should have all the city in flames, and he would rejoice at it;" for it was said he lifted up his hands, and spread them with a circular sweep over his head, after he had pronounced the words (by-and-by) and then concluded with a loud laugh. Whether these figures are thus more properly applied, the reader will hereafter be better able to judge; but the construction of them at that time confirmed many in the notion of a conspiracy; though they could not suspect one of so black a dye, as there were afterwards flagrant proofs of, and will appear by and by.

His honour the lieutenant governor was pleased to order a military watch to be kept this evening, and the same was continued all the summer after.

John Hughson and Sarah his wife were committed to jail by the mayor and three aldermen, being charged as accessories to divers felonies and misdemeanors.

SATURDAY, APRIL 11

The recorder[23] taking notice of the several fires which had lately happened in this city and the manner of them, the frequency of them, and the causes being yet undiscovered; must necessarily conclude, that

[23]Horsmanden.

they were occasioned and set on foot by some villainous confederacy of latent enemies amongst us; but with what intent or purpose, time must discover . . . he therefore moved, "that the board *[The Common Council]* should come to a resolution to pay such rewards as should by them be thought a proper and sufficient temptation to induce any party or parties concerned to make such discovery."

Upon consideration whereof, it was "*ordered,* That this board request his honour the lieutenant governor to issue a proclamation, offering a reward to any white person that should discover any person or persons lately concerned in setting fire to any dwelling-house or storehouse in this city (so that such person or persons be convicted thereof,) the sum of *one hundred pounds,* current money of this province; and that such person shall be pardoned, if concerned therein. Any slave that should make discovery, to be manumitted, or made free; and the master of such slave to receive *twenty-five pounds* therefor; and the slave to receive, besides his freedom, the sum of *twenty pounds,* and to be pardoned; and if a free negro, mulatto,[24] or Indian, to receive *forty-five pounds,* and also to be pardoned, if concerned therein. And that this board will issue their warrant to the chamberlain, or treasurer of this corporation for the payment of such sum as any person, by virtue of such proclamation, shall be entitled unto. And that the mayor and recorder wait on his honour the lieutenant governor, and acquaint him with the resolution of this board."

Many persons in the neighbourhood of the several fires before mentioned, thought it necessary to remove their household goods for safety; and in their consternation, as was natural, suffered any body who offered their assistance, to take them away; by which means, some villains had the cruelty to make prey of them; for there were great complaints of losses upon those occasions, which the magistrates took this day into their consideration: and it being much suspected that there were some strangers lurking about the city, who had upon the supposition only, that by those means, they might have opportunities of pilfering and plundering. A scheme was proposed, that there should be a general search of all houses throughout the town, whereby it was thought probable discoveries might be made, not only of stolen goods, but likewise of lodgers, that were strangers, and suspicious persons. The proposal was approved of, and each alderman and his common council-man, with constables attending them,

[24]*mulatto:* Mixed-race.

undertook to search his respective ward on the south side of the fresh water pond; and the Monday following was the day fixed upon for making the experiment.

The scheme was communicated to the governor, and his honour thought fit to order the militia out that day in aid of the magistrates, who were to be dispersed through the city, and sentries of them posted at the ends of streets to guard all avenues, with orders to stop all suspected persons that should be observed carrying bags or bundles, or removing goods from house to house, in order for their examination; and all this was to be kept very secret till the project was put in execution.

MONDAY, APRIL 13

Pursuant to the scheme concerted on Saturday last, the general search was made; but there were not any goods discovered which were said to have been lost, nor was there any strange lodger or suspicious persons detected. But some things were found in the custody of Robin, Mr. Chamber's negro, and Cuba his wife, which the alderman thought improper for, and unbecoming the condition of slaves, which made him suspect they were not come honestly by; and therefore ordered the constable to take them in possession, to be reserved for further inquiry: and these two negroes were committed.

FRIDAY, APRIL 17

The lieutenant governor, by and with the advice of his majesty's council, issued a proclamation, therein reciting the before mentioned order and resolution of the common council, promising the rewards agreeable thereto.

In the mean while, between the sixth and seventeenth instant,[25] a great deal of time had been spent by the magistrates in the examination of the negroes in custody, upon account of these fires, but nothing could be got out of them.

Cuff (Philipse's) was closely interrogated, but he absolutely denied knowing any thing of the matter. He said he had been at home all that afternoon, from the time he returned from Hilton's fire, where he had been to assist and carry buckets. That he was at home when the bell rung for the fire at Col. Philipse's storehouse. It appeared, upon

[25]*instant:* Of the current calendar month.

inquiry and examination of witnesses, that he, according to his master's orders, had been sawing wood, that afternoon with a white boy; and that when his master came home from dinner, he took him off from that work, and set him to sew on a vane[26] upon a board for his sloop; the white boy testified, "that he stood by him to see him sew it, and that he left him but a little before the bell rung for the fire." And when the alarm of the fire was, and that it was supposed to be at his master's storehouse, it was said, Cuff asked whether he would go out with the buckets, and that he should answer, he had enough of being out, in the morning. Some of the neighbours also declared, that they had seen him looking over his master's door but a little before the bell rung; but an old man who had known Cuffee for several years, deposed, that he had seen him at the fire at the storehouse, and that he stood next him: there seemed to be some objection against the man's evidence; it was thought he might be mistaken, being very near sighted. Upon examination, it was found he could distinguish colours, and he described the clothes he had on, and moreover declared, he spoke to him, and asked him, why he did not hand the buckets; and that thereupon he answered him, and did hand water, and that he knew his voice.

There was very strong proof that he was the negro that leaped out of the window of one of the storehouses as the fire was extinguished, and most of the people drawn away upon the new alarm of a fire; that he was seen to leap over several garden fences, and to run home in great haste.

Upon the whole, it was thought proper Cuff should remain in confinement, to await further discovery.

LARCENY: THE TRIALS OF CAESAR AND PRINCE

When the trial opened, the court's suspicions initially focused on the theft at the Hoggs' and the discovery of the stolen goods at the Hughsons'. Mary Burton's testimony first implicated the Hughsons, Kerry, Caesar, and Prince. With seeming reluctance, she also hinted to the judges that she knew something about a plot larger than a mere theft. With the help of a prison informer named Arthur Price, the court brought a case against the Hughsons and Kerry for receiving stolen goods. Price, a white servant who was in jail for stealing the lieutenant governor's goods from his own

[26]*vane:* A weather vane. Here, a strip of cloth, or tell-tale, that indicates the direction of the wind.

master's house, may have plea-bargained his own case in return for the information. Caesar and Prince were swiftly convicted and executed.

The court also began to collect evidence from Burton, Price, and Peggy Kerry about the involvement of whites in these undertakings. Notice how important the evidence and participation of white women were to the description of the thefts.

As the evidence for an interracial conspiracy mounted, Horsmanden and his colleagues on the bench insisted that the plot was too difficult for slaves to have developed alone, without the help of whites. While the condescending comments of the court make clear the judges' disdain for the slaves, the judges also took great pains to point out the fairness of the trials. The complexity of racial attitudes is apparent, not just in the judges' and lawyers' statements, but also in the depositions of the witnesses and the accused. The relationship between white women and black men is particularly complicated.

It is helpful to take careful note of statements like that of number 9 in Burton's first deposition (see p. 68). Such statements are interesting for two reasons. First, they indicate clearly the sorts of questions that officials were asking: "What white people (or possibly 'other white people') were present?" Such statements are also useful for tracking the movement of the trials from the investigation of a small larceny ring to that of an international conspiracy. Pay attention to how witnesses' statements shifted over time and how judges and juries reconciled or rejected these changes.

The court's inquiries until the middle of May concentrated on stolen goods, but hints of a more destructive and far-ranging conspiracy quickly emerged. Burton's first deposition, in which she refused to discuss the fires even before she was asked about them, immediately whetted the grand jury's interest. Although the trials for conspiracy to commit arson came later, much of the evidence for those trials surfaced earlier. This pattern, of the evidence from one trial leading to the investigation of another, is one that you will find throughout the transcripts.

TUESDAY, APRIL 21, 1741

[The grand jury was called and sworn.]

Mr. Justice Philipse gave the charge to the grand jury, as followeth:

"*Gentlemen of the grand jury,*

"It is not without some concern, that I am obliged at this time to be more particular in your charge, than for many preceding terms there hath been occasion. The many frights and terrors which the good people of this city have of late been put into, by repeated and unusual fires, and burning of houses, give us too much room to suspect, that some of them at least, did not proceed from mere chance, or common accidents; but on the contrary, from the premeditated malice and wicked pursuits of evil and designing persons; and therefore, it greatly behoves us to use our utmost diligence, by all lawful ways and means, to discover the contrivers and perpetrators of such daring and flagitious undertakings: that, upon conviction, they may receive condign[27] punishment. . . .

"I am told there are several prisoners now in jail, who have been committed by the city magistrates, upon suspicion of having been concerned in some of the late fires; and others, who under pretence of assisting the unhappy sufferers, by saving their goods from the flames, for stealing, or receiving them. This indeed, is adding affliction to the afflicted, and is a very great aggravation of such crime, and therefore deserves a narrow[28] inquiry: that so the exemplary punishment of the guilty (if any such should be so found) may deter others from committing the like villainies; for this kind of stealing, I think, has not been often practised among us.

"*Gentlemen,*

"Arson, or the malicious and voluntary burning, not only a mansion house, but also any other house, and the out buildings, or barns, and stables adjoining thereto, by night or by day, is felony at common law; and if any part of the house be burned, the offender is guilty of felony, notwithstanding the fire afterwards be put out, or go out of itself.

"This crime is of so shocking a nature, that if we have any in this city, who, having been guilty thereof, should escape, who can say he is safe, or tell where it will end?

"*Gentlemen,*

"Another Thing which I cannot omit recommending to your serious and diligent inquiry, is to find out and present all such persons who sell rum, and other strong liquor to negroes. It must be obvious to every one, that there are too many of them in this city; who, under pretence of selling what they call a penny dram[29] to a negro, will sell to him as many quarts or gallons of rum, as he can steal money or goods to pay for.

[27] *condign:* Appropriate, fitting.

[28] *narrow:* Strict, precise.

[29] *penny dram:* A small drink, about an eighth of an ounce, that could be bought for one penny. As Philipse explains, a "penny dram" was usually rum.

"How this notion of its being lawful to sell a penny dram, or a pennyworth of rum to a slave, without the consent or direction of his master, has prevailed, I know not; but this I am sure of, that there is not only no such law, but that the doing of it is directly contrary to an act of the assembly now in force, *for the better regulating of slaves.*[30] The many fatal consequences flowing from this prevailing and wicked practice, are so notorious, and so nearly concern us all, that one would be almost surprised, to think there should be a necessity for a court to recommend a suppressing of such pernicious houses: thus much in particular; now in general.[31]

"My charge, gentlemen, further is, to present all conspiracies, combinations, and other offences, from treasons down to trespasses; and in your inquiries, the oath you, and each of you have just now taken will, I am persuaded, be your guide, and I pray God to direct and assist you in the discharge of your duty."

WEDNESDAY, APRIL 22

The grand jury having been informed, that Mary Burton could give them some account concerning the goods stolen from Mr. Hogg's, sent for her this morning, and ordered she should be sworn; the constable returned and acquainted them, that she said she would not be sworn, nor give evidence; whereupon they ordered the constable to get a warrant from a magistrate, to bring her before them. The constable was some time gone, but at length returned, and brought her with him; and being asked why she would not be sworn, and give her evidence? she told the grand jury she would not be sworn; and seemed to be under some great uneasiness, or terrible apprehensions; which gave suspicion that she knew something concerning the fires that had lately happened: and being asked a question to that purpose, she gave no answer; which increased the jealousy that she was privy to them; and as it was thought a matter of the utmost concern, the grand jury was very importunate, and used many arguments with her, in public and private, to persuade her to speak the truth, and tell all

[30]This act, its full title "An Act for the more Effectual Preventing and Punishing the Conspiracy and Insurrection of Negro and other Slaves; for the better regulating them and for repealing the Acts herein Mentioned Relating thereto," was passed on October 29, 1730 and remained the primary slave code. The legislature did not pass a new slave code after the 1741 trials, although they had done so after the 1712 uprising. The 1712 Act was called "An Act for preventing Suppressing and punishing the Conspiracy and Insurrection of Negroes and other Slaves." *New York Colonial Laws,* I: 250, December 10, 1712.

[31]On July 23, the Supreme Court indicted ten people for keeping disorderly houses; all pled guilty and paid fines.

she knew about it. To this end, the lieutenant governor's proclamation was read to her, promising indemnity, and the reward of one hundred pounds to any person, confederate or not, who should make discovery, etc. She seemed to despise it, nor could the grand jury by any means, either threats or promises, prevail upon her, though they assured her withal, that she should have the protection of the magistrates, and her person be safe and secure from harm; but hitherto all was in vain: therefore the grand jury desired alderman Bancker to commit her; and the constable was charged with her accordingly; but before he had got her to jail, she considered better of it, and resolved to be sworn, and give her evidence in the afternoon.

Accordingly, she being sworn, came before the grand jury; but as they were proceeding to her examination, and before they asked her any questions, she told them she would acquaint them with what she knew relating to the goods stolen from Mr. Hogg's, but would say nothing about the fires.

This expression thus, as it were providentially, slipping from the evidence, much alarmed the grand jury; for, as they naturally concluded, it did by construction amount to an affirmative, that she could give an account of the occasion of the several fires; and therefore, as it highly became those gentlemen in the discharge of their trust, they determined to use their utmost diligence to sift out the discovery, but still she remained inflexible, till at length, having recourse to religious topics, representing to her the heinousness of the crime which she would be guilty of, if she was privy to, and could discover so wicked a design, as the firing houses about our ears; whereby not only people's estates would be destroyed, but many persons might lose their lives in the flames: this she would have to answer for at the day of judgment, as much as any person immediately concerned, because she might have prevented this destruction, and would not; so that a most damnable sin would lie at her door; and what need she fear from her divulging it; she was sure of the protection of the magistrates? or the grand jury expressed themselves in words to the same purpose; which arguments at last prevailed, and she gave the following evidence, which however, notwithstanding what had been said, came from her, as if still under some terrible apprehensions or restraints.

Deposition, No. 1.—Mary Burton, being sworn, deposeth,

1. "That Prince* and Caesar† brought the things of which they had robbed Mr. Hogg, to her master, John Hughson's house, and that they

*Mr. Auboyneau's negro.
†Vaarck's negro.

were handed in through the window, Hughson, his wife, and Peggy receiving them, about two or three o'clock on a Sunday morning.*

2. "That Caesar, Prince, and Mr. Philipse's negro man (Cuffee) used to meet frequently at her master's house, and that she had heard them (the negroes) talk frequently of burning the fort; and that they would go down to the fly† and burn the whole town; and that her master and mistress said, they would aid and assist them as much as they could.

3. "That in their common conversation they used to say, that when all this was done, Caesar should be governor, and Hughson, her master, should be king.

4. "That Cuffee used to say, that a great many people had too much, and others too little; that his old master had a great deal of money, but that, in a short time, he should have less, and that he (Cuffee) should have more.

5. "That at the same time when the things of which Mr. Hogg was robbed, were brought to her master's house, they brought some indigo and bees wax, which was likewise received by her master and mistress.

6. "That at the meetings of the three aforesaid negroes, Caesar, Prince, and Cuffee, at her master's house, they used to say, in their conversations, that when they set fire to the town, they would do it in the night, and as the white people came to extinguish it, they would kill and destroy them.[32]

7. "That she has known at times, seven or eight guns in her master's house, and some swords, and that she has seen twenty or thirty negroes at one time in her master's house; and that at such large meetings, the three aforesaid negroes, Cuffee, Prince, and Caesar, were generally present, and most active, and that they used to say, that the other negroes durst not refuse to do what they commanded them, and they were sure that they had a number sufficient to stand by them.

8. "That Hughson (her master) and her mistress used to threaten, that if she, the deponent, ever made mention of the goods stolen from Mr. Hogg, they would poison her; and the negroes swore, if ever she published, or discovered the design of burning the town, they would burn her whenever they met her.

*1st March, 1740. [New Style, 1741.—Ed.]

†The east end of the city.

[32]This is a reference to the 1712 rebellion, in which the slaves also ambushed whites as they came to put out a fire.

9. "That she never saw any white person in company when they talked of burning the town, but her master, her mistress, and Peggy."

This evidence of a conspiracy, not only to burn the city, but also destroy and murder the people, was most astonishing to the grand jury, and that any white people should become so abandoned as to confederate with slaves in such an execrable and detestable purpose, could not but be very amazing to every one that heard it; what could scarce be credited; but that the several fires had been occasioned by some combination of villains, was, at the time of them, naturally to be collected from the manner and circumstances attending them.

The grand jury therefore, as it was a matter of the utmost consequence, thought it necessary to inform the judges concerning it, in order that the most effectual measures might be concerted, for discovering the confederates; and the judges were acquainted with it accordingly.

THURSDAY, APRIL 23

It was considered, that though there was an act of the province for trying negroes, as in other colonies, for all manner of offences by the justices, etc. in a summary way; yet as this was a scheme of villainy in which white people were confederated with them, and most probably were the first movers and seducers of the slaves; from the nature of such a conjunction, there was reason to apprehend there was a conspiracy of deeper design and more dangerous contrivance than the slaves themselves were capable of; it was thought a matter that required great secrecy, as well as the utmost diligence, in the conduct of the inquiry concerning it: and upon the whole, it was judged most advisable, as there was an absolute necessity that a matter of this nature and consequence should be fathomed as soon as possible. . . .

Margaret Kerry, commonly called Peggy, committed for Hogg's Robbery, being impeached[33] by Mary Burton, as one of the conspirators, the judges examined her in prison in the evening; they exhorted her to make an ingenuous[34] confession and discovery of what she knew of it, and gave her hopes of their recommendation to the governor for a pardon, if they could be of opinion that she deserved it, assuring her (as the case was) that they had his honour's permission to give hopes of mercy to such criminals as should confess their guilt, and they should think proper to recommend to him as fit and proper

[33]*impeach:* Give accusatory evidence against.
[34]*ingenuous:* Honest, frank.

objects; but she withstood it, and positively denied that she knew any thing of the matter; and said, that if she should accuse any body of any such thing, she must accuse innocent persons, and wrong her own soul. She had this day been examined by the grand jury, and positively denied knowing any thing about the fires.

FRIDAY, MAY 1

[Caesar and Prince were arraigned on charges of two robberies: the Hoggs' and Abraham Meyers Cohen's, both on March 1, 1740.]

To each of which indictments they pleaded, *not guilty.*

The prisoners upon their defence denied the charge against them. And,

The evidence being summed up, which was very strong and full, and the jury charged, they withdrew; and being returned, found them guilty of the indictments.

SUNDAY, MAY 3

Arthur Price, servant to captain Vincent Pearse, having been committed, upon a charge of stealing out of his master's house several goods belonging to the lieutenant governor, which had been removed thither for safe custody from the fire at the fort; he informed the under-sheriff, that he had some discourse in the jail with Peggy, which he would communicate to a magistrate: the under-sheriff acquainted one of the judges therewith, and he examined Price in the evening, and the following deposition was taken.

Deposition, No. 1.—Arthur Price being duly sworn, saith,

1. "That about the beginning of last week, Peggy Carey, or Kerry, now in jail, came to the hole in the prison door, in which he is confined, and told him, she was very much afraid of those fellows (meaning the negroes, as he understood) telling or discovering something of her; but, said she, if they do, by God, I will hang them every one; but that she would not *forswear** herself, unless they brought her in. Upon which the deponent asked her, Peggy, how *forswear* yourself? To which she answered, there is fourteen sworn. Upon which he further asked her, what, is it about Mr. Hogg's goods? And she replied, no, by G–d, about the fire. Upon which the deponent said to her, what,

*What she meant by forswearing herself, will be better guessed at hereafter. [*Forswear:* To deny an oath or go back on a promise.—Ed.]

Peggy, were you a going to set the town on fire? And she made answer, she was not; but said, by G–d, since I knew of it, they made me swear. Upon which the deponent asked her, was John and his wife in it? (meaning John Hughson and his wife.) And she answered, yes, by G–d, they were both sworn as well as the rest. Then the deponent asked her, if she was not afraid that the negroes would discover her? And she said no; for Prince, Cuff and Caesar, and Forck's (Vaarck's) negro, were all true-hearted fellows. Then he asked her, if Caesar was not Forck's negro? And she answered, no, by G–d, it was the other;* but what other she meant he did not know.

2. "That yesterday in the afternoon the said Peggy came to him again, and told him, she had no stomach to eat her victuals; for that bitch (meaning Hughson's maid† as he understood) has fetched me in, and made me as black as the rest, about the indigo, and Mr. Hogg's goods: but if they did hang the two poor fellows below (meaning Caesar and Prince, as understood) they (meaning the rest of the negroes) would be revenged on them yet; but if they sent them away, it was another case. Upon which this deponent said to Peggy, I don't doubt but they will endeavour to poison this girl that has sworn, (meaning Hughson's maid.) And Peggy replied, no, by G–d, I don't believe that; but they will be revenged on them some other ways: And she further said to the deponent, for your life and soul of you, you son of a b—h, don't speak a word of what I have told you."

WEDNESDAY, MAY 6

[John and Sarah Hughson and Peggy Kerry were all indicted for receiving stolen goods on March 3. All pled not guilty.]

The conviction of Caesar and Prince read.

The examination of Hughson before the justices read.

And the charge against them being fully proved; the evidence summed upon; the arguments closed, and the jury charged, they withdrew; and being returned, found them all guilty.

Sarah Hughson, single woman, daughter of John Hughson and Sarah his wife, was this morning committed as one of the confederates in the conspiracy, being apprehended while the court was sitting.

Jack (Sleydall's negro) was this day committed on suspicion of putting fire to Mr. Murray's haystack.

*Bastian, alias Tom Peal, also belonging to Vaarck.
†Mary Burton.

THURSDAY, MAY 7, A.M.

Deposition taken before the judges—No. 2. Arthur Price being duly sworn, saith,

1. "That yesterday morning having discourse with Sarah, the daughter of John Hughson, about the fires which have lately happened in the town; she told him, that she had been with a fortune teller, who told her that in less than five weeks time, she would come to trouble, if she did not take good care of herself; but after that she would come to good fortune; then he inquired of her father's fortune; and she said, her father would be tried and condemned, but not hanged; but was to go over the water.

2. "That then, after some other discourse, the deponent told her, that some of the negroes who were concerned in the plot about the fires, had discovered; upon which she said, she did not know of any plot; and thereupon he told her, that they that were sworn in the plot, had discovered, and brought them every one in: upon which she coloured, and put her bonnet back, and changed colour several times, and asked him if he knew who it was and when he had heard it? and he told her, he had heard it by the by, and it was kept private: upon which she made a long stop; and then said, it must be either Holt's negro, or Todd's; for, said she, we were always afraid of them, and mistrusted them, though they were as bad as the rest, and were to have set their own master's houses on fire; and then she said, I wish that Todd had sent his black dog away, or sold him, when he was going to do it.*

3. "That then the deponent told her, sure you had better tell every thing that you know; for that may be of some service to your father; upon which she said no, for that they were doing all that they could to take his life away; and that she would sooner suffer death, and be hanged with her daddy (if he was to be hanged) than she would give them that satisfaction of telling or discovering any thing to them; or words to that effect: that she was to have gone up into the country (like a fool that she was that she did not go) but staid to see what

*Dundee. Todd, it seems, did threaten, and was going to send this negro beyond sea last fall; that her intelligence was right. [Robert Todd kept a very respectable tavern that was the frequent meeting place for a social club whose members included Daniel Horsmanden, Chief Justice De Lancey, Adolph Philipse (the brother of the second justice), and other elite lawyers and politicians of the city. See Carl Bridenbaugh, ed., *Gentleman's Progress: The Itinerarium of Dr. Alexander Hamilton, 1744* (Chapel Hill: University of North Carolina Press, 1948), 41–49 and 173–85, especially 175.—Ed.]

would become of her mammy and daddy; but that now she would go up in the country, and that she would be hanged if ever they should get her in York again; but if they (meaning the people of this city, as he understood) had not better care of themselves, they would have a great deal more damage and danger in York, than they were aware of; and if they did hang her daddy, they had better do something else; and as to the fire at the fort, they did not set the saddle on the right horse.[35]

4. "That on Monday last Peggy came to him, and bid him not discover any thing for his life, that she had told him; for if he did, by G–d she would cut his throat.

5. "The deponent further saith, that as to the expression made use of by Sarah Hughson, viz., As to the fire at the fort, they did not set the saddle on the right horse; the occasion of these words was, the deponents telling her, that they had been picking out of him what they could concerning the fire at the fort, and thought that he knew something of it; but he said to her, that he took God to be his judge, that he did not know any thing of it.*

Upon the information by this deposition, Dundee (Todd's negro) was apprehended and committed; but, upon examination, denied knowing any thing of the conspiracy.

The other negro was at this time gone with his master (Holt) a dancing master, to Jamaica, in the West Indies, who thought it proper to remove from hence soon after the fire at the fort.

FRIDAY, MAY 8

[Caesar and Prince, having been found guilty of larceny, were sentenced by Judge Philipse.]

"You, Caesar and Prince, the grand jury having found two indictments against each of you, for feloniously stealing and taking away from Mr. Hogg, and Mr. Meyers Cohen, sundry goods of considerable value. To these indictments you severally pleaded not guilty; and for your trials put yourselves upon God and the country; which country

[35]*set the saddle on the right horse:* To lay the blame on the right person.

*Upon the supposition, that Arthur knew nothing of the secrets of the conspiracy before he came to jail, the reader may be apt to judge, that he acted with more than ordinary acuteness for one of his station, in pumping so much out of Peggy and Sarah, (Hughson's daughter) and their confidence in him, if he were a stranger to them, was somewhat extraordinary on the occasion.

having found you guilty, it now only remains for the court to pronounce that judgment which the law requires, and the nature of your crimes deserve.

"But before I proceed to sentence, I must tell you, that you have been proceeded against in the same manner as any white man, guilty of your crimes, would have been. You had not only the liberty of sending for your witnesses; asking them such questions as you thought proper; but likewise making the best defence you could; and as you have been convicted by twelve honest men upon their oaths, so the just judgment of God has at length overtaken you.

"I have great reason to believe, that the crimes you now stand convicted of, are not the least of those you have been concerned in; for by your general characters you have been very wicked fellows, hardened sinners, and ripe, as well as ready, for the most enormous and daring enterprizes, especially you, Caesar: and as the time you have yet to live is to be but very short, I earnestly advise and exhort both of you to employ it in the most diligent and best manner you can, by confessing your sins, repenting sincerely of them, and praying God of his infinite goodness to have mercy on your souls: and as God knows the secrets of your hearts, and cannot be cheated or imposed upon, so you must shortly give an account to him, and answer for all your actions; and depend upon it, if you do not truly repent before you die, there is a hell to punish the wicked eternally.

"And as it is not in your powers to make full restitution for the many injuries you have done the public; so I advise both of you to do all that in you is, to prevent further mischiefs, by discovering such persons as have been concerned with you, in designing or endeavouring to burn this city, and to destroy its inhabitants. This I am fully persuaded is in your power to do if you will; if so, and you do not make such discovery, be assured God Almighty will punish you for it, though we do not: therefore I advise you to consider this well, and I hope both of you will tell the truth.

"And now, nothing further remains for me to say, but that you Caesar, and you Prince, are to be taken hence to the place from whence you came, and from thence to the place of execution, and there you, and each of you, are to be hanged by the neck until you be dead. And I pray the Lord to have mercy on your souls."

Ordered, that their execution be on Monday next, the eleventh day of this instant, between the hours of nine and one of the same day. And further ordered that after the execution of the said sentence, the body of Caesar be hung in chains.

MONDAY, MAY 11

Caesar and Prince were executed this day at the gallows, according to sentence. They died very stubbornly, without confessing any thing about the conspiracy; and denied they knew any thing of it to the last. The body of Caesar was accordingly hung in chains.

These two negroes bore the characters of very wicked idle fellows; had before been detected in some robberies, for which they had been publickly chastised at the whipping-post, and were persons of most obstinate and untractable tempers; so that there was no expectation of drawing any thing from them which would make for the discovery of the conspiracy, though there seemed good reason to conclude, as well from their characters as what had been charged upon them by information from others, that they were two principal ringleaders in it amongst the blacks. It was thought proper to execute them for the robbery, and not wait for the bringing them to a trial for the conspiracy, though the proof against them was strong and clear concerning their guilt as to that also; and it was imagined, that as stealing and plundering was a principal part of the hellish scheme in agitation, amongst the inferior sort of these infernal confederates, this earnest of example and punishment might break the knot, and induce some of them to unfold this mystery of iniquity, in hopes thereby to recommend themselves to mercy, and it is probable, that with some it had this effect.

ARSON: THE TRIALS OF CUFFEE AND QUACK

Even before Caesar and Prince went to the gallows, the court had begun to turn its attention to uncovering the plot behind the fires. Two other slaves, Quack and Cuffee, had been arrested immediately after the fires, and Burton implicated Cuffee in her first deposition. Like Caesar and Prince, Cuffee and Quack were quickly convicted. Unlike the first two, however, their conviction of arson rather than larceny meant that they were sentenced to death at the stake rather than on the gallows. While the two men were at the stake, prosecutors tried to persuade them to confess and give evidence about the plot, offering them in return the possibility of an amnesty. The men only began to speak after each had been told that the other had given evidence already. Although their testimony was not identical, both seemed to confirm the evidence of a plot.

This trial also introduces Sawney or Sandy, a young man whom Thomas Niblet had intended to sell in Albany, but who was brought back when another slave told the court that Sandy was the one who had torched the fort. Sandy offered the first and most complete slave testimony about the conspiracy to burn down the city. As he unfolded the plot, he particularly stressed the presence of the "Spanish Negroes," some of the black sailors who had been captured by privateers and held in slavery in New York. (See the Introduction.)

The passionate speeches that the attorney general and Justice Horsmanden delivered in this trial indicate some of their ideas about the proper place and relationships in society of slaves, poor white men, and white women. Other evidence, however, indicates that other New Yorkers had different ideas. The testimony of Burton and others reveals a biracial world in which whites did not always look down on blacks. Besides the testimony about the interracial socializing in the taverns, consider the renewed emphasis that the judges put on the fairness of the proceedings. The speeches in this section are also dense with traditional religious language about sin, souls, and repentance before death. Neither Horsmanden nor Philipse makes a distinction between blacks' and whites' ability to seek God's mercy for sins. As the trial of John Ury will show, however, not all whites thought that black souls were so similar to whites.

TUESDAY, MAY 12

Arthur Price having been found by experience to be very adroit at pumping out the secrets of the conspirators, in the two instances of Peggy and Sarah Hughson the daughter, before set forth; the under-sheriff was ordered to put Cuffee (Mr. Philipse's negro) into the same cell with him, and to give them a tankard of punch now and then, in order to cheer up their spirits, and make them more sociable. These directions were accordingly observed, and produced the desired effects; and one of the judges being acquainted that Arthur had something to communicate he went up this morning in order to examine him.

Deposition taken before one of the judges, No. 3.—Arthur Price being duly sworn, saith,

1. "That having discourse on Saturday night last, with Cuffee, a negro slave belonging to Mr. Philipse, he the said Cuffee, amongst other discourse, said, that he was one of the Geneva club* that was

*There was a confederacy of negroes, of which Caesar (Vaarck's) and Prince (Auboyneau's) both hanged yesterday, and Cuffee (Mr. Philipse's) were the heads and

sworn; but being overcome with sleep, he did not go to their meeting at that time: that Cuffee asked the deponent what could be the reason that Peggy was called down so often?* The deponent replied, he thought Peggy was discovering the plot about the fire; Cuffee replied, she could not do that unless she forswore herself, he knew; for that he that had done that was sworn after she (Peggy) was in prison; he (Cuffee) left his master's house in the evening, and went along the wharves to the Fly-Market, and waited there till one Quack came out of his master's house; they two then went to the house of John Hughson, where they met nobody but John Hughson, his wife, and daughter Sarah; that they (the two negroes) called for a tankard of punch; that Hughson swore Quack three times; that they only drank out their punch, and then went down to the Fly. That this deponent then said, I believe I know this Quack, and that he lived with a butcher; Cuffee replied, no; he doth not live with a butcher, but he lived with a painter, who lived within a few doors of a butcher; which painter's name he understood to be Roosevelt, according to the best of his remembrance.

2. "That Cuffee told him, that Quack was married to a negro wench who is cook to the fort, to the governor as he understood; that they were all to meet at Hughson's the Sunday after Quack was sworn; but some came and some did not. That the deponent, upon some further discourse, asked Cuffee how Quack could do it? (meaning the setting fire to the house in the fort) Cuffee answered, he could not tell how he did it; but that Quack was to do it, and did do it.

---

ringleaders; who robbed, pilfered and stole whenever they had an opportunity: and it happened about five or six years ago, a cellar of one Baker, a tavern-keeper in this city, had one night been broken open, and robbed of some Geneva *[gin]*; many of the parties concerned were detected, viz., several negroes, of which Caesar and Prince were two principals; and all that were discovered were chastised at the public whippingpost. From thence it may be supposed they became distinguished among each other by the name of the Geneva Club; for they used frequently to be junketting together at nights with Cuff upon the produce of the spoils of their pilfering. But it came out upon the examination of these negroes, that they had before that time the impudence to assume the style and title of *Free Masons,* in imitation of a society here: which was looked upon to be a gross affront to the provincial grand master and gentlemen of the fraternity at that time, and was very ill accepted: however, from this time the negroes may be supposed to have declined their pretensions to this title; for we heard nothing more of them afterwards under that stile. But it is probable that most of this Geneva Club that were sworn (as Cuffee said) were of the conspiracy; and it is likely that by the swearing, Cuff meant, sworn of the conspiracy. [Eighteenth-century Freemasons were an elite male social club, with none of the negative implications that the term would garner in the nineteenth century.—Ed.]

*She had been frequently sent for to be examined.

3. "That Cuffee said, they were to meet and have a club at John Hughson's in the Easter hollidays, but that the d—d constables hindered them.

4. "That he asked Cuffee, whether he did not think that the firing would be found out; he replied, no, by G–d, he did not think it ever would.

5. "That he further asked Cuffee, if he was not afraid, that the two negroes who were to be executed on Monday, would discover (the affair about the firing of the fort and town meaning) Cuffee answered, he was not afraid of that; for that he was sure they would be burnt to ashes before they would discover it; he would lay his life on it.

6. "That yesterday the deponent having some further discourse with Cuffee, he said, he wondered why they only took up the Long Bridge boys, and did not take up those of the Smith's Fly; for he believed, if the truth was known, they (the Smith's Fly negroes meaning) were as much concerned as they (of the Long Bridge meaning.)"

Upon this deposition, Quack (Roosevelt's) was apprehended and committed; who was one of the *Smith's Fly Boys,* as Cuff called them.

WEDNESDAY, MAY 13

Deposition before the judges, No. 2.—Mary Burton, being duly sworn, deposed,

1. "That a day or two after she was examined before the grand jury, she was coming by Vaarck's door in the Broadstreet of this city, and saw a negro of the said Vaarck's, who (now at the time of her examination being produced) called himself by the name of Bastian, but used to be called by the negroes, Tom Peal, who asked the deponent, whether she had discovered any thing about the fires? To which the deponent answered no. To which he replied, *d—n you, it was not best for you, for fear you should be burnt in the next.*

2. "That Quaco* the negro man now produced to her, she has often seen at Hughson's door along with Philipse's Cuff, Caesar (Vaarck's), and Prince (Auboyneau's), but never saw Quaco within Hughson's house, as she remembers.

3. "That she has seen Jack (Sleydall's, the tallow-chandler) very often at Hughson's house, and believes he was very well acquainted with Hughson's eldest daughter Sarah; but does not remember she ever saw him there at the times of the meetings of the negroes, when

* Roosevelt's.

they talked about fires; but from the kindness shewn to him by Hughson, his wife, and daughter aforesaid, she had great reason to think he was in their secrets.

4. "That she hath often times seen many negroes at Hughson's house, she believes thirty together, especially on a Sunday; many of them playing at dice, whose faces she could remember if she saw them; and she believes there were thirty of them concerned in the conspiracy about the fires; and some country negroes, particularly one Jamaica.

5. "That Hughson and his wife, and Peggy, and Sarah Hughson the daughter, used, at the meetings of the negroes, to be the forwardest of any of them in talking about fires, (that is to say) that they would burn the fort; then they would go to the Fly* and burn the whole town, and destroy all the people; to which all the negroes present were consenting; and by name Cuff,† Caesar and Prince,‡ Albany, Tom Peal, alias Bastian, amongst the rest. . . .

7. "That she knows Jonneau (Vaarck's negro) and has seen him at Hughson's house a drinking with other negroes; but don't remember he was present at any time of the discourse about the fires, or killing the white people."

Jonneau, Albany and Bastian were immediately apprehended and committed.

THURSDAY, MAY 14

This day Sandy alias Sawney (Niblet's negro boy) was brought down from Albany, and committed to jail.

Deposition before the judges—No. 3.—Mary Burton deposed,

1. "That at the time when she saw the meetings of the several negroes at Hughson's house, as mentioned in the deponent's deposition of yesterday, the said Hughson said, *they were all sworn,* meaning the negroes and all the white people present, (as she understood) that is, Hughson himself, his wife, and daughter Sarah, and Peggy, and she understood by Hughson, that the purport of the oath was *that they were not to discover the secrets about firing the fort, the houses at the fly, and the whole town;* and about murdering the white people: and Hughson said to the negroes present, which were Cuff, Caesar and Prince;

*Towards the east end of the town.

†Philipse's.

‡Vaarck's and Auboyneau's.

now you must take care, for you are all sworn; and the deponent at the time saw a bible (as she took it to be) in Hughson's hand; and when the deponent came into the room, he laid it upon the table: and then Caesar spoke to the deponent, and cautioned her not to tell; and Hughson made answer, that she dared not; and Cuff said, *d—n his bl—d, if he would tell of any, if he was burnt;* and so said the other two negroes; and so said Hughson, his wife, their daughter Sarah, and Peggy.

2. "That Hughson asked Caesar if he could get any others (meaning the negroes) to help them? Caesar answered, he could get enough, who dared not but go if he spoke.

3. "That she saw Caesar pay Hughson twelve pounds in eight shilling Spanish pieces,[36] as Hughson said, after counting them; which was paid him, in order to buy guns; and that Hughson afterwards went abroad with his boat, and was about three days, or thereabouts, and brought back with him seven or eight guns, three pistols and four swords, which were hid away under the boards in the garret floor in Hughson's house."

FRIDAY, MAY 22

The grand jury having been informed that Sawney, Niblet's negro boy, was brought to town and committed upon suspicion of being a confederate in the conspiracy, they requested the court that he might be brought before them; which being accordingly done; upon interrogation Sawney denied he knew any thing of the fires, or any conspiracy concerning them. The grand jury for a long time argued with him, to persuade him to speak the truth; being convinced from the evidence of Mrs. Carpenter's negro,* who already had been examined by them, that he could give some account of the fires. They told him if he would speak the truth, the governor would pardon him, though he had been concerned in them; and this was the time for him to save his life by making a free and ingenuous confession; or in words to this purpose. He answered, that the time before† after that the negroes told all they knew, then the white people hanged them. The grand jury assured him, that it was false; for that the negroes which confessed the truth and made a discovery, were certainly pardoned, and shipped off: (which was the truth)—and upon this assurance he began to open, and gave the following evidences.

[36]Eight-shilling Spanish pieces were Spanish pieces of eight.
*A young man not accused of the conspiracy.
†Hinting at the conspiracy in 1712.

Examination of Sawney (Niblet's negro) before the grand jury, No. 1.—He said,

1. "That about three weeks before the fire at the fort, Quack (Mr. Roosevelt's negro) asked him to assist him to set the fort on fire; and that he answered no, he would not run the risk of being hanged; but that he might go to hell and be d—d.

2. "That he heard the said Quack and Mr. Philipse's Cuffee say, they would set fire to Mr. Philipse's storehouse.

3. "That Cuffee said, d—n him, that hang him or burn him, he would set fire to the town.

4. "That William (capt. Lush's Spanish negro) told him, that if they did not send him over to his own country, he would ruin the city.

5. "That Curracoa Dick said, he would set fire to Mr. Van Zant's storehouse; and that he was to be a captain.

6. "That Juan (capt. Sarly's negro) said, he would set fire or help to set fire to Hilton's house; and was to be captain of the fly company.

7. "That Francis (capt. Bosch's negro) threw fire into Mr. Bancker's yard, and told him so.

8. "That Anthony (Mr. Peter Delancey's negro Spaniard) said, he would burn his master's house.

9. "That Augustine (McMullen's Spanish negro) said, he would burn his master's house; and was to have been an officer.

10. "That Jack and an old man* (Gerardus Comfort's) said, they would set fire to their master's house, and assist in their designs.

11. "That Cuffee (Gomez's) said, he would burn his master's house; and was to have been an officer in the Fly company; said so to a country fellow, and he heard him.

12. "That just by Coenties-market he heard Patrick (English's negro) and Cato (col. Moore's) say, they would set fire to their master's houses.

13. "That Fortune (Wilkins') was to set fire to his master's house.

14. "Sawney being asked what the negroes proposed by rising and doing all this mischief? He answered, 'that their design was to kill all the gentlemen, and take their wives;' and that Quack† and Cuffee (Philipse's) were particular persons that talked so.

15. "That while he was in jail, Francis (capt. Bosch's) said, he would kill him if he told any thing; and that when Mr. Mills came for him,‡ several negroes winked as he came out.

* Cook.

† Roosevelt's.

‡ To bring him down to be examined.

16. "Being asked if Quack (Mr. Walter's negro) was knowing or concerned in the affair: he answered, no, though he was always cursing the white people.

17. "Being asked if he had much acquaintance with Danby, the governor's negro, and if he knew any thing? he answered, he had very little; and he believed not.

18. "That Caesar (Vaarck's) that was hanged, was concerned and was to have been captain of the Long Bridge company.*

19. "That about a fortnight before the fire at the fort, at Comfort's house, he overheard Jack and the old man (Cook) in company with four other negroes he did not know, talk about the rising of the negroes; and Jack said, that there was not enough of them, and he would stay longer, or to that purpose."

FRIDAY, MAY 29

[Quack (Roosevelt's) and Cuffee (Philipse's) were indicted for conspiracy to murder the inhabitants of New York and to commit arson. The two pled not guilty.

Burton repeated her first deposition of April 22, in which she testified that Cuffee, like Caesar and Prince, were often at the Hughsons' when they were planning the uprising.]

Court: Did the prisoner Cuffee ever threaten you so?
M. Burton: Yes, he, Caesar and Prince, and the rest.

"That about three weeks after she came to Hughson's, which was about midsummer last, the negroes were there talking of the plot and some of them said perhaps she would tell; and Coffee said no, she would not, he intended to have her for a wife; and then run up to her;

*It seems that the conspirators had divided the city, as it were, into two districts, and the confederates in each were distinguished by the denominations of the Fly Boys, and the Long Bridge Boys; being remarkable places, the one towards the east, and the other towards the west end of the town. This may be drawn from Cuffee's confession to Arthur Price, set forth in this deposition, 12th May, No. 3, section 6. And in these districts, it should seem, were several companies; for several of the officers were appointed captains. . . . These were the two lodges in the two districts (as may be concluded from the course of the evidence) where the conspirators met; though the ringleaders, or heads of the negroes such as Caesar (Vaarck's) Prince (Auboyneau's) and Cuffee (Philipse's) might resort to both places, for transacting those deeds of darkness and inhumanity, in combination with the most flagitious, degenerated and abandoned, and scum and dregs of the white people, and others of the worse hearts, if possible because of abler heads, who entitled themselves to be ten times more the children of Belial, than the negroes themselves.

and she had a dishclout[37] in her hand, which she dabbed in his face, and he ran away.

"That at a meeting of the negroes at Hughson's house, Hughson said they were all sworn, negroes and white people present, as she understood; that is, Hughson, his wife, daughter Sarah, and Peggy, and that the purport of the oath was, that they were not to discover the secrets about firing the fort, the houses at the Fly, and the whole town, and about murdering the white people; and Hughson said to the negroes present, which were Coffee, Caesar and Prince, now you must take care, for you are all sworn; and at the same time the witness saw a bible, as she took it to be, in Hughson's hand, and when the witness came into the room he laid it upon the table; and then Caesar spoke to the witness and cautioned her not to tell, and Hughson made answer that she dared not; and Coffee said, d—n his bl—d, if he would tell of any, if he was burnt; and so said the other two negroes, and so said Hughson, his wife, daughter Sarah, and Peggy."

[Arthur Price also restated an earlier deposition of May 12 (no. 3), in which he testified that Cuffee had confessed to being part of a sworn conspiracy and to being part of a theft ring. He added:]

"That after Quack, the other prisoner at the bar, was committed, Cuffee never mentioned any thing concerning the former discourse to the witness, but read sometimes, and cried very much."[38]

[Six white witnesses testified that they had seen Cuffee at the fire at Col. Philipse's storehouse. One claimed he had seen Cuffee whistling and dancing and purposely spilling the buckets of water with which the brigade was attempting to put out the fire. A slave (Fortune) testified that he had seen Cuffee the night before the fire outside the storehouse, and that Quack had told him that he was going to burn down the fort. Another slave (Sandy) said that Quack had admitted to burning the fort.]

Witnesses called at the request of the prisoners.—Jacob Bursen, Peter Jay, Lewis Parent, Gerardus Beckman, Mr. Niblet, Captain Rowe, John Roosevelt and his son, Catherine Wells, Adolph Philipse, esq.

Adolph Philipse, esq. (Cuffee's master) said, that all he could declare about him was, "that the afternoon his nephew's (col. Philipse's)

[37]*dishclout:* A dishcloth.
[38]Notice here and elsewhere the evidence of literacy among some of the slaves.

storehouse was on fire, he had left him at home not long before the alarm of the fire at work, sewing a vane upon a board for his boat; that as to his character he could say nothing."

Quack's master (Mr. Roosevelt) and his son, both declared, "that Quack was employed most part of that morning the fort was fired, from the time they got up, in cutting away the ice out of the yard; that he was hardly ever out of their sight all that morning, but a small time while they were at breakfast; and that they could not think he could that morning have been from their home so far as the fort."

Captain Rowe and Beckman said, "Quack was employed last year to work at the new battery, and that he minded his business very well." The other witnesses called at the request of the prisoners, said nothing more material.

The Prisoners being asked what they had to offer in their defence, they offered nothing but peremptory denials of what had been testified against them, and protestations of their innocency.

Mr. Smith *[William Smith Sr., a lawyer for the prosecution]* then proceeded to sum up and remark upon the evidence, and spoke as followeth:

"*May it please your honours, and you, gentlemen of the jury,*

"The part assigned to me on this trial, is to sum up the evidence which you have heard; and in general it may be observed, that a most horrid conspiracy has been formed, to burn this city, and to destroy the white people.

"That great numbers of persons have been concerned in the plot; some whites, and many blacks. That the place of their general rendezvous was the house of John Hughson. That there thirty negroes have met at a time. That their meetings were chiefly on Sundays. That Hughson, as the captain of this hellish band, swore himself and others into this dark confederacy. That some arms and ammunition were provided by Hughson for the purpose; and that the night season was agreed on for the putting it in execution.

"*Gentlemen,* no scheme more monstrous could have been invented; nor can any thing be thought of more foolish, than the motives that induced these wretches to enter into it! What more ridiculous than that Hughson, in consequence of this scheme, should become a *King*! Caesar, now in gibbets,[39] a *Governor*! That the white men should be all killed, and the women become a prey to the rapacious lust of these

[39]*in gibbets:* On the gallows. The bodies of criminals were publicly displayed after execution as a warning.

villains! That these slaves should thereby establish themselves in peace and freedom in the plundered wealth of their slaughtered masters! It is hard to say whether the wickedness or the folly of this design is the greater; and had it not been in part executed before it was discovered, we should with great difficulty have been persuaded to believe it possible, that such a wicked and foolish plot could be contrived by any creatures in human shape.

"Yet, gentlemen, incredible as such a plot would have seemed to have been, the event has in part proved it to be real. Whence else could so many fires have been lighted up all around you in so short a time, with evident marks of wilful design? A design that could not be executed but by several hands.

"Now gentlemen, the prisoners at the bar stand charged with being principal parties in this tragical design, and two of the prime incendiaries: Quack for burning his majesty's house in the fort, and Cuffee for burning col. Philipse's storehouse."

Then concluded,

"Thus, gentlemen, I have distinguished the several points of the evidence against the prisoners, and have repeated the substance of what each witness has said to each point, and shall leave it to you to determine whether the prisoners are guilty or not. I have endeavoured to lay no more weight upon any part of the evidence, than it will well bear; and I hope I have not urged any consequence which the fact proved will not fairly warrant.

"*Gentlemen,* the prisoners have been indulged with the same kind of trial as is due to free men, though they might have been proceeded against in a more summary and less favourable way. The negro evidence, in the manner in which it has been produced, is warranted by the act of assembly that has been read to you; the law requires no oath to be administered to them, and indeed it would seem to be a profanation of it, to administer it to a Heathen in the legal form. You have seen that the court has put them under the most solemn caution, that their small knowledge of religion can render them capable of. The being and perfections of an Almighty, all knowing, and just God, and the terrors of an eternal world, have been plainly laid before them, and strongly pressed upon them. Unless they were professed Christians, and had taken upon them the bonds and obligations of that religion, their word, with the cautions that have been used, I suppose will be thought by you, as satisfactory as any oath that could have been devised. But, gentlemen, the court has no power to administer an oath, but in the common form, and if Pagan negroes could not be received as witnesses against each other, without an oath in legal form, it is easy to perceive that the greatest villanies would often pass with impunity."

Then the jury were charged, and a constable was sworn to attend them as usual; and they withdrew; and being soon returned, found the prisoners guilty of both indictments. The prisoners were asked, what they had to offer in arrest of judgment, why they should not receive sentence of death? and they offering nothing but repetitions of protestations of their innocence; the third justice *[Horsmanden]* proceeded to sentence, as followeth:

Quack and Cuffee, the criminals at the bar,

"You both now stand convicted of one of the most horrid and detestable pieces of villainy, that ever satan instilled into the heart of human creatures to put in practice; ye, and the rest of your colour, though you are called slaves in this country; yet you are all far, very far, from the condition of other slaves in other countries; nay, your lot is superior to that of thousands of white people. You are furnished with all the necessaries of life, meat, drink, and clothing, without care, in a much better manner than you could provide for yourselves, were you at liberty; as the miserable condition of many free people here of your complexion might abundantly convince you. What then could prompt you to undertake so vile, so wicked, so monstrous, so execrable and hellish a scheme, as to murder and destroy your own masters and benefactors? nay, to destroy root and branch, all the white people of this place, and to lay the whole town in ashes.

"I know not which is the more astonishing, the extreme folly, or wickedness, of so base and shocking a conspiracy; for as to any view of liberty or government you could propose to yourselves, upon the success of burning the city, robbing, butchering, and destroying the inhabitants; what could it be expected to end in, in the account of any rational and considerate person among you, but your own destruction? And as the wickedness of it, you might well have reflected, you that have sense, that there is a God above, who has always a clear view of all your actions, who sees into the utmost recesses of the heart, and knoweth all your thoughts; shall he not, do ye think, for all this bring you into judgment, at that final and great day of account, the day of judgment, when the most secret treachery will be disclosed, and laid open to the view, and every one will be rewarded according to their deeds, and their use of that degree of reason which God Almighty has entrusted them with.

"Ye that were for destroying us without mercy, ye abject wretches, the outcasts of the nations of the earth, are treated here with tenderness and humanity; and, I wish I could not say, with too great indulgence also; for you have grown wanton with excess of liberty, and your idleness has proved your ruin, having given you the opportunities of forming this villainous and detestable conspiracy; a scheme compounded of the blackest and foulest vices, treachery, blood-thirstiness, and ingratitude. But be not deceived, God Almighty only can and will proportion punishments to men's offences; ye that have shewn no mercy here, and have been for destroying all about ye, and involving them in one general massacre and ruin, what hopes can ye have of mercy in the other world? For shall not the judge of all the earth do right? Let me in compassion advise ye then; there are but a few moments between ye and eternity; ye ought therefore seriously to lay to heart these things; earnestly and sorrowfully to bewail your monstrous and crying sins, in this your extremity; and if ye would reasonably entertain any hopes of mercy at the hands of God, ye must shew mercy here yourselves, and make what amends ye can before ye leave us, for the mischief you have already done, by preventing any more being done. Do not flatter yourselves, for the same measure which you give us here, will be measured to you again in the other world; ye must confess your whole guilt, as to the offences of which ye stand convicted, and for which ye will presently receive judgment; ye must discover the whole scene of iniquity which has been contrived in this monstrous confederacy, the chief authors and actors, and all and every the parties concerned, aiding and assisting therein, that by your means a full stop may be put to this horrible and devilish undertaking. And these are the only means left ye to shew mercy; and the only reasonable ground ye can go upon, to entertain any hopes of mercy at the hands of God, before whose judgment seat ye are so soon to appear.

"Ye cannot be so stupid, surely, as to imagine, that when ye leave this world, when your souls put off these bodies of clay, ye shall become like the beasts that perish, that your spirits shall only vanish into the soft air and cease to be. No, your souls are immortal, they will live forever, either to be eternally happy, or eternally miserable in the other world, where you are now going.

"If ye sincerely and in earnest repent you of your abominable sins, and implore the divine assistance at this critical juncture, in working out the great and momentous article of the salvation of your souls; upon your making all the amends, and giving all the satisfaction which is in each of your powers, by a full and complete discovery of the conspiracy, and of the several persons concerned in it, as I have observed to ye before, then and only upon these conditions can ye reasonably expect mercy at the hands of God Almighty for your poor, wretched and miserable souls.

"Here ye must have justice, for the justice of human laws has at length overtaken ye, and we ought to be very thankful, and esteem it a most merciful and wondrous act of Providence, that your treacheries and villanies have been discovered; that your plot and contrivances, your hidden works of darkness have been brought to light, and stopped in their career; that in the same net which you have hid so privly[40] for others your own feet are taken: that the same mischief which you have contrived for others, and have in part executed, is at length fallen upon your own pates,[41] whereby the sentence which I am now to pronounce will be justified against ye; which is,

"That you and each of you be carried from hence to the place from whence you came, and from thence to the place of execution, where you and each of you shall be chained to a stake, and burnt to death; and the lord have mercy upon your poor, wretched souls."

Ordered, that the execution of the said Quack and Cuffee be on Saturday the 30th of this instant, between the hours of one and seven o'clock in the afternoon of the same day.

SATURDAY, MAY 30

This day Quack and Cuffee were executed at the stake according to sentence.

The spectators at this execution were very numerous; about three o'clock the criminals were brought to the stake, surrounded with piles of wood ready for setting fire to, which the people were very impatient to have done, their resentment being raised to the utmost pitch against them, and no wonder. The criminals shewed great terror in their countenances, and looked as if they would gladly have discovered all they knew of this accursed scheme, could they have had any encouragement to hope for a reprieve. But as the case was, they might flatter themselves with hopes: they both seemed inclinable to make some confession; the only difficulty between them at last being, who should speak first. Mr. Moore, the deputy secretary, undertook singly to examine them both, endeavouring to persuade them to confess their guilt, and all they knew of the matter, without effect; till at length Mr.

[40]*privly:* Secretly.
[41]*pates:* Heads.

Roosevelt came up to him, and said he would undertake Quack, whilst Mr. Moore examined Cuffee; but before they could proceed to the purpose, each of them was obliged to flatter his respective criminal that his fellow sufferer had begun, which stratagem prevailed: Mr. Roosevelt stuck to Quack altogether, and Mr. Moore took Cuff's confession, and sometimes also minutes of what each said; and afterwards upon drawing up their confessions in form from their minutes, they therefore intermixed what came from each.

Quack's confession at the stake. He said,

1. "That Hughson was the first contriver of the whole plot, and promoter of it; which was to burn the houses of the town; Cuffee said, to kill the people.

2. "That Hughson brought in first Caesar (Vaarck's); then Prince (Auboyneau's); Cuffee (Philipse's); and others, amongst whom were old Kip's negro; Robin (Chambers's); Cuffee (Gomez's); Jack (Codweis's) and another short negro, that cooks for him.

3. "That he Quack did fire the fort, that it was by a lighted stick taken out of the servants hall, about eight o'clock at night, that he went up the back stairs with it and so through Barbara's room, and put it near the gutter, betwixt the shingles, and the roof of the house.

4. "That on a Sunday afternoon, a month before the firing of the fort, over a bowl of punch, the confederates at Hughson's (amongst whom were the confederates above named, Albany, and Tickle, alias Will, Jack and Cook (Comfort's); old Butchell;* Caesar, and Guy (Horsfield's); Tom (Van Rants's); Caesar (Peck's); Worcester, and others) voted him Quack, as having a wife in the fort, to be the person who should fire the fort,† Sandy, and Jack (Codweis's); Caesar, and Guy (Horsfield's); were to assist him in it.

5. "That Hughson desired the negroes to bring to his house, what they could get from the fire, and Hughson was to bring down country people in his boat to further the business, and would bring in other negroes.

6. "That forty or fifty to his knowledge were concerned, but their names he could not recollect (the mob pressing and interrupting).

7. "That Cuffee (Gomez's); and Caesar (Peck's), fired Van Zant's storehouse.

* It was not discovered who this negro was.

†The reader may perceive hereafter, that the whole current of the testimony of the witnesses, white and black, do agree, that there was a great meeting of the negroes at Hughson's, on a Sunday evening, about a month before the fort was burnt.

8. "That Mary Burton had spoke the truth, and could name many more.

9. "Fortune (Wilkins's) and Sandy, had done the same; and Sandy could name the Spaniards, and say much more, which Cuffee particularly confirmed.

10. "Being asked what view Hughson had in acting in this manner? He answered, to make himself rich.

11. "That after the fire was over, Quack was at Hughson's house, Jack (Comfort's), a leading man, Hughson, wife and daughter present, and said, the job was done, meaning the fire; that he went frequently to Hughson's house, and met there Tickle and Albany.

12. "Quack said his wife was no ways concerned, for he never would trust her with it: and that Denby* knew nothing about the matter.

13. "Jamaica (Ellis's) not concerned that he knew of, but was frequently at Hughson's with his fiddle.

14. "Said he was not sworn by Hughson, but other were."

McDonald (the witness against Quack upon the trial) at the stake desired Mr. Pinhorne to ask Quack, whether he had wronged him in what he had said of him at court? He answered no; it was true he did pass him at the fort gate, about eleven o'clock that morning.

Cuffee's confession at the stake.—He said,

1. "That Hughson was the first contriver of all, and pressed him to it: that he Cuffee was one of the first concerned.

2. "The fire was intended to begin at Comfort's shingles, and so through the town.

3. "Old Kip's Negro; Robin (Chambers's); Jack (Comfort's); and Cuffee (Gomez's); were of the conspirators: Albany and Tickle were concerned.

4. "That he was sworn, and Caesar and Prince† also by Hughson.

5. "That Cuffee (Gomez's) and Caesar (Peck's); burnt Van Zant's storehouse.

6. "That Sandy set fire to Mr. Machado's house; Niblet's Negro wench can tell it; and Becker's Bess‡ knows it.

7. "That he set fire to the storehouse as sworn against him, that when his master went to the Coffee-House, he ran out of the other

*The governor's negro boy. Quack's wife was the governor's cook.
†Vaarck's and Auboyneau's.
‡This wench not apprehended.

door, and went the back way into the storehouse, having lighted charcoal in his pocket between two oyster shells, he put the fire between the ropes and the boards, and leaving it on fire, went home.

8. "That Hughson's people were to raise a mob to favour[42] the design.

9. "That the evidence that Peterson, did see him (was true); that Fortune did see him the night before.*

10. "That Fortune knew and was as deeply concerned as he; and Sandy was concerned, and knew the Spaniards.[43]

11. "There was about fifty concerned;† and that all were concerned that a constable who stood by‡ had seen all at Hughson's house."

After the confessions were minuted down (which were taken in the midst of great noise and confusion) Mr. Moore desired the sheriff to delay the execution until the governor be acquainted therewith, and his pleasure known touching their reprieve; which, could it have been effected, it was thought might have been means of producing great discoveries; but from the disposition observed in the spectators, it was much to be apprehended, there would have been great difficulty, if not danger in an attempt to take the criminals back. All this was represented to his honour; and before Mr. Moore could return from him to the place of execution, he met the sheriff upon the common, who declared his opinion, that the carrying the negroes back would be impracticable; and if that was his honour's order it could not be attempted without a strong guard, which could not be got time enough; and his honour's directions for the reprieve being conditional and discretionary, for these reasons the execution proceeded.

MONDAY, JUNE 1

Examination of Sandy (Niblet's negro) before one of the judges—No. 3.—He said,

1. "That he heard by captain Lush's house, about six of the Spaniards (about fourteen days before the fort was burnt) say, that if

[42] *favour:* To aid or support.

* See Fortune's evidence on the trial and his examination. . . .

[43] The Spanish negro conspirators.

† This seems to be a random guess under great confusion, for it is most probable he knew more.

‡ North, the whitsuntide [*Whitsuntide:* The seventh Sunday after Easter.—Ed.] before, he had interrupted a number of negroes feasting at Hughson's, and cudgelled them away.

the captain would not send them to their own country,[44] they would ruin all the city; and the first house they would burn should be the captain's, for they did not care what they did: He (Sandy) stood by Arden's door, and they did not (as he thought) see him; and that (pointing to Lush's house) they said, d—n that son of a b—h, they would make a devil of him: which was the first time he ever heard of the conspiracy.

2. "That the second time Quack* called to him by Coenties Market, and told him he wanted to speak to him; and said, will you help to burn the fort? and answered as he said at the trial, and in his examination before the grand jury; said that Quack told him the first time he met him, he would make an end of him.

3. "That the third time, at Comfort's house, one Sunday, when Comfort's Jack called to him to come to him, and he went in, Sarah (Burk's negro wench) d—d him, and bid him drink, having before refused.

4. "That there was a great number of negroes present, and about six Spanish negroes among them; but none of them were the same that he saw at Lush's. That he did drink.

5. "That Comfort's Jack brought out about eleven penknives, which were rusty; some complained their knives were dull and would not cut, which they went to sharpen on a stone; Jack (Comfort's) said his knife was so sharp, that if it came a-cross a white man's head, it would cut it off; on which he (Sandy) said, if you want to fight, go to the Spaniards, and not fight with your masters.

6. "That they asked him (and Comfort's Jack in particular) if he would help to burn some houses; he cried: on which Jack (Comfort's) said, d–n you, do you cry? I'll cut your head off in a hurry, and surrounded him; on which Burk's wench said he deserved it, if he would not say yes, on which he consented, and said yes; whereupon they did not threaten him, but bid him say nothing to black or white about it, and every one would do his part, and take a round, and fire the town.

7. "That Jack (Comfort's) said they had not men enough this year, but next year would do it, every one present was to set his master's house on fire first, and then do the rest at once, and set all the houses

[44]These Spaniards had been taken off Spanish ships by privateers and brought to British ports. Most of them spent most of the war trying to return to their homes in the Spanish Caribbean. See the Introduction.

*Roosevelt's negro.

on fire in the town, which when they had done, they would kill all the white men, and have their wives for themselves. . . .

9. "That Augustine and Wilkins' Fortune were to burn their master's houses, which he heard them say, as they were talking by Frazier's corner, about a week before the fort was burnt.

10. "That at the aforesaid meeting at Comfort's Jack, the old man, and the old woman, and three of the Spaniards were sworn to the effect, that the first thunder that came, might strike them dead, if they did not stand to their words.

11. "That they asked him to come again the next day to be sworn; the rest said they would come to be sworn the next day."

CONSPIRACY: THE TRIAL OF THE HUGHSONS AND PEGGY KERRY

In some ways, this trial lies at the heart of Horsmanden's account. His particularly careful notes of his conversations with John Hughson and Peggy Kerry and of the details of the trial itself indicate the importance of the trial. The trial is unusual in other respects as well. It is the only place in the account that records laughter in the courtroom. Horsmanden notes a number of jokes and sly remarks, especially about the three women on trial. More courtroom dialogue and more comments on nonverbal behavior appear here than anywhere else in the transcript. Although the legal focus of the trials is on John Hughson, the textual focus of Horsmanden's account is on the three female defendants. Notice the special emphasis put on white women serving black men. Thus, from Horsmanden's attention to nonlegal detail, scattered but valuable evidence emerges about gender relationships. In this context, consider why the court puts off the execution of the younger Sarah Hughson.

Horsmanden's rage at John Hughson colors the trial from beginning to end, and the attorney general's vehemence is equally noticeable. Moreover, the biases of Horsmanden's text come through clearly in the difference between the verbatim copies of the longer speeches that he must have gotten from the prosecuting lawyers and the brief mention of the prisoners' defense that included no direct quotations at all. Notice how carefully Horsmanden shaped his summary of the prisoner's defense ("The prisoners asked the witnesses no material questions, such only as seemed rather to imply their guilt"). Can one reconstruct the defense from the prosecution's version?

Despite the clear focus on the white conspirators at this stage in the trials, other themes also come to the fore. The tenor of the conspiracy becomes increasingly violent. Guns and ammunition, hinted at in earlier testimony, take center stage in Burton's evidence in this trial. Several slaves who were tried during the week between Kerry's and the Hughson's conviction and execution (a trial not reproduced here) attempted to win pardons from the court by giving evidence. One extensive deposition of Comfort's Jack sets the stage for the prosecution of the Spanish sailors whom Sandy had previously implicated. This deposition is also packed with details about the gatherings at the Hughsons'.

MONDAY, JUNE 1

About noon this day, the under-sheriff informed the recorder, that John Hughson wanted to speak to the judges, and (as he had said) to open his heart to them, and they should know more, and was very urgent that somebody should go to them to acquaint them therewith. Pursuant to Hughson's desire, the recorder did go up to the City-Hall in the afternoon, expecting he would make some material discovery, and having sent for him, he was asked, what it was that he wanted with the judges? Whereupon Hughson asked if there was a bible, and desired that he might be sworn. He was told that no oath would be administered to him; if he had any thing to say, he had free liberty to speak, but he wanted very much to be sworn.[45] The recorder thereupon reproached him with his wicked life and practices, debauching and corrupting of negroes, and encouraging them to steal and pilfer from their masters and others, and for shewing his children so wicked an example, training them up in the highway to hell. He further observed to him, that he, his wife, and Peggy, then stood convicted of a felony for receiving stolen goods of negroes; and that now nothing remained but to pass sentence to death upon them, and to appoint a day for their execution for that fact; but that it was now determined, that he, his wife and daughter, and Peggy, should also be tried for being confederated in this most horrible conspiracy; that the evidence would appear so strong and clear against them in this particular, that

[45]Given the solemnity of oaths in the seventeenth and eighteenth centuries, common law forbade confessions to be made under oath, in order to protect a defendant from self-incrimination. If a confession was made under oath, it could not be used as evidence in a trial against the confessor. As one legal handbook explained, an individual's guilt was not "to be wrung out of himself." Dalton, *Countrey Justice* (1677), c. 165, no. 6, cited in Goebel and Naughton, *Law Enforcement,* 656.

there was little doubt of their being all convicted upon that head also; that it would appear undeniably that he was a principal, and head agent in this detestable scheme of villainy; the chief abettor, together with the rest of his family, of this execrable and monstrous contrivance for shedding the blood of his neighbours, and laying the whole city in ashes, upon the expectation of enriching himself by such an inhuman and execrable undertaking. He therefore admonished him, if he would entertain the least hopes of recommending himself to the mercy of God Almighty, before whose tribunal he must soon appear, that he would ingenuously tell the truth, and lay open the whole scene of this dark tragedy, which had been brooding at his house, and discover the several parties he knew to have been engaged in it; in doing which he would make some atonement for his past villainies, by preventing that slaughter, bloodshed and devastation, which he and his confederates had intended; or the recorder expressed himself in words to this purpose. But hereupon Hughson put on a soft smiling air of innocence upon his countenance, again desiring that he might be sworn, which was refused him, and he then declared, he knew nothing of all of any conspiracy, and called God to witness his protestations, that he was as innocent with respect to that charge as the child unborn, and also his wife, daughter and Peggy, for aught he knew.

Whereupon the Recorder remanded him to jail.

Whether the man was struck with a compunction, or flattered himself with making a merit by his discovery, and thereby recommended himself to mercy, and that he should so save his life; or whether he imagined that if he could be sworn, and then make the most solemn protestations with the sanction of an oath, that this would give such strong impressions of his innocence, as might make way for his escape; what his view was can only be guessed at; but several who were by him in the jail when he expressed his desire of having the opportunity of speaking with the judges, as above mentioned, concluded from his condition and behaviour at that instant, that he was then really in earnest to lay open this scene of villainy; but it was thought that in two or three hours afterwards, his wife or others had got the better of him, and prevailed with him to change his mind, and desist from his former resolution.

[The next day, June 2, the Hughsons (John and Sarah) and Kerry were indicted on a second charge of aiding and abetting the burning of the fort. The three had previously, on May 6, pled not guilty to the charge of

receiving stolen goods. On June 4, the Hughsons' daughter Sarah, along with her parents and Kerry, was indicted for aiding and abetting the burning of Philipse's storehouse. They pled not guilty to all charges.]

THURSDAY, JUNE 4

The King against John Hughson, Sarah his wife, Sarah their daughter, Margaret Sorubiero alias Kerry.

Clerk in court: Cryer, make proclamation.

Cryer: O yes![46] Our sovereign lord the king doth strictly charge and command all manner of persons to keep silence upon pain of imprisonment.

Cryer: If any one can inform the king's justices or Attorney General for this province, or the inquest now to be taken on the behalf of our sovereign lord the king, of any treason, murder, felony, or any other misdemeanor committed or done by the prisoners at the bar, let them come forth, and they shall be heard, for the prisoners stand upon their deliverance.

Clerk: Cryer, make proclamation.

Cryer: O yes! You good men that are impanelled to inquire between our sovereign lord the king and John Hughson, Sarah his wife, Sarah Hughson the daughter, and Margaret Sorubiero alias Kerry, the prisoners at the bar, answer to your names, etc.

Clerk: John Hughson, Sarah the wife of John Hughson, Sarah the daughter of John Hughson, Margaret Sorubiero, alias Kerry, hold up your hands.

These good men that are now called and here appear, are those which are to pass between you and our sovereign lord the king, upon your lives or deaths, if you, or any, or either of you challenge any of them, you must speak as they come to the book to be sworn, and before they are sworn.

Court: You the prisoners at the bar, we must inform you that the law allows you the liberty of challenging peremptorily twenty of the jurors, if you have any dislike to them, and you need not give your reasons for so doing; and you may likewise challenge as many more as you can give sufficient reasons for; and you may either all join in your challenges, or make them separately.

[46]*O yes* (or *oyez*): This call by a court official to order silence in the courtroom for a proclamation or beginning of a trial is traditionally translated as "hear ye."

The prisoners agreed that John Hughson should challenge for them all.

[At Hughson's challenging (among others) a young gentleman, merchant of the town, Peggy seemed out of humour, and intimated that he had challenged one of the best of them all; which occasioned some mirth to those within the hearing of it.]

Clerk: Cryer, make proclamation.

Cryer: O yes! Our sovereign lord the king doth strictly charge and command all manner of persons to keep silence, upon pain of imprisonment.

Clerk: You, gentlemen of the jury that are sworn, look upon the prisoners and hearken to their charge.

The Attorney General, after opening to the court and jury the charge against the prisoners, proceeded as followeth.

"*Gentlemen,*

"I shall in the first place, on the trial of the prisoners upon these indictments, shew you, that the negroes Quack and Cuffee, mentioned in the second and third of them, have already been tried, found guilty, and executed for the felonies and burnings which these indictments charge them to have been guilty of: that they confessed the same at the place of their execution; and that the evidence which Mary Burton gave against them at their trial, was true, in every respect.

"In the next place, gentlemen, I am to shew you, what share each of the prisoners at the bar had in these most horrible felonies.

[The Attorney General opened by accusing the three women of being sworn members of the plot to destroy New York and of aiding and abetting others who were also involved.]

"I shall now endeavour to represent to you the part which Hughson himself has acted in this tragedy.

"Gentlemen, it will appear to you in the course of the evidence for the king upon this trial, that John Hughson was the chief contriver, abetter and encourager of all this mystery of iniquity; that it was he who advised and procured secret and frequent meetings of the negroes, and the rest of the conspirators at his house, there to form and carry on these horrible conspiracies. That it was he that swore the negroes Quack and Cuffee, with many others, and himself too, into this direful plot. That it was he who devised firebrands, death and destruction to be sent among you. That it was he who received of negroes twelve pounds in money, stolen money, no doubt (and what he could not but know to be so) to buy arms and ammunition, to kill and destroy his neighbours: and that he in pursuance thereof, made a journey on purpose to buy, and did procure arms and ammunition, and hid them in his house, against such time as this unnatural and bloody scheme should be ripe for execution.

"Gentlemen, such a monster will this Hughson appear before you, that for the sake of the plunder he expected by setting in flames the king's house, and this whole city, and by the effusion of the blood of his neighbours, he, murderous and remorseless he! counselled and encouraged the committing of all these most astonishing deeds of darkness, cruelty and inhumanity.—Infamous Hughson!

"*Gentlemen,* This is that Hughson! whose name and most detestable conspiracies will no doubt be had in everlasting remembrance, to his eternal reproach; and stand recorded to latest posterity.—This is the man!—this that grand incendiary!—that arch rebel against God, his king, and his country!—that devil incarnate, and chief agent of the old Abaddon of the infernal pit, and Geryon of darkness.[47]

"*Gentlemen,* behold the author and abettor of all the late conflagrations, terrors, and devastation that have befallen this city.—Was not this Hughson sunk below the dignity of human nature! was he not abandoned to all sense of shame and remorse! to all sense of feeling and dreadful calamities he has brought on this city, and his own guilt, his monstrous guilt, be so confounded, as not able to look up, or stand without the greatest confusion of face, before this court and audience; but would openly confess his, and the rest of his wretched confederates' guilt, and humbly ask pardon of God, the king, and his injured country.

"*Gentlemen,* we shall now call, and examine the witnesses, who will prove the crimes charged upon each of the four criminals; and when we have so done, I doubt not but you will find all of them guilty."

Witnesses for the king.—Mr. George Joseph Moore, clerk in court, and Mr. John Roosevelt called and sworn.

Mr. Moore proved[48] the arraignment and conviction of the two negroes, Quack and Cuffee, for burning the king's house in the fort,

[47] *Abaddon:* The angel of the "bottomless pit" of hell, from Rev. 9:11. *Geryon:* A monstrous character from Dante's *Inferno* (Canto XVII) and the symbolic embodiment of fraud. Geryon had the face of a just man but the body of an enormous snake.

[48] *prove:* A technical term for establishing the legal validity of documents to be introduced into the evidence of a trial.

and Mr. Philipse's storehouse. Both witnesses proved the confessions of these two negroes, taken in writing at the stake, "that they declared, that Hughson was the first contriver and promoter of the plot, and urged them into it; and that they should never have thought of it, if he had not put it into their heads. That Quack said, the plot was to burn the houses."

Mr. Moore proved Cuffee's confession, more particularly taken in writing by him, "that, as Quack said, the plot was to burn the houses of the town; Cuffee said likewise, that the plot was, to kill the people; and that both of them declared, that what Mary Burton had given in evidence upon their trials, was true; and that she could name many more (persons) concerned: all which Mr. Roosevelt confirmed."*

Court to the prisoners: Have you any questions to ask these witnesses? the prisoners answered, nothing.

Joseph North, Peter Lynch, and John Dunscomb, called and sworn. North and Lynch proved, "that there was a cabal[49] of negroes at Hughson's last Whitsuntide was twelve months, ten, twelve, or fourteen of them; which they having intelligence of went down thither in order to disperse them; and when they came there, they went into the room where the negroes were round a table, eating and drinking, for there was meat on the table, and knives and forks; and the negroes were calling for what they wanted; and at their appearance, the negroes were making off as fast as they could, and North laid his cane about them, and soon cleared the room of them: they said, they thought that Peggy was waiting upon them, and had a tumbler in her hand for them to drink in; that they saw the negro who was then hanged in gibbets† at that time waiting at the door, in order to get in as they took it: that they had heard frequent complaints of Hughson's entertaining negroes there; they said, that John Hughson was at the door, and as they came away, they reproached him therewith; and he answered them, that he could not help it, it was his wife's fault."

Court to the prisoners: Have you any questions to ask these witnesses?—They had nothing to ask.

Mary Burton called and sworn.—She said, "that there were many negroes frequently at Hughson's at nights, ever since she came to the

*See the confessions before annexed to the trials of Quack and Cuffee, 30th May.
[49]*cabal:* A secret meeting of people gathered to form a plot.
†Vaarck's Caesar.

house, eating and drinking; that she has seen twenty and thirty at a time there, but most of a Sunday; that the negroes used to bring provisions there, particularly Carpenter's negro;* that Hughson, his wife and daughter, and Peggy used, at such meetings, frequently to be amongst the negroes; and that they talked of burning the town and killing the people."

(While Mary Burton was delivering her evidence, Hughson and his wife were crying and bemoaning themselves, and embracing and kissing their daughter Sarah; and Hughson the father, intimated what care they had taken in catechizing her, and the rest of their children, and teaching them to read the bible, and breeding them up in the fear of the Lord. And in order (as may be supposed) to move compassion in the court and jury, Hughson's wife brought thither a sucking child at her breast, which was ordered to be taken away.)

Mary Burton further said, "that at such great meetings of negroes at Hughson's, Caesar (Vaarck's) and Prince (Auboyneau's) negroes (that were hanged) and Cuffee (Philipse's) were usually amongst them.

"That Hughson swore the negroes into the plot, and the Hughsons swore themselves and Peggy; that one of Hughson's daughters carried a bible up stairs, and the Hughsons carried the negroes into a private room; and when they came down again to the rest of the negroes, Hughson said they were all sworn; but the witness said, she did not see them sworn."

(Upon the witness saying, that a bible was carried up stairs, Hughson's wife interrupted and said to her, as if much surprised, now you are found out in a great lie, for we never had a bible in the world; which the audience, considering what her husband declared but a little before, were much diverted with.)[50]

Mary Burton further said, "that she saw Vaarck's Caesar pay John Hughson twelve pounds in silver Spanish pieces of eight, to buy guns, swords and pistols; and that Hughson thereupon went up into the country; and when he returned, he brought with him seven or eight guns and swords, and that he hid them in the house; that she had seen a bag of shot and a barrel of gunpowder there; that the negroes were sworn to burn the fort first; and that they were to go down to the Fly, and so to burn the whole town; and the negroes were to cut their masters' and their mistresses' throats; and when all this was done, Hughson was to be king, and Caesar (Vaarck's) governor: that the

*His mistress was a butcher.

[50]*diverted with:* Amused by.

negroes used to say to Hughson, when she (the witness) was in the room and heard them talking of burning the town and killing the people, that perhaps she (the witness) would tell; and Hughson said, no, that she dared not; and the negroes swore that if she did, they would burn or destroy her.

"That the Hughsons often tempted her to swear, and offered her silks and gold rings, in order to prevail with her, but she would not."

(The prisoners asked the witnesses no material questions, such only as seemed rather to imply their guilt; but some of them threw up their hands, and cast up their eyes, as if astonished, and said, she was a very wicked creature, and protested all she said was false.)

Arthur Price called and sworn.

His evidence was the substance of his deposition, No. 1, 2, 3, of the third, seventh and twelfth May, as to what passed in conversation in the jail between him and Peggy, Sarah Hughson the daughter, and Mr. Philipse's Cuffee separately; and therefore to avoid repetition, the reader is referred to them.

Court to the prisoners: If you have any questions to ask these witnesses, now is your time to propose them; or if you have any witnesses to produce to your characters, let them be called.

Witnesses for the prisoners.—Eleanor Ryan, Mr. Blanck and Peter Kirby called.

Eleanor Ryan* said, "that she and her husband lodged two months in Hughson's house last winter; that she saw no negroes there but Cuff (Philipse's) and the negro that was hung in gibbets, three or four times; that she never saw any entertainments there for negroes, but said that she lay sick in bed in the kitchen almost day and night all that time."

Mr. Blanck said, "he saw Hughson give a dram[51] to a negro, but that he thought him a civil man."

Peter Kirby said, "that he knew nothing of the character of Hughson's house, but he never saw no harm of him."

Francis Silvester called and sworn for the king. He said, "that when John Hughson lived next door to him upon the dock, he kept a very disorderly house, and sold liquor to, and entertained negroes there; he had often seen many of them there at a time, at nights as well as in

*Wife of Andrew Ryan, a soldier, afterwards charged as one of the conspirators, and committed.

[51]*dram:* A small drink of about an ounce.

the daytime: once in particular he remembers, in the evening, he saw a great many of them in a room, dancing to a fiddle, and Hughson's wife and daughter along with them. That he often reproached Hughson with keeping such a disorderly house, which very much offended his neighbours; and Hughson replied to him, that his wife persuaded him to leave the country, where he subsisted his family tolerably well by his trade* and his farm; but his wife said, they would live much better in town, though then he wished they had returned to the country again, for he found their gains were so small, and his family so large, that they soon run away with what they had got: that his wife was the chief cause of having the negroes at his house, and he was afraid some misfortune would happen to him, and that he should come to some untimely end, or that Hughson expressed himself in words to that effect."

Court to the prisoners: Have you any more witnesses?

Prisoners: Yes sir; we desire that Adam King and Gerardus Comfort may be called.

Adam King and Gerardus Comfort called.

King said "that of late he took Hughson's house to be disorderly; for he saw whole companies of negroes playing at dice there, and that Wyncoop's negro once carried a silver spoon there that was hammered down;[52] that he saw no harm of the man himself."

Attorney General (to Hughson): Have you any more such witnesses as this?

Comfort said "that he saw nothing amiss of him; his business was a cooper,[53] and that he was often abroad, and went very seldom to his house."

Court: Mr. Comfort, you are a next door neighbour to Hughson: you live opposite to him, and surely you must have seen negroes go in and out there often, as the witnesses have testified, that there were frequent caballings with the negroes there; pray what have you observed of the house since Hughson came to live there?

Comfort: I have seen nothing amiss; I have seen no harm there.

*He was by trade a shoemaker.

[52]Stolen goods of silver or gold were often melted or beaten into another shape to escape recognition.

[53]*cooper:* A barrel- or cask-maker.

Court [to the prisoners]: Have you any more witnesses?
Hughson: We have no more, sir.
Court: Then now is the time for you the prisoners, severally to offer what you can in your own defence, that then the counsel for the king may sum up the evidence.

Then the prisoners severally spoke in their justification in their turns, protested their innocence, and declared that all the witnesses said against them was false, and called upon God to witness their asseverations.[54]

[William Smith, one of the prosecuting attorneys, summed up the evidence of the prosecution. He put particular emphasis on Hughson as the "principal contriver" and urged the jury to find all four guilty.]

A constable being sworn to attend the jury, they withdrew, and being returned in a short time, found Hughson, his wife, and Kerry, *guilty* of all three indictments; and Sarah Hughson the daughter, *guilty* of the second and third.

MONDAY, JUNE 8

The King against John Hughson, Sarah his wife, Margaret Hughson (Sorubiero), alias Kerry, Sarah the daughter.

The prisoners being called up to judgment upon their conviction for the conspiracy, and placed at the bar, the second justice proceeded to pass sentence, as followeth.

"John Hughson, and you the rest of the prisoners at the bar.

"You are now brought before this court to receive that sentence which the law has appointed for your offences; though I cannot say the punishment is adequate to the horrid crimes of which you stand convicted. The Roman commonwealth was established some hundred years before any law was made against parricide,[55] they not thinking any person capable of so atrocious a crime; yours are indeed as singular, and unheard of before, they are such as one would scarce believe any man capable of committing, especially any one who had heard of a God and a future state; for people who have been brought up and

[54]*asseveration:* An emphatic or solemn declaration.

[55]*parricide:* The murder of a father or a parent, but often used to describe the crime of treason against one's country. The Roman punishment for parricide was to sew the offender into a bag with a rooster, a monkey, and a dog, and throw the bag into the river.

always lived in a Christian country, and also called themselves Christians, to be guilty not only of making negro slaves their equals, but even their superiors, by waiting upon, keeping with, and entertaining them with meat, drink and lodging, and what is much more amazing, to plot, conspire, consult, abet and encourage these black seed of Cain,[56] to burn this city, and to kill and destroy us all. Good God! when I reflect on the disorders, confusion, desolation and havock, which the effect of your most wicked, most detestable and diabolical councils might have produced (had not the hand of our great and good God interposed) it shocks me! for you, who would have burnt and destroyed without mercy, ought to be served in like manner; and although each of you have with an uncommon assurance, denied the fact, and audaciously called upon God as a witness of your innocence; yet it hath pleased him, out of his unbounded goodness and mercy to us, to confound your devices, and cause your malicious and wicked machinations and intentions to be laid open and clear before us, not only to the satisfaction and conviction of the court, the grand and petty jury,[57] but likewise to every one else that has heard the evidence against you: all are satisfied the just judgment of God has overtaken you, and that you justly merit a more severe death than is intended for you, having, in my opinion, been much worse than the negroes: however, though your crimes deserve it, yet we must not act contrary to law."

Ordered, That the said condemned prisoners be executed on Friday the twelfth day of June instant, between the hours of nine and one of the same day; and that the body of John Hughson be afterwards hung in chains.

[Six slaves were tried and found guilty; five were condemned to death by burning at the stake and the sixth to death by hanging.]

This evening captain Jack (Comfort's negro) condemned, amongst others *[in a trial of June 6–8],* to be executed to-morrow afternoon,

[56]Cain, the first murderer in the Bible, and Ham, the son of Noah, who had seen his father naked and therefore been cursed by him, were often confused for each other in the Middle Ages and Early Modern period. Noah's curse to Ham, that his descendents would be subject to all the other races, was often conflated with Cain. The curse of Ham/Cain was an Early Modern explanation for racial slavery. See Benjamin Braude, "The Sons of Noah and the Construction of Ethnic and Geographical Identities in the Medieval and Early Modern Periods," *William and Mary Quarterly,* 3rd ser., 54, no. 1 (January 1997): 103–42.

[57]*petty jury:* Petit jury.

had caused to be signified to the judges, that if his life might be spared, he would discover all that he knew of the conspiracy. From the course of the evidence, there was reason to conclude that he had been a most trusty and diligent agent for Hughson; he lived very near him, and his master was frequently absent from home for days and weeks together, which left him too much at liberty; and there was a well in his yard whereto many negroes resorted every day, morning and afternoon, to fetch tea water; and Hughson, no doubt, thought he had carried a great point when he had seduced captain Jack to his infamous schemes, for this gave him the greatest opportunities of corrupting his fellow slaves; and Jack was a crafty, subtle fellow, very well qualified for such an enterprize, and might be captivated with the fine promises and hopes given him of being not only a free, but a great man; a commander in this band of fools, of whom the greatest knaves perhaps (like fools too) projected to make a prey in the end. It was therefore thought proper, as this mystery of iniquity was yet but beginning to be unfolded, so far to accept Jack's offer as to respite his execution, till it was found how well he would deserve further favour.

Jack was examined before the judges this afternoon, and was under examination the next day, when his fellow criminals were carrying from the City-Hall to their execution. He was advised not to flatter himself with the hopes of life, without he would do the utmost in his power to deserve it, and that would be by telling freely all that he knew of the matter, and discovering all the parties concerned, to the best of his knowledge. He was told we were already let so far into this secret, as to persons and things, as to be able to give a good guess, whether he spoke the truth, and he would but deceive himself in the end if he told falsehoods. Jack looked very serious, and at length began to open, but his dialect was so perfectly negro and unintelligible, it was thought that it would be impossible to make any thing of him without the help of an interpreter. There were two young men, sons-in-law of Jack's master, who were aware Jack would not be understood without their aid, and they signified their desire of being by when he was examined, from a supposition that they might be of service in interpreting his meaning, as he had been used to them, having often worked in the same shop together at the cooper's trade, whereby he was so familiarized to them, they could make a shift to understand his language, and they thought they had such an influence over him, that they were persuaded, they could also prevail upon him to make an ingenuous confession; and to do them justice, they were very serviceable in both respects, and the event well answered the expectation they had given. But notwithstanding this assistance, his examination took up as much time of three successive days, morning and afternoon, as could conveniently be spared him from other business.

Several negroes concerned in the conspiracy, having been discovered by Jack in this first sitting, were apprehended the next morning early, pursuant to orders then immediately given, but there was not time to commit his confession to writing this evening, yet it is thought proper to set the same forth as of this day. Jack desired he might be removed from the cell where his fellow criminals, condemned with him, were lodged, and his request was granted.

Examination and Confession of Jack (Comfort's) before one of the judges, No. 1.—He said,

1. "That a little after new year, on a Monday, about four in the afternoon, Ben* (Capt. Marshall's) came to Comfort's house to fetch tea water, where he left his keg in the shop, and went to Hughson's house (Hughson and his wife then gone into the country); Ben staid about two hours there, and then returned to Comfort's, and told Jack that he had met there six Spaniards, among whom were Anthony and Wan† (now in jail) and said to him, countryman, I have heard some good news: what news said Jack? Ben said there were Spanish negroes at Hughson's, who told him they had designs of taking this country against the wars came; what would they do with this country? said Jack, to which Ben answered, oh! you fool, those Spaniards know better than York negroes, and could help better to take it than they, because they were more used to war; but they must begin first to set the house [i.e. the houses] on fire.

2. "That the Sunday following Hughson and his wife came home, and brought a goose, a quarter of mutton, and a fowl home. That Ben came a little after church out, in the afternoon, to Comfort's, and told him, brother go to Hughson's, all our company is come down: he went with Ben thither, and went round the house and went in at the back door; when he came there they sat all round the table, and had a goose, a quarter of mutton, a fowl, and two loaves of bread: Hughson took a flask of rum out of a case and set it on the table, and two bowls of punch were made; some drink dram; a cloth was laid:

*Jack's description of Ben:—His master live in tall house Broadway. Ben ride de fat horse.

†Mr. Peter DeLancey's and Capt. Sarly's.

"Quash (H. Rutgers's negro); Caesar (Koertrecht's); Powlus, a Spanish negro; Toby, or Cato (Provoost's); Cato (Shurmur's); Cook (Comfort's); John (Vaarck's); York and London (Marschalk's); Ticklepitcher (Carpenter's); Francis (Bosch's); Bastian, alias Tom Peal; Scipio (Mrs. Van Borsom's); Ben (captain Marshall's) were all present, and also six Spanish negroes, among whom were Wan and Anthony, and a negro lately belonging to John Marschalk, the three others he should know if he saw them; Hughson, and his wife, and daughter sat down on one side of the table, and the negroes on the other: two or three tables were put together to make it long; Hughson's daughter brought in the victuals, and just as he came in Sarah brought the cloth and laid it; Mary Burton did not come into the room, but Hughson said she was above making a bed; Peggy came down stairs and sat down by Hughson's wife at the table, and eat with them; when they were eating they began all to talk about setting the houses on fire, and Hughson asked Ben, who would be the head man or captain for to rise? Ben said yes, he would stand for that, and said he could find a gun, shot and powder, at his master's house, that his master did not watch him, he could go into every room: Ben asked Quash, what will you stand for? he said he did not care what he stood for, or should be, but he could kill three, four, five white men before night.

3. "That Quash said he could get two half dozen of knives in papers, three or four swords; and that he would set his master's house on fire, and when he had done that, he would come abroad to fight.

4. "That Marschalk's York said that his mistress had scolded at him, and he would kill her before he went out to fight.

5. "London (Marschalk's other negro) said that before he went out to fight, he would set his master's house on fire.

6. "Scipio (Van Borsom's negro) said he would set his mistress's house on fire before he would go out to fight.

7. "Cato (Shurmur's negro) said he would set his mistress's house on fire, and that as the houses stand all together, the fire would go more far.

8. "Cato alias Toby (John Provoost's negro) said he would get his master's sword, and then set the house on fire, and go out to fight.

9. "The Spanish negroes he could not understand.

10. "Caesar (Kortrecht's negro) said he would set his master's bakehouse on fire.

11. "Ben said (when it was proposed to burn his master's house) no, if they conquered the place, he would keep that to live in himself.

12. "That Dick came in just as they had done eating, but victuals

enough were left for him, and he sat down and eat: when Dick had done eating, he said every one must stand to his word, and that he would get his master's gun, and after that would set his stable on fire.

13. "He (Jack) being asked to set his master's house on fire, said no, he would set his master's shingles on fire, and then go out to fight.

14. "Hughson said he would stand by what the Spanish and York negroes should do; and he would go before and be their king, and would mix them one amongst another when they came to fight.

15. "Hughson sat the negroes upon this discourse, and design, at the said meeting; on which the Spanish negroes agreed all to join with the York negroes.*

16. "That they all swore; some said d—n, some said by G—d, and other oaths; a Spanish negro swear by thunder;[57] Hughson swore by G—d, if they would be true to him, he would take this country; and Jack swore by G—d for his part.

17. "That Peggy went away after they had done eating, before they swore.

18. "Mary Burton took away the dishes and plates, and Sarah (Hughson's daughter) took away the cloth; Sarah (Hughson's wife) sat down by her husband, and continued there all the time. . . .

25. "Says, they agreed to wait a month and half for the Spaniards and French to come; and if they did not come then, they were to begin at Wenman's, next to Mr. DeLancey's, and so on down the Broadway.

26. "That they waited until this month and half was expired, and then the fort was burnt.

27. "Says, that every negro then present was to do what they engaged to do, on one and the same Sunday, when church was gone in of the morning; and if all was not done in that one day, they were to go on the Saturday following; and so, if the Spaniards and French did not come, they were to do all themselves. . . .

29. "That same Sunday's Monday (the next day) about sun down, all the same negroes came to Hughson's again; some brought money and gave to Hughson for drink and dram; Ben played on the fiddle; Hughson's wife and daughter danced together in one part of the room, and the negroes in another; staid there until about seven that night: that they came there that night to frolick and merry make, and did not talk about fires, for they had agreed upon that the day before. . . .

*See the confessions of Quack and Cuffee, 30th May.

[57] Swearing by thunder was a common West African oath.

33. "This conversation began, and was most talked of before Sandy came in; Sandy came into the kitchen first, being called in by him (Jack) but was loth to come; Jack asked him to drink a dram, Sandy said no; Sarah (Burk's negro wench) who was then present, said he must drink, and made him drink; and having drunk the dram, Jack asked him if he would stand to, and help them burn houses, and kill the white people? Sandy seemed afraid, they all drank a dram round, and he (Jack) brought in nine clasp knives in a paper; those that had not knives before, took knives from the paper; some went into the shop; and some came into the kitchen, and all the knives were distributed: being asked how he came by those knives, said he asked Powlus, a Spanish negro, about a week before this meeting, to give him a knife; Powlus said he would get some for him, and sell him; Powlus appointed him to meet him the Wednesday before this meeting, at the meal-market, about dusk; that Powlus came, and he gave him two shillings and six pence for them.

34. "When they saw Sandy afraid, they whetted their knives in order to frighten him to say yes, to stand by them; and Jack said, if he did not stand by them he would cut his head off; to which Sarah said, he deserves it if he don't say yes; then Sandy said yes."

THURSDAY JUNE 11

The king against Sarah Hughson, daughter of John Hughson.

As to this miserable creature under sentence of death, to be executed with her father and mother and Margaret Kerry to-morrow, the judges wished that she would have furnished them with some colour or pretence for recommending her as an object of mercy, but they waited for it hitherto in vain: she was a wretch stupified and hardened in wickedness, and seemed void of all sense of a future state;[58] however it was thought proper to respite her execution to Friday, 19th June, which was ordered accordingly, in hopes that after her father and mother had suffered, she might be molified to a confession of her own guilt, and raise some merit by making a further discovery; or at least, configuring what had hitherto been unfolded concerning this accursed scheme.

FRIDAY, JUNE 12

This day John Hughson, Sarah his wife, and Margaret Kerry, were executed according to sentence.

[58]*sense of a future state:* That is, concern for her soul after death.

The under-sheriff had often advised John Hughson, to make a confession about the conspiracy, but he always denied he knew any thing of the matter; said he had deserved death for receiving stolen goods. The wife was ever sullen; said little or nothing, but denied all.

The sheriffs observed John Hughson, when he was brought out of jail to be carried to execution, to have a red spot on each cheek, about the bigness of a shilling, which at that time thought very remarkable, for he was always pale of visage: these spots continued all along to the gallows. Amongst other discourse it seems he had said, he did not doubt but some remarkable sign would happen to him, to show his innocence; concerning which more will be observed upon hereafter. He stood up in the cart all the way, looking round about him as if expecting to be rescued, as was by many conjectured from the air he appeared in: one hand was lifted up as high as his pinion[59] would admit of, and a finger pointing, as if intending to beckon.

At the gallows his wife stood like a lifeless trunk, with the rope about her neck, tied up to the tree; she said not a word, and had scarce any visible motion.

Peggy seemed much less resigned than the other two, or rather unwilling to encounter death; she was going to say something, but the old woman who hung next to her, gave her a shove with her hand, as was said by some, so Peggy was silent.

But they all died, having protested their innocence to the last, touching the conspiracy.

This old woman, as it has been generally reported, was bred a Papist; and Peggy was much suspected of the same persuasion, though perhaps it may seem to be of little significance what religion such vile wretches professed.

From the scanty room in the jail for the reception of so many prisoners, this miserable wretch, upon her conviction with the Hughsons for the conspiracy, was put in the same cell with them; which perhaps was an unfortunate incident; for though she had to the time of their trial screened them from the charge of the conspiracy; yet there was reason to expect, that upon the last pinch, when she found there was no hopes of saving her own life if she persisted, the truth as to this particular would have come out; and indeed it was upon this expectation, that she was brought upon trial for the conspiracy; for her several examinations before set forth, and what Arthur Price had sworn to have dropt from her in accidental talk in jail, had put it beyond doubt,

[59]*pinion:* Manacles; handcuffs.

that she was privy to many of the Hughsons' secrets concerning this detestable confederacy; but when she was admitted to the Hughsons, under the circumstances of conviction and condemnation for the conspiracy, they most probably prevailed with her to persevere in her obstinacy, to the end to cover their own guilt, since they were determined to confess nothing themselves; and they might drive her to desperation by subtle insinuations, that the judges she saw after they had picked all they could out of her, whatever expectations she might have raised from her confessions, or hopes she flattered herself with of saving her life upon the merit of them; yet after all, she was brought to trial and condemned for the conspiracy, as well as they; and why should she expect pardon any more than they: and by such like artifices it is probable they might stop her mouth, and prevent her making further discovery; and not only so, but then of course prevail with her to recant, as to what she had confessed already.

John Hughson's body was hung in chains according to sentence.

FOREIGN THREATS: THE TRIAL OF THE SPANISH PRISONERS

The trial of the Spanish prisoners, as the governor's proclamation of June 10 makes clear, convinced the court that the leading slaves of the conspiracy were Spanish rather than British. Burton gave evidence of the bloodthirstiness of the Spanish, as did the slave witnesses. The fact that they were both national and religious enemies prejudiced the courts against them as well.

The Spanish slaves mounted the most vigorous (and best-documented) defense of any of the accused slaves. Their initial strategy was two-pronged: first, that they were not slaves and thus could not be convicted on the basis of slave testimony and, second, that Mary Burton did not speak Spanish and thus could not testify against them, since she did not know what they said. When the courts dismissed these two arguments, the Spaniards changed their defense. They then asserted either that they did not understand enough English to plot with New York slaves, or that their feet were so frostbitten from the winter that they could not walk. Most of their owners seemed to support their defense and believe in their innocence. Despite the fact that all five were convicted, in the end, only one was executed (in August). The rest were transported out of New York. One was sent to Newfoundland, the only one of the British colonies to which convicted slaves were sent. The other four were sent to Spanish possessions. They may have been sold into a life of brutal labor on sugar plantations, where slaves were often worked literally to death, but it is also possible, given their owners' support of them, that they were sent to Cuba or other Spanish possessions. Horsmanden does not say.

SATURDAY, JUNE 13

The King, against DeLancey's Antonio, Mesnard's Antonio, Pablo alias Powlus, Juan alias Wan, Augustine.

The five prisoners being Spanish negroes, lately imported into this city as prize slaves, were put to the bar, and arraigned upon an indictment for the conspiracy, and thereto severally pleaded, *not guilty.*

MONDAY, JUNE 15

This being the day appointed for the trial of these prisoners as slaves upon an indictment for the conspiracy, on which they were arraigned on Saturday last, they were brought to the bar in order to proceed thereon: but they complained (as it is supposed they were advised) that they had great injustice done them by being sold here as slaves, for that, as they pretended, they were free men in their own country, and gave in their several surnames.

The indictment was grounded upon an act of the assembly* which enumerated several offences; and conspiracies amongst the rest, and made one slave evidence against another, so that this fetch[60] might probably be calculated to take off the negro evidence: the prisoners all protested they could not speak English, and as Mary Burton was the only white evidence against them, and should it be credited that they could speak only in a tongue which she did not understand, how could she tell what passed between them in conversation at Hughson's? Thus their advisers might think they would stand the best chance for the jury to acquit them.

The court deferred their trial till Wednesday the 17th instant.

WEDNESDAY, JUNE 17

The King against DeLancey's Antonio, Mesnard's Antonio, Becker's Pablo, Sarly's Juan alias Wan, McMullen's Augustine, Spanish negroes.

*4th Geo. II. For the more effectually preventing and punishing the conspiracy and insurrection of negro and other slaves, etc. before mentioned on trial of Quack and Cuffee, 29th May. [This refers to the 1730 slave code that established the slave courts. See the Introduction.—Ed.]

[60]*fetch:* A trick or strategem.

The prisoners being set to the bar, were arraigned upon a second indictment, for counselling and advising the negro Quack, to burn the fort, etc. by the names of Antonio de St. Bendito, Antonio de la Cruz, Pablo Ventura Angel, Juan de la Sylva, Augustine Gutierez; whereto they severally pleaded, *not guilty,* etc.

Then the court proceeded upon their trials on both indictments.

Mr. Gomez sworn interpreter.

Witnesses for the king called.

Mary Burton sworn. She said that she had seen many meetings of the negroes at Hughson's, and especially about new-year, and that it was the common talk among them and the Hughson's, that they would burn the town and murder the people, that Hughson swore the negroes to be true to him, and to each other, and not to discover; that they were to burn the fort, then the Fly, and murder the people: that Hughson said they would burn Lush's house, and tie Lush to a beam and roast him like a piece of beef: that there were several great meetings there, and that she had seen Anthony (DeLancey's) often there at nights, that he was there when they talked about fires, and some of them said, the Spaniards could fight well; that she thought the said Anthony was there about new-year, but was sure she saw him there often in March, and that he often spoke to her in English, and that she heard him say, while the York negroes killed one, the Spaniards could kill twenty: that he used to come upon the shingles and get into Peggy's window: that she had seen all the prisoners at Hughson's, when they were talking about the plot, and they were consenting.

[Sawney (Sandy) summarized his depositions of May 22 and June 1.]

Mr. George Joseph Moore, called and sworn. He proved the confessions of Quack and Cuffee at the stake.

He said, that they declared the Spanish negroes were most of them concerned in the plot; that they did not name any names but referred to Sawney, who, they said, could name them all.

[Slaves who had given depositions earlier to the court here repeated their testimony.]

Jack (Comfort's negro) said, that after new-year there was a great company of negroes at Hughson's on a Sunday evening; that he went with captain Marshall's Ben thither, and he supped there, and all the prisoners were present, which was in February; that all present agreed to burn the town, and they were all sworn.—That ten days before the fort was burnt, they had a meeting at his master's (Comfort's) and there they all swore to burn the town, and kill the people; that they were first to begin at Mr. DeLancey's and so to go to the fort; that they sharpened their knives, and he let nine have knives that had none; that he bought the knives of Pablo for half a crown; that there was only two Spaniards there, to wit, Antonio (Mr. DeLancey's) and Pablo (Becker's) and that Mr. DeLancey's negro said, he had stuff to throw on the houses to make them get fire, which Hughson had talked about before: that they were to stay a month and a half for the Spaniards, and if they did not come, to begin themselves.

Ticklepitcher said, that about three weeks after new-year, he saw all the prisoners at Hughson's on a Sunday evening with one Spanish negro more; and Mr. DeLancey's negro (Antonio) had something black, which he said was to throw on houses to set them on fire; and he cut it in pieces and gave to several of the negroes: that he (the witness) did not then stay at Hughson's, so did not hear what they talked of. That afterwards there was a great meeting of the negroes at Comfort's, and he saw Juan and Augustine there; and it was agreed by those present to set the town on fire, and kill the white people; and there they sharpened their knives: that Mr. Niblet's Sawney was also there, and Burk's Sarah, who told him that they were making a plot to kill the white people, burn the houses, and to steal the money and goods and go off; there were two rooms full of them, some were in the kitchen and some in the shop.

Richard Nichols, esquire, deputy register of the admiralty, sworn.

He said, that the nineteen negroes and mulattoes, taken and brought in by captain Lush, were libelled in the court of admiralty, as Spanish slaves, and condemned as such in May, 1740; and Pablo (Becker's) was condemned as a slave taken by captain Kierstead.[61]

[61]When privateers brought foreign ships and cargoes back to British ports, they had to declare their prizes before the local vice-admiralty court. There the British captain would ask the court to consider their prize legitimate and legally able to be sold, or "libelled." The prize was sold at auction (or vendue) and the profits were then shared among the ship's owners, captain, and crew. Black and mixed-race sailors were assumed to be slaves and thus foreign property belonging to French or Spanish subjects. Although sailors could protest their enslavement and sale in court, few freedom suits were successful during King George's War (1739–1748). Condemned sailors were sold at auction along with the ship and its cargo. The capture of the nineteen sailors by John Lush was first reported in the *New York Weekly Journal,* May 5, 1740. For Benjamin Kierstead's case in the vice-admiralty court, see "Benjamin Kierstead and company, etc. agt. Twenty one serons of cocoa, two Negro Slaves and other Goods in the Lybell Mentioned," March 12, 1740–41. Vice-Admiralty Minute Books, National Archives, Northeast Division.

John Cruger, esquire, vendue-master.—He said, that he afterwards sold Antonio, DeLancey's; Antonio, Mesnard's; and Juan, Sarly's, at vendue.

Captain John Lush sworn.—He said, that Juan, Sarly's, could speak English, and Antonio, DeLancey's, could speak a little so as to be understood.

William Douglass, sworn.

He said he was taken in captain Hinman's vessel with Mr. DeLancey's Antonio's brother; that they were carried into the Havanna, and that a gentlemen there bought Antonio's brother as a slave, and said he knew him and his family at Carthagena, and that they were slaves.

Mr. Benson, partner with Mr. Becker, Pablo's master, sworn.

Being asked whether he had any such clasp knives as Jack (Comfort's) had described, and said he had bought of Pablo? he answered, that he had had a parcel of clasp knives, but whether he had sold them, or whether he had them still, he could not say; but that he would go home and see, if the court pleased; and he going accordingly and being returned, said that upon search he found that he had none of those knives left but one; that his wife told him that they had brought but three of them when they came to Becker's. He said that Pablo talked very broken English, but he could make a shift to understand him.

Witnesses for the prisoner Antonio (DeLancey's).—Mr. Peter DeLancey, merchant, said that his negro went to his farm in the country last fall, and did not return till two days after the fire at the fort; that he was not there all the while himself, but was frequently there, and saw him lame, his feet being frozen, and he did not think he could have been in town in that time.

Witnesses for Antonio (Mesnard's).—Dr. Depuy, senior, said that Antonio (Mesnard's) feet were frozen, and that he dressed them during December and January last.

Dr. Depuy, junior, said that the latter end of November and December last, this negro was ill, and he saw his toes in December, and then they were bad, so that he could not walk, but he did not know whether he was able to walk in February or not: that he (Antonio) came to his father's house the beginning or middle of March, the time he could not exactly say, but it was before the fire at the fort.

Mrs. Mesnard, this negro's mistress, said he was not down stairs from November till the 17th of March, and she believed it was not possible for him to be abroad at that time.

Witness for Juan.—Captain Jacob Sarly, his master, said that when the fire was at Mr. Thomas's, Juan, his negro, first discovered it to his wife, as she told him, and that he never had a more faithful servant, and when he was home, the negro could not be out after nine at night. That one Don Juan told him by an interpreter, that he heard that his negro was free. Further, that he was not always at home himself, but he did not believe his negro had been out.

Witness for Pablo.—Frederick Becker, Pablo's master, said that his negro was brought into this country by captain Boyd, in January last, and was sick in his house till some time in March.

Witnesses for Augustine.—McMullen, his master, said that his negro was sick all the winter, and did not know that he was abroad all the winter. In February he had an ague, as the Doctor said, that he kept his bed most of the time, but not constant but about a week: that he always behaved very well, and captain Warren gave him a very good character: that he was brought by capt. Warren into this country, who offered to sell him to him for 70 pounds but they did not agree.

Thomas Palmer said to the same purpose.

The prisoners, upon their defence, denied all in general that was alleged against them, and made great protestations of their innocence, and most of them pretended to have been sick or lame, so that they were incapable of going abroad from new year to the time of the fire at the fort (the eighteenth of March), neither could they speak English.

Antonio (DeLancey's) said in particular, that his master and the overseer could prove that he had been lame, and was in the country all the winter, and that his master had him to town a little after the fort burnt, and that he had not kept company with any negroes since he came to the country.

Augustine said he had been sick ever since he came here; that he knew no negroes; kept no company but McMullen's apprentices.

Pablo or Powlus, said that he kept no company with Negroes since he came here; he had not been used to keep company with negroes (or slaves) in his own country.

Juan or Wan spoke much to the same purpose; he did not use to keep company with negroes (or slaves.)

Antonio (Mesnard's) was sick and lame, etc.

The court charged the jury as followeth:

Gentlemen of the jury,

The prisoners at the bar stand charged upon two several indictments, for conspiring to burn and destroy this city, and murder the white people.

The one indictment is grounded upon an act of assembly of this province, supposing them to be slaves, by which act the testimony of one negro slave shall be legal evidence against another.

But it has been made a question, whether these prisoners, now before us, are slaves or not; and the prisoners themselves pretend to be free subjects of the king of Spain, with whom we are now at war, from whom they have been taken and made prize, and have been condemned and adjudged as such in the court of admiralty here, without any plea being offered there, or so much as any claim or pretence of the prisoners being entitled to any privilege, as being free subjects of Spain; and surely there never could have been a more proper time and season for them to have set up such pretence, as when their case was depending before the court of admiralty, where they should have offered it by way of plea; especially considering, that by their neglect of that opportunity, they must well know the consequence would be, their being adjudged as part of the goods and chattels of the subjects of Spain, would be condemned as lawful prize, and would also be sold as slaves; but if this pretence had been offered there, (as was not) and they could not have proved the truth of the plea it would not have availed them, but they must have been adjudged to be slaves.

But they have made that pretence in this court, and what has been offered in support of it? Why there has been several witnesses that have spoke to the point; and what is the amount of their testimony? Why, it is no more than the hearsay of an hearsay of a person, who imagined or believed, that they or most of the Spanish negroes taken by capt. Lush, were freemen; but which of them were or were not, he could not say, nor does it appear that the prisoners at the bar, or any of them, are such of capt. Lush's prize prisoners, as that the said Spanish gentleman imagined were free; for it was no more than his imagination, as to any of them being such.

You have heard the adjudication and decree of the court of admiralty read, by which it appears, they were condemned as prize, and that they were sold as slaves, has been proved by the vendue-master; therefore for what appears now before the court, it should seem that they really are slaves; and as nothing appears; no sufficient or proper evidence appears to the contrary, then if you take them upon these considerations, to be slaves, all the negro evidence which has been given upon this trial against them, is legal evidence, and so you are to consider of that testimony, and let it have its full force; and if you should have sufficient reason in your own consciences to discredit them, and that notwithstanding the weight of that evidence, you can think them, or any of them, not guilty, you will then say so and acquit them, or such of them as you think innocent as to the charge of this indictment, upon the act of assembly.

Gentlemen, the prisoners having started this pretence, of being free subjects of the king of Spain, in case it should have happened upon this trial, as we think it has not, that there should be sufficient evidence to shew that the prisoners were freemen, if we could take them to be such, is it fit that persons guilty of so atrocious and enormous crimes (let them be free or bond) such execrable villains should miss of their deserved punishment and escape the justice of the law? Surely that would be very unbecoming, that such wickedness should be suffered with impunity in any well regulated government or society: therefore be they freemen, or be they slaves, the main question before you is, whether they, or any, or which of them are guilty of the charge against them, in the second indictment, of conspiring with other slaves and persons to burn the house in the fort, to burn the town and murder and destroy the people.

To prove the charge in this indictment, there was the testimony of Mary Burton: I must observe to you, that her testimony, as to the charge in this indictment, is single, there is no other witness; but nevertheless gentlemen, one witness is sufficient, and if you give credit to her testimony, you will no doubt discharge a good conscience, and find them guilty; if you should have sufficient reason in your own minds to discredit her testimony, if you can think so, you must then acquit them: the prisoners seem all to be equally involved by her testimony, in this unparalleled and hellish conspiracy, and there is no room to make any difference between them; therefore you will either acquit them all, or find them all guilty.

Then the jury withdrew, and in about half an hour returned, and found them all guilty.

The judges having advised with his honour the lieutenant governor, ordered, the execution of Sarah Hughson be further respited until next Friday seven-night;[62] though with respect to Sarah this was a mere act of mercy, for she yet remained inflexible.

FRIDAY, JUNE 19

The lieutenant governor having this day issued a proclamation with the advice of his majesty's counsel, the same was read in court, taking

[62]*seven-night:* One week.

notice of the conspiracy which had been set on foot, abetted, encouraged and carried on by several white people in conjunction with divers Spanish negroes brought hither from the West-Indies, and a great number of other negroes within this city and country, for the burning and destroying this whole city, and murdering the inhabitants thereof; to the end that mercy might be shewn to such as might merit the same, his honour thought it necessary, and did thereby in his majesty's name, offer and promise his majesty's most gracious pardon, to any and every person and persons, whether white people, free negroes, slaves, or others, who had been or were concerned in the said conspiracy, who should on or before the first day of July then next, voluntarily, freely and fully discover, and confession make, of his, her or their confederates, accomplices, or others concerned in the said conspiracy, and his, her and their part or share, actings and doings therein, so that the person or persons making such discovery and confession, were not thereof before convicted, arraigned, or indicted for the same.

Confession of Wan, Indian man of Mr. Lowe, before the grand jury.

1. He said that about twelve months ago he met at the water-side, John, a free Indian, late of Cornelius Cosine, who carried him to Hughson's, where they drank a mug of beer, and paid for it: when John went away, but Hughson stopped him (Wan) and told him a law was made to sell no liquor to slaves, bid him not tell: Wan said he would not; then Hughson bid him swear on a book he held to him, to do what he should tell him, and Wan said he would; and he put his hand on the book and swore after what Hughson said, to burn his master's house, and to kill his master and mistress, and to assist to take the town.

2. That Ticklepitcher and Bastian were there when he swore; and being asked if any one else? he said none.

3. That John, the Indian, met him afterwards, and seeing him melancholy, asked him what was the matter? He (Wan) told him what he had done, on which John said it was good for him.

4. That Cuffee (Gomez's) and Francis (Bosch's) told him, they were to set their master's house on fire, and one day asked him if he was ready, and he told them yes.

5. That being asked what they were to do when they took the town? he answered, they were to kill the white people, the men, and take their wives to themselves.

SATURDAY, JUNE 20

Confession of York, negro of Marschalk's.

1. He acknowledged that what the witnesses said on the trial yesterday was true.

2. That he went one Sunday morning early about two years ago, to Hughson's house with Kip's Samuel, who has been dead two years, and bought a quart of rum, and went with it to Mr. Bayard's.

3. That Comfort's Jack, about Christmas last, informed him first of the plot: Jack met him by his gate and told him of it, and appointed him to meet him at Hughson's, that he went to Hughson's; was there the Sunday the feast was, as mentioned by the witnesses in court.

4. Has been twice at Hughson's and once at Comfort's.

5. Was to be a captain, and was sworn; that many negroes were present, and all sworn and consented.

6. Agreed to the circumstances told of the plot in general; Spanish negroes were there; Furman's Harry, Moore's Cato, all the prisoners who were tried with him were there; Ben Moore's Tom and Mink there, Gabriel Crooke's Prince there, Ben and Quash there.

7. Hughson, his wife and daughter swore first, then those who were at the upper end of the table, near Hughson, swore upon the book, and the others at a distance without book, by thunder, etc.

8. He agreed to set his master's house on fire, but said he would not do it until he saw somebody else begin, and then he would; he was to kill his mistress: went to Hughson's just after church out.

9. That he believed that meeting was about six weeks before the fort burnt.

10. London (his fellow slave) was to be a private man under him.

11. Comfort's meeting was two weeks after this: at Comfort's he and Kip's Harry were in the shop, about twenty there; Gabriel Crooke's Prince there, London there, Marshal's Ben there, Hermanus's Quash; Jack went backwards and forwards from the shop to the kitchen, Furman's Harry there.

12. Hughson proposed to them to get as many other negroes in as they could.

13. Mr. Moore's Cato, Shurmur's Cato, at Comfort's; he did not go into the kitchen, but heard that a great many were there.

14. Hughson told him at his house, that the Spaniards knew better than York negroes how to fight, and they were all to stand by one another and assist the French and Spaniards, they were to wait

for them sometime, if they did not come, they were to do all themselves.

15. Every one in the shop (at Comfort's) had knives, and they were sharpening of them; and they were to cut white men's heads off.

WEDNESDAY, JULY 1

The five Spanish negroes convicted of the conspiracy on the seventeenth of June last, were this day called up to judgment, viz.—Mr. De Lancey's Antonio, Mesnard's Antonio, Becker's Pablo, Sarly's Juan or Wan, McMullen's Augustine; and having nothing to offer in arrest, but protestations of their innocence, Mr. Gomez* was directed to interpret what the court delivered.

[The court found them to be slaves and sentenced them to be hanged.]

PAPIST PLOT: THE TRIAL OF JOHN URY

The trial of the Spanish sailors brought to the fore the fear of international conspiracy. Between the time of the sailors' trial and sentencing, officials scoured the city for reputed Catholics, and arrested John Ury. The next day, Burton reversed her initial testimony of April 22, in which she asserted that Kerry and the Hughsons were the only whites involved. She now testified that Ury had been frequenting the Hughsons' house since the previous Christmas.

In the person of Ury, the court at last found the mastermind it had been seeking. An itinerant teacher, with some unorthodox religious beliefs (or possibly, as his friend Joseph Webb testified, simply incomprehensible ones), Ury seemed a suspicious character. His ability to read Latin, the language of the Catholic Church, made him yet more suspect. When Burton and others testified that he claimed to be able to "forgive sins," they were referring to the Catholic practice of absolution, a practice that most Protestant churches did not uphold. It was assumed that any man who said he was able to perform absolution in the anti-Catholic world of eighteenth-century New York could be nothing other than a priest. When New York's lieutenant governor received a letter from the governor of Georgia warning him that itinerant teachers and dancing masters were in fact Catholic priests spying for the Spanish government,

*He had been interpreter upon the trial.

Ury's fate was sealed. Irish soldiers from the fort who were suspected to be Catholic were also accused as conspirators.

The emphasis on religion did not replace Horsmanden's concerns about racial upheavals. In a tone both admonitory and bemused, he reported that the bodies of Caesar and Hughson, then decomposing on the gallows, swapped races. Since he refuses to give his own explanation for this phenomenon, he allows his readers to draw their own conclusions about the relationship of race and color.

As a result of the proclamation of June 19, by which the governor promised a pardon to anyone who would confess to his or her involvement in the conspiracy or give information about others', enormous numbers of slaves offered confessions. Only one, Jack's (Murray's), is reproduced at length here, since most were simply confirmation of evidence that Burton, Sandy, and others had already given. Jack's confession encapsulates almost every theme, plot, and participant since the trials began in April.

The pressure to confess, however, undoubtedly created false and exaggerated testimony, if not outright lies. The constable, John Schultz, gave evidence of several pieces of false testimony. Caesar (Horsefield's) is also caught in contradictions during his confession. Adam's testimony indicates that some slaves recognized the dangers to them of false accusations and tried to divert them. Consider the reasons the witnesses gave both for their initial testimony and for their retractions. Whites, too, in their eagerness to give evidence, accused more and more people, including, finally, an unnamed gentleman "with a pigtail wig," an indication of gentility and high social status. The court decided not to pursue that particular piece of evidence. As the anonymous writer to Cadwallader Colden noted in his letter (Document 4), when the accusers in Salem, Massachusetts, began to charge elites (including the governor's wife) with witchcraft, those trials quickly ended. The same pattern is evident in New York.

WEDNESDAY, JUNE 24

Intimation having been given for some time past, that there had of late been Popish priests lurking about the town, diligent inquiry had been made for discovering them, but without effect; at length information was given, that one Ury alias Jury, who had lately come into this city, and entered into partnership with Campbell, a school-master, pretending to teach Greek and Latin, was suspected to be one, and that he kept a private conventicle;[63] he was taken into custody this day, and not giving a satisfactory account of himself, was committed to the city jail.

THURSDAY, JUNE 25

Deposition of Mary Burton, taken before one of the judges. No. 4.—Mary Burton being duly sworn, deposed,

1. That the person yesterday shewn to her in prison, lately taken into custody on suspicion of being a Roman Catholic priest, is the same person she has often seen at the house of John Hughson; that to the best of her recollection she saw him there first, some time about Christmas last, and that then for a fortnight together he used to come there almost every night, and sometimes used to lie there, but was always gone in the morning before she the deponent got up, but she well remembers he used to go by different names, but whether by the name of Jury or Ury, or Doyle, she cannot now depose positively, but to the best of her remembrance, some of his names consisted only of one syllable, and believes she heard him called by all the said three names.

[Burton also testified that Ury was present when Hughson and others discussed the conspiracy. She said that he had joined with the others to pressure her to swear an oath, although they would not tell her to what she would be swearing. Despite their bribes of money and silk fabrics, she refused.]

9. That one day at Hughson's, some of the negroes had behaved rudely towards her, and being in a passion, she was provoked to swear at them, in the presence of Jury alias Ury, above mentioned, and upon recollecting herself she said, God forgive me; whereupon the said Jury answered her, that was a small matter; he could forgive her a great deal more sins than that; that was nothing.

10. That at another time when the negroes had provoked her, she wished those black toads at the devil; oh, said Jury, let them be black, or what they will, the devil has nothing to do with them; I can forgive them their sins, and you yours too.

[63]*conventicle:* A religious meeting of Protestant dissenters from the Anglican Church of England. Although all forms of Protestant dissent were legal in New York, sects other than Anglicans or Dutch Reform Lutherans were often viewed with suspicion.

FRIDAY, JUNE 26

Examination and confession of Jack, Mr. Murray's negro, before one of the judges.—He said,

1. That soon after new-year holidays he went to Comfort's to fetch tea-water, and as he was coming from thence he saw Vaarck's Caesar standing at Hughson's door, who called to him to come thither, and when he came to the house he saw John Hughson in the entry, who asked him to come in, and he went in, and Caesar followed him; and Hughson asked him to set his keg of tea-water down and stay there a little, but he (Jack) said that he could not stay; Hughson then told him that he had better carry his keg of tea-water home, and then return again and bring a gun and powder and bullets, and some negro with him, and then asked him to drink some punch, and he drank a small draught and was then going, but Hughson made him promise to come back, and said when he returned they would talk about a plot, and so he went away: there were present in the room at this time, Hughson, his wife and daughter, and Peggy, Vaarck's Caesar, Walter's Quack, Pintard's Caesar, old Mr. Jay's Ben, Auboyneau's Prince, Philipse's Cuffee, and the Chief justice's Othello, and three Spanish negroes.

2. That as he was going home with the tea-water he met Adam, his fellow servant by old Mr. DeLancey's house, and he told Adam where he had been and what had been talked of, and what company was at Hughson's, as before mentioned; Adam thereupon ordered him to set his keg down, which he did, and gave it in charge to one of Mr. DeLancey's negro wenches, and said they would go down there and drink some punch, and they went accordingly.

3. When they came to Hughson's, they found the same company Jack had left, and the cloth was laid and the supper getting: he heard them talking when he came into the entry, of burning the houses and killing the white people, and of taking all the gentlewomen for their wives.

4. That when Adam and he came into the room, Hughson asked them whether they would do as they were going to do; which he said was to set the town on fire and to kill the white men and to keep the white women for their wives, to get all their master's guns and swords and pistols, and when their masters came to put out the fires to kill them all? Adam answered he would do the same, and he (Jack) said he would do the same: then Hughson carried Adam and him up stairs, and brought a book to swear them, but he (Jack) would not swear by

the book, but kissed his hand and said he would stand to it, but Adam put his hand upon the book and kissed it, and said he would stand to it; then Hughson produced a paper, and said it was an agreement of the blacks to kill the white folks, and he put his (Jack's) and Adam's names down in it, as he (Jack) understood him.

5. That after this they went down stairs again to the rest of the company, and there they found two negro men a fiddling to them, before whom Hughson and the blacks talked of the like discourse: one fiddler belonged to Holt, named Joe, the other Kiersted's Braveboy; the negroes shook hands with Adam and him, and wished them joy, and Hughson did the like to them up stairs; and they all said they must keep every thing secret and stand to their words.

6. They said they expected the French and Spaniards here, and then they would fire and plunder the houses and carry all to Hughson's, who was to carry them off into another country, and make them a free people, but they were to stay about two months before they began to set fire, and then all of them were to begin at once.

7. That he (Jack) and Adam staid and eat some supper and drank some punch, and as soon as they had supped went home together, and left the rest of the company behind: this meeting was of a Sunday evening.

8. That he (Jack) went afterwards to Hughson's several times as he went to fetch tea-water, and was there twice afterwards with Adam; that they always talked with Hughson and the negroes present about the plot, and when was the time to begin.

9. That Jay's Brash carried him (Jack) once to Hughson's, and another time Pintard's Caesar; and that it was usual for them at such by-meetings to swear without book, that they all stand to their words and keep all secret.

10. That on Easter Sunday he (Jack) and Adam went down to Hughson's after church in the afternoon; he (Jack) was to go to Comfort's for tea-water; Adam went in before, and he (Jack) went to Comfort's and left his keg there, and soon followed him thither after he had filled his keg; and there they met with Walter's Quack, Pintard's Caesar, Ward's Bill, Jay's Ben, Philipse's Cuffee, Auboyneau's Prince, Brash, Vaarck's Caesar, Mrs. Sim's Billy, Albany, Othello, Hughson, his wife and daughter Sarah; and then John Hughson proposed to all the negroes last mentioned, and to him (Jack) and Adam, that they should meet at Mr. Murray's house that night, that he (Jack) was to be in the kitchen, and to open the back gate whereat all those negroes

were to come in, and Adam and he were to come down stairs to them, and they were to proceed to set fire to the house, murder his master and mistress, and the white people in the house, but he was interrupted by Mrs. Dimmock's* accidentally coming down into the kitchen and sending him up to bed.

11. That after Mrs. Dimmock discovered him in the kitchen and sent him up to bed, a second time he came down again, went into the yard and opened the back gate, and staid in the yard half an hour, expecting the aforesaid negroes coming according to the appointment aforesaid; and they not coming after his waiting so long time, he (Jack) went up to Mr. Cruger's (the Mayor's) corner, and there saw Quack (Walter's) and the other negroes who had engaged to come to his master's house as before mentioned, but they said they could not come then, for they must go down to Hughson's; and he (Jack) returned home and went in at the kitchen window and there slept, and staid till the first cock-crowing, and then opened the kitchen door and fetched in wood to make the fire, intending thereby to make the family believe that he got up early and came down stairs to make it.

12. That Hughson at the same meeting proposed to the said negroes, that they should destroy Mr. Murray, Mrs. Murray and all the family with knives, and Hughson asked them all if they had got knives? and they all said they had, and pulled them out of their pockets; and Adam pulled out a long knife, and all the rest had long knives; but he (Jack) had a short one, which he calls a pen-knife, a clasped-knife which he eats his victuals with; he had seen Adam's before, he was whetting it one day upon the broad stones in the yard, and made it very sharp, and eat meat with it in his master's kitchen before all the servants; but he observed he generally kept it in his chest, and it was the same knife which was found upon the general search for stolen goods.†

13. That when the snow was upon the ground, about Christmas last, he was at Hughson's, having been at Comfort's for tea-water, and Caesar (Vaarck's) standing at Hughson's door, called him in to drink; Prince (Auboyneau's), Cuffee (Philipse's), Quack (Walter's), and Bill (Sims') were in the entry; Hughson called him (Jack) aside, and told him, after he (Jack) and Adam had murdered the whole family, that

* Mr. Murray's house-keeper.

† There was such a knife found in Adam's chest upon the general search.

he (Jack) should steal the plate out of the beaufets,[64] the kitchen furniture, wearing apparel, linen, guns, swords, and every thing that was of value, and bring them to his (Hughson's) house; that the aforesaid negroes should assist him to bring them, and that they should bury them under ground; Hughson and his wife were both together with him (Jack) when he received these directions. Jack was unwilling at first, but at length consented to undertake it.

14. That Adam was to kill his master and mistress, Mrs. Dimmock and her daughter; and that he (Jack) was to kill Caesar, Congo and Dido* and after that they were to take the above mentioned goods and carry them to the place appointed, after which they were to return to the house and set fire to it, then go down again to Hughson's and make ready for the general attack.

15. That this proposal last above said was made by Hughson, before that of the Easter Sunday before mentioned,† and that Adam was not present.

SATURDAY, JUNE 27

[The day after Murray's Jack confessed, his fellow-slave Adam was brought to the magistrates.]

It was observed by several in Mr. Murray's family, some time before Adam's commitment, that his behaviour was such as betokened strong symptoms of guilt, he appeared very uneasy and disturbed in his mind, and much more so when Jack his fellow servant was taken up as one concerned in the conspiracy, for the next morning he came several times into the clerk's office, with a seeming intention to disclose some secret; the young gentlemen at last took notice of it, and shutting the door too, asked him, whether he knew any thing concerning the plot? he denied he did, but said he was afraid some dog or another would owe him a spite, and bring him in, for that people talked a great deal of him.

In the afternoon, Mr. Murray having been present and assisting at his negro Jack's examination, upon his return home found Adam running backwards and forwards like a distracted creature, he called him into his study and charged him as one concerned in the conspiracy,

[64]*beaufets:* Buffet or sideboard where silver was kept.
*Three other of Mr. Murray's negroes.
†See #10, of this confession.

which he absolutely denied, and protested his innocence; his master endeavoured and used many arguments to prevail with him to confess if he was guilty, but to no purpose, and then he delivered him to the constable.

In the evening two of Mr. Murray's clerks went to see Adam in the jail, to try how far they could prevail upon him; and as soon as he knew they were come, he desired leave to speak with them privately, which being granted, he began with exclamations and protestations of his innocence, declaring it was nothing but damned lies that brought him there, and that he knew who was the author of them, and would be revenged if he died for it: the young gentlemen reasoned with him, telling him if he was innocent to insist upon it, and not be afraid, for he might be assured of having justice done him; but if he was guilty, his denying of it would signify nothing, for that they knew as much about the plot as they that were concerned in it, and the only way to recommend himself to favor, was by making a full confession; he then considered awhile, and desired to know his accuser, they told him they believed it was Jack, which as soon as he heard, he said then I am a dead man, striking his head against one of the beams of the jail; and said further, he was afraid the dog would have served him so. Then he gave the young gentlemen his shoe and knee-buckles (being silver) and some other things, desiring they might be delivered to his brother Caesar (another negro of Mr. Murray's.) In this manner they parleyed with him a full hour, till at length tired with his obstinacy, they concluded to leave him, but he pressed them to stay, still giving them some hopes of his confession; they told him they had no occasion to stay to hear him repeat the same things over again: he then asked them what they would have him say? upon which they told him they would have him speak sincerely, whether he was guilty or not: why then said he to speak sincerely, I am guilty.

Now many negroes began to squeak, in order to lay hold of the benefit of the proclamation;[65] some who had been apprehended but not indicted; and many who had been indicted and arraigned, who had pleaded *not guilty,* were disposed to retract their pleas and plead *guilty,* and throw themselves on the mercy of the court; so that confessions were like to be numerous, and business to multiply upon our bands,

[65]*proclamation:* See the lieutenant governor's announcement of June 19 promising pardons to anyone who confessed or informed on conspirators.

which made it necessary to call in some gentlemen of the law to our assistance upon the occasion, who very readily undertook the task.

Before the issuing of the proclamation of the 19th instant, for the encouragement of the conspirators to come in, and make voluntary and free confession and discovery, etc. there were betwixt sixty and seventy negroes in jail, who had been already impeached, many of whom after publishing the proclamation, not only confessed their own guilt, in order to entitle themselves to the benefit of it, as may appear by the foregoing examination, but also discovered many of their accomplices who were at large; who were thereupon immediately taken into custody by order of the judges, or grand jury, as the case happened before whom such confessions were made; so that between the 19th and this day, there were upwards of thirty slaves more added to the former, insomuch that the jail began to be so thronged, it was difficult to find room for them; and we were apprehensive that the criminals would be daily multiplying on our hands; nor could we see any likelihood of a stop to impeachments, for it seemed very probable that most of the negroes in town were corrupted.

[The lawyers in the city met and agreed to share the work of taking down the depositions of the slaves in shorthand, which explains some of the scantier notes of some of the depositions. They found that most of the slaves testified to the same thing. Just two are excerpted here.]

The negroes in general that came to a confession, agreed in the impeachment of Hughson and his family; that the drift of the plot was to burn the town and destroy the inhabitants; that they were sworn into the confederacy at Hughson's, or by Hughson, or some person intrusted by him for that purpose.

Confessions taken this day by Mr. Nicholls and Mr. Lodge, of the fifteen following negroes:

No. 1. Jack (Breasted's) said that Vaarck's Caesar (hanged) carried him to Hughson's; that Hughson told him he must join with them in a plot they were making, and swore him to set his master's house on fire, and to cut his mistress's throat.

No. 11. Scipio (Abrahams's) said, that he was at Hughson's at the great Supper; that Hughson swore him to burn the houses and kill the people.

[Horsmanden recorded thirteen other short confessions like Jack's and Scipio's.]

Confession taken by Mr. George Joseph Moore:

Caesar (Horsefield's) said, that Roosevelt's Quack, about new year, of a working day, met him in the meal-market, and told him he must go with him to some company on the North river; he went there and drank, and Quack asked him to stay supper; he consented; they supped; had a goose and some mutton; the supper on the table before they went there. Albany and Caesar (Vaarck's) were there.

Being asked several questions about this meeting, and not answering so as to be believed, nor making out any thing, he seemed very much concerned, and said, he understood that Roosevelt's Quack had used his name at the fire, and therefore thought he should be condemned, but declared what he had before said he did because he was afraid of his life, and that he should die if he did not say something, but could not tell what to say, not knowing any thing at all of the plot.

WEDNESDAY, JULY 1

Deposition, No. 1—John Schultz made oath, that whereas by the judge's orders he took a confession in writing from the mouth of Pedro, belonging to Pierre De Peyster, wherein he accused two negroes, the one belonging to Cornelius Van Horn, called Kid, the other to Dr. Henderson, called Caesar, that they Kid and Caesar, with some other negroes and him the said Pedro, were sworn at Hughson's, and there agreed to set fire to houses and destroy the people inhabiting this city: and whereas the said Pedro did, on the 30th day of June 1741 acknowledge voluntarily to the said John Schultz, Francis Barrow being present, and likewise in the evening of the same day, John Schultz, Pierre De Peyster and Stephen Courtlandt being present, that the words which he spoke relating to himself and the others which he had said were present and all sworn at Hughson's, viz. Kid, Caesar, etc. was not true, and that Will, a negro belonging to one Ward, a watch maker, being in the same prison with him, had told him that he understood these affairs very well, and that unless he the said Pedro did confess and bring in two or three, he would either be hanged or burnt, and did likewise name the aforesaid as proper ones to be accused, and he the said Pedro did say that Will was the cause of his making that false confession, which he can prove by four negroes which are in the same prison with him.

[Will was reputed to have taken part in the 1736 uprising in Antigua, where he supposedly informed on eighty-eight of his fellow-conspirators.]

FRIDAY, JULY 3

This day Duane's Prince, Latham's Tony, Shurmur's Cato, Kip's Harry, and Marshalk's York, negroes, were executed at the gallows, according to sentence; and the body of York was afterwards hung in chains, upon the same gibbet with John Hughson.

Some few days after this the town was amused with a rumour, that Hughson was turned negro, and Vaarck's Caesar a white; and when they came to put up York in chains by Hughson (who was hung upon the gibbet three weeks before) so much of him as was visible, viz. face, hands, neck, and feet, were of a deep shining black, rather blacker than the negro placed by him, who was one of the darkest hue of his kind; and the hair of Hughson's beard and neck (his head could not be seen for he had a cap on) was curling like the wool of a negro's beard and head, and the features of his face were of the symmetry of a negro beauty; the nose broad and flat, the nostrils open and extended, the mouth wide, lips full and thick, his body (which when living was tall, by the view upwards of six feet, but very meager) swelled to a gigantic size; and as to Caesar (who, though executed for a robbery, was also one of the head negro conspirators, had been hung up in chains a month before Hughson and was also of the darkest complexion) his face was at the same time somewhat bleached or turned whitish, insomuch as it occasioned a remark, that Hughson and he had changed colours. The beholders were amazed at these appearances; the report of them engaged the curiosity of many, and drew numbers of all ranks, who had curiosity, to the gibbets, for several days running, in order to be convinced by their own eyes, of the reality of things so confidently reported to be, at least wondrous phenomenons, and upon the view they were found to be such as have been described; many of the spectators were ready to resolve them into miracles; however, others not so hasty, though surprized at the sights, were willing to account for them in a natural way, so that they administered matter for much speculation.

The sun at this time had great power, and the season as usual very hot, that Hughson's body dripped and distilled very much, as it needs must, from the great fermentation and abundance of matter within him, as could not but be supposed at that time from the extraordinary bulk of his body; though considering the force of the sun, and the natural meagreness[66] of his corpse, one would have been apt to imagine

[66] *meagreness:* Leanness or emaciation.

that long ere[67] this it would have been disencumbered of all its juices. At length, about ten days or a fortnight after Hughson's mate, York, hung by him, Hughson's corpse, unable longer to contain its load, burst and discharged pail fulls* of blood and corruption;[68] this was testified by those who were near by, fishing upon the beach when the irruption happened, to whom the stench of it was very offensive.

SATURDAY, JULY 4

This day Will, Ward's negro, was executed according to sentence, and made the following confession at the stake.

1. He said that William Kane, a soldier belonging to the fort, knew of the plot, and he heard the said Kane say, he did not care if the fort was burnt down; that since the plot was discovered he told Kane he would make a discovery, on which Kane gave him three pounds in bills and told him not to discover; part of which money his young mistress found in his chest.

2. That his mistress lost a silver spoon, which he, Will, stole and carried to Kane's wife, who gave it her husband in his presence, and he sold it to Peter Van Dyke, a silversmith, and gave him, Will, eight shillings of the money.

[At the stake, Will also accused Edward Kelly, another solider, of knowing about the plot. He accused two other slaves of pressing him to become involved, and he absolved De Peyster's Pedro of any knowledge.]

The pile being kindled, this wretch set his back to the stake, and raising up one of his legs, laid it upon the fire, and lifting up his hands and eyes, cried aloud, and several times repeated the names, Quack Goelet and Will Tiebout, who he had said first brought him into this plot.

This evening William Kane, soldier, Goelet's Quack and Tiebout's Will, negroes, were apprehended and committed.

SUNDAY, JULY 5

[The court examined William Kane on Sunday, July 5. He admitted that his wife had once brought home a silver spoon that she said she had gotten

[67] *long ere:* Long before.
*Which may be understood to mean a surprizing quantity.
[68] *corruption:* The decomposition that is a result of death.

from a sailor. He and his wife had brought the spoon to the silversmith Van Dyke to sell. He denied even knowing where Hughson's house was or ever being at Kelly's house. He also denied any acquaintance with John Ury.]

While Kane was under examination, the under-sheriff came and informed the judges, that Mary Burton had declared, that she had often seen him at Hughson's, amongst Hughson, his wife, etc. and the negroes, when they were talking of the conspiracy, and that he was one of the confederates: whereupon she was ordered to be brought in, and being confronted with Kane, she immediately declared to the effect in the following deposition. The Chief Justice, who was a stranger to the transactions concerning the detection of the conspiracy (having been absent attending the execution of his majesty's special commission at Providence) he thought proper to admonish the witness in an awful and solemn manner, concerning the nature of an oath, and the consequences of taking a false one, more especially as it affected a man's life: she answered, she was acquainted with the nature of an oath very well, and that she would not take a false one upon any account, and repeated the same charge against Kane over and over, and persisted in it, that what she said was truth; all which Kane as positively denied: whereupon she was sworn, and the following evidence taken.

Deposition No. 5.—Mary Burton being duly sworn and produced before William Kane, soldier, said that she had seen the said Kane at Hughson's very often, talking with Hughson, his wife and daughter, Peggy Salingburgh alias Kerry, Caesar, Vaarck's; Galloway, Rutgers'; Prince, Auboyneau's; and Cuffee, Philipse's, negroes; and the discourse amongst them was, that they would burn the town, the fort first, the governor and all his family in it, and kill all the white people, and that she heard the said William Kane say, that he would help them all that lay in his power.

Then Mary Burton was ordered to withdraw, and Kane was apprized of the danger he was in, and told he must not flatter himself with the least hopes of mercy, but by making a candid and ingenuous confession of all that he knew of the matter, or to this purpose: but he still denied what had been alleged against him by Mary Burton, till upon most solemn admonition, he began to be affected; his countenance changed, and being near fainting, desired to have a glass of water, which was brought him, and after some pause, he said he would tell the truth, though at the same time he seemed very loth to do it; but after some hesitation began to open, and several hours were spent in taking down heads of his confession, which were afterwards drawn out at large, and distinctly read over to him, and being duly sworn, he made oath that the same was true, and (not knowing how to write) he put his mark to it.

Further *examination and confession* of William Kane, the same day—No. 2.

[In this confession, Kane admitted to being at two meetings at the Hughsons', where he heard the plot discussed to burn the city, take the goods, and wait six weeks for the Spanish or the French to come and take the city. He also claimed to have met the priest, John Ury, who tried to convert him to Catholicism on the grounds that Catholics could "forgive sins." He described one particularly vivid scene of the swearing of the oath that differed substantially from the slave descriptions of being "sworn" into the conspiracy.]

18. That at the second meeting he was at Hughson's about the plot, there was present about eight negroes, viz. Walter's Quack, Vaarck's Caesar, Philipse's Cuffee, Auboyneau's Prince, Carpenter's Albany, Chambers's Robin, Comfort's Jack, and Niblet's Sandy,* he saw all the negroes sworn, and the following ceremony was used: there was a black ring made on the floor about two feet and a half diameter, and Hughson bid every one pull off the left shoe and put their toes within the ring, and Mrs. Hughson held a bowl of punch over their heads as the negroes stood round the circle, and Hughson pronounced the oath above mentioned, and every negro severally repeated the words after him, and then Hughson's wife fed them with a draught out of the bowl.

FRIDAY, JULY 10

Deposition taken before the Chief Justice—John Schultz maketh oath, that a negro man slave, called Cambridge, belonging to Christopher Codwise, esquire, did on the ninth day of June last, confess to this deponent in the presence of the said Mr. Codwise and Richard Baker, that the confession he had made before Messrs. Lodge and Nicholls, was entirely false, viz. that he had owned himself guilty of the conspiracy, and had accused the negro of Richard Baker, called Cajoe, through fear; and said, that he had heard some negroes talking together in the

*Though Sandy always denied he ever was there.

jail, that if they did not confess, they should be hanged; and that was the reason of his making that false confession: and that what he had said relating to Horsefield's Caesar was a lie: that he did not know in what part of the town Hughson did live, nor did not remember to have heard of the man until it was a common talk over the town and country, that Hughson was concerned in a plot with the negroes.

TUESDAY, JULY 14

Examination of John Ury, before the Chief Justice and third justice, apprehended upon suspicion of being a Romish priest, and a confederate in the conspiracy.

John Ury, school-master, denies being any wise concerned in the conspiracy for burning the town and killing the inhabitants, says, that he never was any wise acquainted with John Hughson or his wife, or Margaret Kerry, nor did he ever see them in his life, to his knowledge.

[William Kane testified that he had seen Ury at Hughson's house, along with a number of white men; all had sworn to help burn the city. He also testified as follows.]

6. That a young gentleman with a pigtail wig, used frequently to come there with Corry, Ury the priest, and Holt;[69] but never saw him in company with any negroes, as those other white people used to be when he was absent.

WEDNESDAY, JULY 15. A.M.

[Ury was indicted first for aiding and abetting the plot to burn down the fort, second for being a Catholic priest and celebrating mass.]

The king against John Ury alias Jury.

[69]John Corry and Henry Holt were both dancing masters. Dancing masters in the eighteenth-century colonies were itinerant peddlers of gentility. They moved from city to city in order to teach the children of elites manners, posture, and dance steps. As itinerants, they were often seen as dangerously unrooted men, although they were also a necessary part of a genteel upbringing. Some dancing masters boarded with or were otherwise patronized by one or two local elite families, which gave them intimate connections to influential households. Little is known of John Corry, but Holt came to New York in 1737, and quickly became a Freemason. He had left New York for Jamaica in the middle of March 1741. See also Arthur Price's deposition of May 7.

SATURDAY, JULY 18

About noon Othello, Walter's Quack, Venture, Frank, Walton's Fortune, and Galloway, negroes, were executed according to sentence.

Walton's Fortune behaved at the gallows like a mountebank's fool, jumped off the cart several times with the halter around his neck, as if sporting with death. Some conjectured he was intoxicated with rum.

WEDNESDAY, JULY 22

The further examination of Sarah Hughson, before the chief justice, No. 2.

1. She said that she had often seen Ury the priest at her father's house, who used to come there in the evenings and at nights, and has seen him in company with the negroes, and talking with them about the plot of burning the town and destroying the white people.

2. That she has seen him several times make a round ring with chalk on the floor, and make all the negroes then present stand round it, and he (Ury) used to stand in the middle of the ring, with a cross in his hand, and there swore all the negroes to be concerned in the plot, and that they should not discover him, nor any thing else of the plot, though they should die for it.

3. That William Kane used often to come there with the negroes, and once, as she remembers, he came there with Ury the priest, who swore him into the plot, and several negroes, in particular, Vaarck's Caesar, Comfort's Jack, Auboyneau's Prince, Walter's Quack, Philipse's Cuffee, Peggy, and the examinant herself, and her father and mother; that all this was done the last winter, and she thinks before Christmas.

4. That she saw him, the said Ury, baptize the above named negroes, or some of them, and told them he made them christians, and forgave them all their sins, and all the sins they should commit about the plot, and preached to the negroes; Kane being there also.

5. That she has heard Vaarck's Caesar, Philipse's Cuffee, and other negroes say, that they used to go to Ury's lodging, where they used to pray in private after the popish fashion, and that he used to forgive them their sins for burning the town and destroying and cutting of the people's throats.

6. That Ury afterwards told the examinant that she must confess what sins she had been guilty of, to him, and he would forgive her them; that she told him that she had been guilty of no other sins but cursing and swearing in a passion; upon which he told her, as she had

taken the oath to be concerned in the plot, he pardoned her her sins; she replied that she did not believe any body could forgive her sins but God; and he said yes, he and all priests could, if the people did but do what the priests bid them, and followed all their directions; that Peggy used to confess in private to Ury, and she heard him tell her, if she would confess all the wickedness she had done in the world, he would forgive her, and particularly about the plot, and she says that Peggy has often told her she was a strong papist.

7. "That several of the soldiers used often to come to their house and call for liquors, but she does not know whether they knew of or were concerned in the plot, or not.

MONDAY, JULY 27

Joseph Web [or Webb] of the city of New-York, carpenter and house joiner, being duly sworn, deposed, *[that he had met Ury, heard him teach Latin and English, and asked Ury if he would be willing to teach one of his children]*.

4. That Ury in some of his conversations with him upon religious topics, expressed himself in such a dark, obscure, and mysterious manner, that the deponent could not understand him; he would give hints that he could neither make head nor tail of. . . .

6. That one day the conversation between Ury and deponent was about negroes; deponent having said they had souls to be saved or lost as well as other people: Ury said they were not proper objects of salvation; deponent replied what would you do with them then, what would you damn them all? no says Ury, leave them to that Great Being that has made them, he knows best what to do with them; says Ury, they are of a slavish nature, it is the nature of them to be slaves, give them learning, do all the good you can, and put them above the condition of slaves, and in return they will cut your throats.*

7. That after Campbell removed to Hughson's house, Ury removed thither about a week or ten days after him, and the deponent went thither three times, and heard him read prayers, in the manner of the church of England, but in the prayers for the king he only mentioned our sovereign lord the king, and not king George; the drift of his first sermon was against drunkenness and debauchery of life, and against deists; the first part of his second sermon was much to the same pur-

*Ury seemed to be well acquainted with the disposition of them.

pose with the former, and the latter part was an admonition to every one to keep to their own minister; they that were of the church of England, to the English minister, those that were of the Lutheran persuasion to keep to that, and those of the Presbyterian to keep to their minister: that he did not propose to set up a society for preaching to them, that he only gave a word of admonition at the request of the family where he was.

[The judges recommended Sarah Hughson for a pardon, even though they were frustrated that she had not revealed more of the conspiracy. Feeling, however, that she would be able to provide material evidence against Ury, they sent the request to the governor.]

Trial of John Ury alias Jury

WEDNESDAY, JULY 29

[The attorney general opened for the prosecution by arguing that Ury was involved in the plot, was a Catholic priest who offered absolution to whites and blacks involved in the plot, and had taken part in the mysterious rite of the chalk circle described by Kane on July 5. He ended by asserting that the whole plot was a scheme supported by the Catholic Church.]

Mary Burton sworn.

Mr. Chambers: Mary, give the court and jury an account of what you know concerning this conspiracy to burn down the town and murder and destroy the inhabitants, and what part you know the prisoner at the bar has acted in it: tell the whole story from the beginning, in your own method, but speak slow, not so hastily as you usually do, that the court and jury may the better understand you.

Prisoner: You say you have seen me several times at Hughson's, what clothes did I usually wear?

Mary Burton: I cannot tell what clothes you wore particularly.

Prisoner: That is strange, and know me so well.

M. Burton: I have seen you in several clothes, but you chiefly wore a riding coat, and often a brown coat trimmed with black.

Prisoner: I never wore any such coat.

Prisoner: What time of the day did I use to come to Hughson's?

M. Burton: You used chiefly to come in the night time, and when I have been going to bed I have seen you undressing in Peggy's room, as if you were to lie there; but I cannot say that you did, for you were always gone before I was up in the morning.

Prisoner: What room was I in when I called Mary, and you came up, as you said?

M. Burton: In the great room up stairs.

Prisoner: What answer did the negroes make when I offered to forgive them their sins, as you said?

M. Burton: I don't remember.

[William Kane then testified that he once saw Ury christening a child using salt, that Ury had tried to convert him to Catholicism, and that he had seen him at the Hughsons helping to swear slaves into the plot.]

Sarah Hughson sworn.*

Mr. Chambers [counsel for the king]: Sarah, do you give the court and jury an account of what you know of Ury's being concerned in this conspiracy.

Mr. Murray (counsel for the king): If your honours please, I have a piece of evidence, which I would not offer until I have opened the nature of it; which is a letter from general Oglethorpe to the lieutenant governor, informing him, that a party of Indians had returned

*The behaviour of this miserable wretch was, upon this occasion, beyond expectation, composed and decent. She seemed to be touched with remorse and compunction. What came from her was delivered with all the visible marks and semblance of sincerity and truth; insomuch, that the court, jury, and many of the audience, looked upon her at this instant to be under real conviction of mind for her past offences, which was somewhat surprizing to those who were witnesses to the rest of her conduct, since her condemnation and several reprieves. Her evidence, as the reader may observe, was regular and uniform, and agreed with the account of the plot, as to the persons and things she spoke to, and was chiefly confirmed by many concurring evidences; and therefore, for once, it seems but reasonable and just to allow, that she spoke the truth. She was brought this morning to plead her pardon out of the condemned hole, where she had been confined from the time of her condemnation; and when her pardon was pleaded, she was taken from court into a room in custody of the undersheriff, where she was to be near at hand for call upon this trial, and there she remained till wanted and was sent for: and the witnesses delivered their testimony in the order of time they are here placed, out of the hearing of each other, till each respective person had given their evidence—which is mentioned, that the reader may more particularly observe the correspondence and remarkable agreement between her evidence, Kane's and Mary Burton's, which must be seen by every one that will be at the pains to make the comparison: and Sarah was under ground before and all the time Kane had been committed, so that there could have been no confabulation between them, nor could Mary Burton have intercourse with either, who was the first white evidence that impeached Kane, and Kane by his confession confirmed her evidence, and now all three confirm each other.

to Georgia, on the eighth of May last, from war against the Spaniards, who in an engagement with a party of Spanish horse[70] near Augustine, had taken one of them prisoner, and had brought him to the general; that the Spaniard in his examination before the magistrates of Georgia, had given some intelligence of a villainous design of a very extraordinary nature, that the Spaniards had employed emissaries to burn all the magazines and considerable towns in the English North America, thereby to prevent the subsistence of the English fleet in the West-Indies; and that for this purpose, many priests were employed, who pretended to be physicians, dancing-masters, and other kinds of occupations; and under that pretence to endeavour to gain admittance and confidence in private families.

Court: Mr. Murray, have you any more witnesses?

Mr. Murray: Sir, we shall rest here at present.

Court: Mr. Ury, have you any witnesses; for now is your time to produce them?

[Horsmanden copied Ury's speech from a draft written by Ury himself. The original, Horsmanden explained, was written with no punctuation, and so he "would not risk altering the sense by printing it with any."]

Prisoner: May it please the King's judges, and the gentlemen of the jury—It is very incongruous to reason to think that I can have any hand or be any way concerned in this plot, if these things be duly weighed: that after the discovery of the conspiracy and the execution of many for it, that I should act such a lunatick part if I were guilty as to continue in this city, join with Mr. Campbell, and not only so, but publicly advertise myself for teaching of grammar* yea further, that I should still continue even after the caution Mr. Webb gave me a week and a few days before I was taken into custody he told me Mr. Chambers told him that the eyes of this city were fixed on me, and that I was suspected to be a Roman priest and thought to be in the plot I answered my innocency would protect me I valued not what the world said, again another instance that must free me from this plot is when Mr. Campbell went to take possession of Huson's [*sic*] house his daughter refusing to go out and she swearing like a life guardman I took up the cause Mr. Campbell not exerting himself as I thought was proper at that time and told her if

[70]*Spanish horse:* Spanish cavalry.
*There was no name to his advertisement as he remarked.

she would not go out quietly I would take another method with her for I would have no such wicked person (as she was said to be) live where I was to dwell now reason must pronounce me innocent for had I been engaged in their scheme of guilt my fears would have forced me to have acted in a very different manner rather to have soothed her and gave her liberty to stay till provided for instead of not shewing her the least countenance[71] and further what corroborates my non knowledge of this plot is that the negro who confessed as it is said that he set fire to the fort did not mention me in all his confession doubtless he would not have neglected and passed over such a person as I am said to be namely a priest and if he was bound by any oath or oaths as he confest it shewed he thought it or them of no value and therefore would have confessed and laid open the whole scheme and all the persons he knew concerned in it but more especially the priest as it is said I am and what is still more strong for my innocency is that neither Huson his wife nor the creature that was hanged with them and all that have been put to death since did not once name me certainly gentlemen if I am a priest as you take me to be I could not be so foolish as to engage myself in so absurd a contrivance as to bind myself with a cord for negroes or what is worse profligate whites the scum of this earth superior in villany to the knights of the post[72] to make an halter for me gentlemen as there is a great unknown and tremendous being whom we call God I never knew or saw Huson his wife or the creature that was hanged with them to my knowledge living dying or dead or the negro that is said to have fired the fort excepting in his last moments but put the case I had known Huson's and had been at his house is it to be inferred from thence that I must be acquainted with his villainy or knew his secrets and as he kept a public house which is open and free for all is it reasonable to think that all or any man being seen at Huson's must make him or them culpable or chargeable with his villainy surely no for if so said would be the case of many gentlemen who in travelling the countries in England who have used bad houses or inns and lit into the company of highwaymen who by their garb and conversation they took for some honest country gentleman or tradesman and yet these have not been in the least suspected but I fear all this trouble

[71] *least countenance:* The smallest amount of support or encouragement.

[72] *knight of the post:* One who makes his living from giving false evidence at trials, an infamous perjurer.

of mine springs from and is grounded upon, the apprehensions of my being a Roman priest, and therefore must be a plotter some believing there can be no mischief in a country but a priest (if there) must be in it say they that in the chain of general woes the first and the last link must be tied to the priest's girdle. But gentlemen I must assure you from reading and conversation I believe no priest would hold a confederacy with negroes they are too wise too cunning to trust such sort of gentry it is not men of fortune good sense and learning they care to meddle with or entrust in such affairs as plots excepting they be men of their own kidney[73] of their own way of thinking in religion supposing a priest could be so foolish or become non compos mentes[74] as to plot in short a priest a joint contriver of firing a fort a celebrater of masses a dispenser of absolutions as it is said I am so long passed by such a particular person forgotten No gentlemen you must think and believe he would have been the next person after the discovery of the plot that would have been brought on the carpet And further what is of great note is that Huson was sworn to be the whole projector and carrier on of the plot and if these witnesses knew me so well as they pretend to how came it about what reason can be assigned why they did not bring me out before what not any thing of me before I came to prison, doubtless they would have been eager to have betrayed me when the scheme was discovered, for being a priest and consequently artful and cunning they would have been afraid of my escaping. No if I had been engaged they would have soon informed thinking to have saved their own lives knowing how this government stands affected to such gentlemen. And as to the second indictment wherein—

Court: Mr. Ury, if you have any witnesses to examine, it is more proper you should do that now, and make your defense afterwards.

Prisoner: If that be the pleasure of the judges, I have several witnesses; I desire Mr. Croker may be called.

[Croker told the court that Ury had taught his son Latin in exchange for room and board. He testified that he had never seen slaves seek Ury out, and in fact had once heard him say that they were not "proper objects of salvation."]

[73]*kidney:* In its figurative use, *kidney* can refer to kind, class, or sort.

[74]*non compos mentes:* Correctly, *non compos mentis,* meaning "not in one's right mind."

Joseph Webb called for the prisoner and sworn.

Prisoner: Mr. Webb, I desire you will give an account of what you know of me.

Webb: I have known Mr. Ury since November last, I was then at work at John Croker's, at the fighting cocks, and hearing him reading Latin and English, and thinking he read well, enquired of Croker who he was? he told me he was a schoolmaster lately come from Philadelphia; and from this I became acquainted with him, and I asked him if he would teach a child of mine: and he said he would, if Croker would give him liberty of coming to his house; which Croker agreed to; and I sent my child to him, and he taught him Latin; and after this I recommended him to Col. Beekman,[75] to teach his daughter to write and cypher; and he and I growing more intimate, and I observing a poor and mean appearance in his habit, I thought his pocket might be answerable to it; and I gave him an invitation to my house, and told him he should be welcome at my table noon and night, at any time, when he saw proper; and he frequently came to my house accordingly all the winter: that he used often to stay at my house late in discoursing, sometimes on one subject, sometimes on another; and has stayed there now and then till eleven or twelve o'clock at night, and I have often gone home with him to his lodging at those hours. Mr. Ury told me he was a non juring[76] minister; having asked him who ordained him, he answered me, the senior non juror in England: I have heard him preach, and have heard him say, such a day is my sacrament day, and he must be at sacrament.

Attorney General: Did he say he must take the sacrament, or be at sacrament, or administer the sacrament?

Webb: I cannot be sure, but I remember he said it was his sacrament day.

Attorney General: Was it Sundays or working days he said were his sacrament days?

Webb: I cannot be sure, but I think I have heard him name both.

[75]Colonel Henry Beekman was a prominent New York merchant and politician.

[76]A non-juring minister was an Anglican priest who refused to acknowledge the British sovereign as the spiritual head of the Church of England. By the middle of the eighteenth century, the influential British legal authority Sir William Blackstone thought that all who refused to swear oaths of loyalty should be considered papist dissenters.

Attorney General: Do you know any thing of his buying of wafers,[77] or going to a confectioner's?

Webb: He asked me for a confectioner's shop, and I showed him Mr. De Brosse's, where he went along with me; and after he asked for several sorts of sweetmeats, he asked for wafers; which being shown to him, he asked Mr. De Brosse if he made wafers for the Lutheran minister, and he was told he did, but I do not remember that he bought any of them: I have heard him pray and preach several times, but do not remember that ever I heard him pray for king George, but in general terms for the king. I am by trade a carpenter, and Ury applied to me to make him up something in Hughson's house, which I have heard since called an altar; that Ury gave me directions for making it, and said it was a place to lay books on to read, or to put a candle or a bottle and glass on, or other such like common uses; it was two pieces of board, which formed a triangle, and was raised against the wall, at the bottom of which was a shelf; on each side there was a place to hold a candle.

Attorney General: Do you think if a man wanted a shelf or other place to lay a book on to read, or set a bottle or glass on, he would make it in that form?

Webb: I can't say; people may have odd humours, but I should not.

Attorney General: Do you know any thing of Ury's being imprisoned in England?

Webb: Ury did tell me that he was imprisoned in England: for he said he had wrote a book there, and that the critics laid hold of it, picked a hole in it, and construed it treason; but if it was, he said, it was contrary to his intentions.

Attorney General: Mr. Webb, in your conversations together, what have you heard him say about negroes?

Webb: We were one day talking about negroes, and I said I thought they had souls to be saved or lost as well as other people: Ury said he thought they were not proper objects of salvation; I replied, what would you do with them then; what, would you damn them all? No, says he, leave them to that Great Being that has made them, he knows best what to do with them; says he, they are of a slavish nature, it is the nature of them to be slaves, give them learning, do

[77]*wafer:* Thin piece of unleavened bread used for communion by Roman Catholics, Lutherans, and some Anglicans.

them all the good you can, and put them beyond the condition of slaves, and in return, they will cut your throats.

Court: Mr. Ury, would you ask this witness any more questions?

Prisoner: No, sir, I have nothing more to ask.

[John Campbell, who was Ury's partner in their school, testified to his good character, as did Campbell's wife.]

Attorney General: If your honours please, as the prisoner has been endeavouring to prove he is not a Romish priest, and has already insisted on it as a part of his defence; I shall beg leave to examine a witness or two to that point.

[Joseph Hildreth, schoolmaster, repeated several conversations he had had with Ury, including one in which Ury implied that he acknowledged Charles Stuart, the Catholic claimant to the British throne, as the true king of England. He also gave some evidence that Ury was sympathetic to Catholicism and practiced some strange religious rituals of his own.]

At another time, says he *[Ury]*, you talk so much against popery, I believe though you speak so much against it, you will find you have (or I think will have) a pope in your belly, for says he the absolution of the church of Rome is not half so bad as that of the church of England at the visitation of the sick: but says I, I don't approve of their confessing to priests, etc. says I there is a deal of wickedness and deceit in it: says he, no, no, for when any person makes confessions the priest does not know who they be, for he does not so much as see them, but only hears and absolves them: Then says I, I was mistaken. Oh! says he, they speak against the church of Rome, but don't know them; their priests says he, are the most learned of men; the articles of the church of England were made in distracted times. And I observed several times he said, we priests. Says he, your Roman priests will make you believe, and prove by the plain rules of grammar, that black is white, and white black, and that the wafer and wine is the real body and blood of Christ.

Council: Mr. Ury, would you ask this witness any question?

Prisoner: No sir, I have nothing to ask him.

[The attorney general also called Mr. Norwood, who had previously employed Ury to teach his children. Norwood explained that he had fired Ury because he frequently neglected his teaching. He also reported that

Campbell had told him Ury was a popish priest. Ury did not challenge any of Norwood's testimony. The prosecution then read evidence from Catholic tracts to show that Ury's religious practices were Catholic in nature, and Ury responded with a rebuttal.]

Mr. Smith summed up the evidence for the king, and addressing himself to the court and jury, proceeded as followeth.

"Though this work of darkness, in the contrivance of a horrible plot, to burn and destroy this city, has manifested itself in many blazing effects, to the terror and amazement of us all; yet the secret springs of this mischief lay long concealed: this destructive scene has opened by slow degrees: but now, gentlemen, we have at length great reason to conclude, that it took its rise from a foreign influence; and that it originally depended upon causes, that we ourselves little thought of, and which, perhaps, very few of the inferior and subordinate agents were intimately acquainted with.

"Gentlemen, if the evidence you have heard is sufficient to produce a general conviction that the late fires in this city, and the murderous design against its inhabitants, are the effects of a Spanish and popish plot, then the mystery of this iniquity, which has so much puzzled us, is unveiled, and our admiration ceases: all the mischiefs we have suffered or been threatened with, are but a sprout from that evil root, a small stream from that overflowing fountain of destruction, that has often deluged the earth with slaughter and blood, and spread ruin and desolation far and wide.

"We need not wonder to see a popish priest at this bar, as a prime incendiary; nor think it strange that an Englishman of that religion and character should be concerned in so detestable a design. What can be expected from those that profess a religion that is at war with God and man; not only with the truths of the Holy Scriptures, but also with common sense and reason; and is destructive of all the kind and tender sensations of human nature? When a man, contrary to the evidence of his senses, can believe the absurd doctrine of transubstantiation;[78] can give up his reason to a blind obedience and an implicit faith; can be persuaded to believe that the most unnatural crimes, such as treason and murder, when done in obedience to the pope, or for the service of the holy church, by rooting out what they call heresy, will

[78]*doctrine of transubstantiation:* The Roman Catholic belief that the wine and bread of communion convert into the blood and body of Christ, with only the external appearance of the wine and bread remaining.

merit heaven: I say, when a man has imbibed such principles as these, he can easily divest himself of every thing that is human but his shape, he is capable of any villainy, even as bad as that which is charged on the prisoner at the bar."

Then the chief justice charged the jury, and a constable being sworn to attend them, they withdrew; and having staid out about a quarter of an hour, returned, and found the prisoner guilty of the indictment.

TUESDAY, AUGUST 4

[John Ury was sentenced to be hanged the following Saturday, August 15.]

SATURDAY, AUGUST 15

This being the day appointed for the execution of John Ury, his honour the lieutenant governor, was pleased, upon the humble petition of the said Ury, to respite the same till Wednesday following.

Juan alias Wan de Sylva, the Spanish negro, condemned for the conspiracy, was this day executed according to sentence; he was neatly dressed in a white shirt, jacket, drawers, and stockings, behaved decently, prayed in Spanish, kissed a crucifix, insisting on his innocence to the last.

SATURDAY, AUGUST 29

This day John Ury was executed according to sentence. Being asked by the sheriff whether he had any speech or paper to deliver? he answered he had given one to his friend, or Webb (the person who attended him at the gallows:) he repeated somewhat of the substance of it before he was turned off: a copy of this paper was made in the jail (from one delivered by Ury himself in his own hand writing) from which the following was taken.

The Last Speech of John Ury

Fellow Christians—I am now going to suffer a death attended with ignominy and pain; but it is the cup that my heavenly father has put into my hand, and I drink it with pleasure; it is the cross of my dear redeemer, I bear it with alacrity; knowing that all that live godly in Christ Jesus, must suffer persecution; and we must be made in some degree partakers of his sufferings before we can share in the glories of his resurrection: for he went not up to glory before he ascended

Mount Calvary; did not wear the crown of glory before the crown of thorns. And I am to appear before an awful and tremendous God, a being of infinite purity and unerring justice, a God who by no means will clear the guilty, that cannot be reconciled either to sin or sinners; now this is the being at whose bar I am to stand, in the presence of this God, the possessor of heaven and earth, I lift up my hands and solemnly protest I am innocent of what is laid to my charge: I appeal to the great God for my non-knowledge of Hewson [*sic*], his wife, or the creature that was hanged with them, I never saw them living, dying, or dead; nor never had I any knowledge or confederacy with white or black as to any plot; and upon the memorials of the body and blood of my dearest lord, in the creatures of bread and wine, in which I have commemorated the love of my dying lord, I protest that the witnesses are perjured; I never knew the perjured witnesses but at my trial. But for the removal of all scruples that may arise after my death I shall give my thoughts on some points.

First—I firmly believe and attest, that it is not in the power of man to forgive sin; that it is the prerogative only of the great God to dispense pardon for sins; and that those who dare pretend to such a power, do in some degree commit that great and unpardonable sin, the sin against the Holy Spirit, because they pretend to that power which their own consciences proclaim to be a lie.

Again, I solemnly attest and believe, that a person having committed crimes that have or might have proved hurtful or destructive to the peace of society, and does not discover the whole scheme, and all the persons concerned with them, cannot obtain pardon from God: and it is not the taking any oath or oaths that ought to hinder him from confessing his guilt, and all that he knows about it; for such obligations are not only sinful, but unpardonable, if not broken: now a person firmly believing this, and knowing that an eternal state of happiness or misery depends upon the performance or non-performance of the above-mentioned things, cannot, will not trifle with such important affairs.

I have not more to say by way of clearing my innocence, knowing that to a true christian unprejudiced mind, I must appear guiltless; but however, I am not very solicitous about it. I rejoice, and it is now my comfort (and that will support me and protect me from the crowd of evil spirits that I must meet with in my flight to the region of bliss assigned me) that my conscience speaks peace to me.

Indeed, it may be shocking to some serious Christians, that the holy God should suffer innocence to be slain by the hands of cruel and bloody persons; (I mean the witnesses who swore against me at my trial), indeed, there may be reasons assigned for it; but, as they may be liable to objections, I decline them; and shall only say, that this is one of the dark providences of the great God, in his wise, just and good government of this lower earth.

In fine, I depart this waste, this howling wilderness, with a mind serene, free from all malice, with a forgiving spirit, so far as the gospel of my dear and only redeemer obliges and enjoins me to, hoping and praying, that Jesus, who alone is the giver of repentance, will convince, conquer and enlighten my murderers' souls, that they may publicly confess their horrid wickedness before God and the world, so that their souls may be saved in the day of the Lord Jesus.

And now, a word of advice to you, spectators: behold me launching into eternity; seriously, solemnly view me, and ask yourselves severally, how stands the case with me? die I must: am I prepared to meet my Lord when the midnight cry is echoed forth? shall I then have the wedding garment on?[79] Oh, sinners! trifle no longer; consider life hangs on a thread; here to-day and gone to-morrow; forsake your sins ere ye be forsaken forever: hearken, now is God awfully calling you to repent, warning you by me, his minister and prisoner, to embrace Jesus, to take, to lay hold on him for your alone saviour, in order to escape the wrath to come; no longer delay, seeing the summons may come before ye are aware, and you standing before the bar of a God who is consuming fire out of the Lord Jesus Christ, should be hurled, be doomed to that place, where their worm dies not, and their fire is never to be quenched.

CONCLUSION

In February 1742, another fire was discovered on the roof of a shed. The court immediately began to interrogate the slaves living in the neighborhood, and the first one they questioned, Tom, confessed immediately. At first, he claimed that several other slaves had told him to set the fire as part of a plot, but after he was questioned publicly by his master and mistress, he recanted the part of his testimony in which he accused other slaves of aiding and abetting him. Tom was convicted of arson. At the gallows on March 15, 1742, he again accused four other slaves of con-

[79] *wedding garment:* A long line of Christian thought portrayed the true meeting of the mortal soul and God as a marriage between a woman (the soul) and a man (Christ).

spiring with him. Yet despite the court's further interrogation of the newly accused slaves, and its investigation of several other fires that spring, the courts never brought another case to trial.

All that remained now was for Mary Burton to collect her reward and for Daniel Horsmanden to reflect on the previous year's events. Burton's credibility had suffered considerably by the end of the trials, but the reward (and the death of her master) made her one of the most independent young women in the city. She quickly disappeared from the historical record.

Concluding the trials was more difficult for Horsmanden. In his conclusion, he attempted to weave all of the testimony that was presented before the court into a coherent whole. Consider whether his conclusion is satisfying, either to him or to the reader.

THURSDAY, SEPTEMBER 2 [1742]

At a common council Mary Burton, the evidence who detected the conspirators, having applied to the board for the reward offered by the proclamation, issued pursuant to an order of the common council of the 11th of April, 1741, promising the sum of one hundred pounds to any white person that should discover any person or persons concerned in setting fire to any dwelling houses, store-houses, or other buildings within this city: It was ordered, that the mayor should issue his warrant to the treasurer to pay to Mr. Moore, for Mary Burton's use and benefit, the sum of eighty-one pounds, which with the sum of nineteen pounds before paid by the corporation for the freedom and other necessaries to and for the use of the said Mary, made in the whole the sum of one hundred pounds, in full of the reward offered.

The mayor accordingly issued his warrant, and the money was paid to Mary Burton.

Conclusion By the course of the evidence, it appears, that a design was conceived to destroy this city by fire, and massacre the inhabitants: that fire was to be put to several quarters of the town, at one and the same time; that the English church was to be set on fire at a time when it was most likely there would be the fullest congregation, and the avenues from the church were to be guarded by these ruffians, in order to butcher those that should attempt to escape the flames; this part of the scheme, it seems, Ury, the priest, had particularly at heart.

The winds were consulted which would be most proper to attempt the fires with. They were to begin at the east end of the town with a strong easterly wind, which (as it was projected) according to the course of its situation, would probably destroy the whole town; but the king's fort was first to be burnt, because most likely to annoy these furies when their hellish devices were put in execution. The negro confederates were each of them to set fire to his master's house, and proceed to the assassinating their respective masters and families; and these fires were calculated for the night. St. Patrick's night was the time appointed. Accordingly we find, as a proof that they were in earnest, the attempt upon the fort was made on St. Patrick's night, though, through the providence of God, the fire did not take effect until the next day at noon, when the villain who first put it, had renewed his effort, by blowing up the same brand[80] that he had placed for the purpose the night before.*

If it be considered, that many of the Irish catholics, unknown to the captains, runagates,[81] or perhaps purposely sent out, had been enlisted in some of the independent companies posted here, some whereof were detected of being confederated with the conspirators; they could not have pitched upon a fitter season for perpetrating their bloody purposes; for on this night, according to custom, their commemoration of their saint might be most likely to excite in those of the infernal league, boldness and resolution, for the execution of this horrible enterprize, and others innocently partaking of their jollity, might in such an event, be thereby incapacitated for service; so that, according to this device, all (it might seem probably to them) would lie at their mercy. But the fire at the fort happening in the day, contrary to the purpose of the conspirators, and the town having been much alarmed at the misfortune, though not apprehending the treachery; yet, a military watch being kept all the night following, the villains were thereat somewhat intimidated, and stopt their progress for a while: nevertheless, from the nightly cabals of the conspirators, at Hughson's, and the encouragement given by Ury the priest, the night after the fort burnt, who told them, now God had prospered them in the beginning, in burning the fort, they need not fear; we must be resolute and proceed in the work, and no doubt God will prosper us in all; execrable wretch! From hence they took courage again, and it was

[80]*brand:* A burning piece of wood.

*See the note upon Quack's confession at the stake.

[81]*runagates:* Deserters, fugitives, or runaways.

resolved amongst them, that they should proceed. Accordingly after one week had passed, they did, we see, set fire to several houses within the compass of a fortnight, sometimes many in a day, undiscovered; and made several other attempts, in which they were frustrated, till at length some Spanish prize negroes having been seized and committed upon suspicion, a stop was put to their career. But more than a fortnight passed after the last of these fires, before the least intimation was given touching the occasion of them, that they were the effects of a diabolical conspiracy; till Mary Burton, servant to John Hughson, was brought before the grand jury, as a witness to a different matter, concerning which she had testified before the magistrates; she at first refusing to be sworn to give her evidence in that case to the grand jury, at length rather than go to jail, submitted, but withal bolted out, that she would give no evidence concerning the fires; this hint afforded sufficient handle to the gentlemen of the grand jury, to exert their diligence in sifting out her meaning, and to prevail with her to disclose the secret; which, after much entreaty and persuasion, they effected, though at the same time, the girl disburthened herself with apparent dread and great unwillingness, from the apprehension of the danger she should be in of being murdered by the conspirators for the discovery, as she afterwards declared.

By the evidence of this girl, it appears, that her master Hughson was a principal engine, agent and instigator of these deeds of darkness amongst the slaves here, ever since she came into his service; and by the evidence of others, whites and blacks, it also appears, that he having kept a public house for some years, had long since made it a practice to entertain numbers of negroes, often 20, 30, 40, or 50 at a time, and by degrees deluded them to engage in the conspiracy, upon his promises that they should all be freemen, and that other fine things should be done for them; that upon their consenting, Hughson always bound them to their engagements by horrible oaths, not only to perform what they undertook to do, viz. to burn and massacre, but also to keep all secret, though they were to die for it; that these oaths were reiterated at all future meetings, in order to confirm them; and for their encouragement, Hughson often swore himself over again, and had sworn his wife and daughter into the confederacy also. That Hughson provided arms and gunpowder, further to convince these deluded wretches how much he was in earnest; but the butchery to be executed by the negroes after they had set fire to their master's houses, was calculated to be done with knives; for those weapons, it seems, they judged would make no noise: this the whole current of negro evidence agrees in, and it is corroborated by whites. That a knife designed for this purpose was actually found in the chest of one of the negro conspirators, and most others of them were provided with knives.

That Hughson employed some of the head negroes as agents under him, to decoy other negroes, and their instructions were, not to open the conspiracy to any but those that were of their own country (as they are brought from different parts of Africa, and might be supposed best to know the temper and disposition of each other) and when they brought a convert to Hughson, or one likely to become such, Hughson always gave them drams till they were intoxicated, and then the conspiracy was proposed to them; and they generally consented without much difficulty, upon his specious promises, and sometimes upon the bare proposal; but if they were unwilling to engage, they were terrified by threats of being murdered, till they complied; then all such were constantly sworn, invited to Hughson's feasts, and these commissioned to seduce others. Many, before they knew any thing of the secret, were invited to Hughson's by himself or others: for, by way of introduction, as well as confirmation, Hughson, it seems, kept open house for the negroes, and entertained them at all times, those that had no money at free cost; he assured them, they should be always welcome to him: these compliments be artfully placed as he judged most proper; for as to such as were his special agents and dexterous fellows, they were to pay in money if they had it, or money's worth, by pilfering and stealing as they could, to raise supplies for carrying on the common cause; and they were to bring all to him: more especially upon the grand catastrophe, when the town should be all in flames, and the negroes had butchered their respective families, the most valuable things easiest to be removed (particularly plate) were to be brought to Hughson's, and it seems they had already carried on so successful a trade, and Hughson's house was become a mart of so great note amongst the negroes, that with them it had obtained the name of Oswego, after the province trading-house. They were likewise enjoined to steal their master's arms, powder, etc. and lodge all in Hughson's custody: he had many barrels of gunpowder at a time. It appears that this hellish project was set on foot here, by agent Hughson, four or five years before it was ripened for execution; and it must needs have been a work of time to seduce so many slaves as have been detected.

The white conspirators were sworn by Ury the priest in chief, and the negroes sometimes by Hughson, and sometimes by Ury in a ring surrounded by them, and he, while the oath administering, holding a crucifix over their heads. They were persuaded that the French and Spaniards were soon to come and join them; and if they did not come in a set time, they were to begin and do all themselves. Further to encourage the town negroes, they were told the confederates had many whites and blacks to come out of the country to their assistance, particularly from Long-Island, and Hughson was to give the word when they were to begin. The negroes were flattered they were to be formed into companies, several officers of them were named for the purpose, captains, etc. and the town was divided into districts. Thus all was to be their own; and if any of them were squeamish, Ury the priest could forgive them all they had committed, or should commit, provided they performed what they had engaged in, and kept all secret to their last breath.

But however true these matters have been found to be, so chimerical,[82] wicked, abominable and inhuman was the device, that those at a distance might have been apt to think it all a dream, or a fiction, were it not for the last proof of a reality, which cannot be withstood, the several fires which did happen in the manner we saw; which consideration was a great motive to this publication. The witnesses, whites and blacks, that gave any evidence, or made any confession at all, agree in the most considerable article concerning it; the design of burning the town, and murdering the inhabitants; and that popish priests were concerned in it; which verified, what is sarcastically cited in Ury's defence as proverbial, that there can be no mischief in a country, but a Roman priest (if there) must be in it; but we may venture to go one step further, and say, if such priests had not been here (and some of capacities much superior to Ury's) there would have been no such plot; for upon this and no other footing can it be accounted for. Let us suppose then (and we shall find just grounds for the supposal) that such priests or monks etc. call them what you please, had conceived a design for such a horrible, detestable purpose, as the devastation of this city, and the massacre of its inhabitants, to be perpetrated by the hands of our own slaves, in conjunction with the most abandoned whites, the dregs and disgrace of their complexion; and that at a critical time, when their successful wickedness would have frustrated the supply of provisions and necessaries to his majesty's fleet, then upon an expedition against his enemies in the West-Indies, upon which perhaps their subsistence was in some measure to rely; and that for the

[82]*chimerical:* Fantastic, unreal.

purpose, emissaries of these kind of gentry were despatched into his majesty's colonies in several different disguises, as those of dancing-masters, school-masters, physicians, etc. who under these colourable[83] appearances, might not be likely to gain admittance and confidence in private families, and thereby have opportunities of debauching[84] their slaves, and acquainting themselves of such white people as might be most likely to be seduced to their detestable purposes: who then so seemingly proper instruments to be pitched upon amongst us, by such infernal agents, as John Hughson and such like? for as the way to hell must be trod by gradual steps, and no one commences consummate villain in an instant; so Hughson had already taken some hopeful degrees in the school of wickedness; he had for many years entertained negroes at his house in all hours of darkness; and to support that expense, and promote his own lucre, encouraged them to pilfer and steal what they could from their masters, and he readily received their spoils: this might be thought a promising earnest of his qualifications: sure such a one must be judged by these craftsmen, a hopeful tool to make experiments upon; for he that could consort with slaves in one kind of villainy, would probably make the less difficulty of going some steps further. But then his religion! why truly, from what has already been observed, it might be thought to little purpose to talk about that: but his wife (good woman!) was already a professed papist, as common fame[85] has it; so the business might be near half done; for her persuasion joined to a Roman priest's assistance, artifice and dainty-fine promises, free and full remission, pardons, indulgences, and absolution for sins past, present, and to come, and a passport for heaven on the condition of performing engagements (to do the devil's business) bound with the sanction of reiterated oaths, to keep all secret to the last breath; he might perhaps (as others before him have been) be buoyed up in full expectation of becoming rich and great here, and of a fool's paradise hereafter, and thus be seduced to enter into their abominable measures.

But we may remember, that the principal witness in this shocking case, and happy instrument of this detection, was Mary Burton, Hughson's indented servant; who (however it was) no one so much as insinuated to have been sworn of the confederacy. As she was the prime cause of the discovery, as before related, their envenomed arrows

[83] *colourable:* Specious or counterfeit.
[84] *debauching:* Perverting, corrupting, or morally depraving.
[85] *fame:* Rumor or report.

have been chiefly pointed at her; and no doubt, say they, she must have been the wickedest of mortals, to bring so many innocents to this shameful, miserable and untimely end. And what have they to impute to her, sufficient to invalidate her testimony? Why, one particular, say they, enough to outweigh all: she deposed, in her first examination before the grand jury, that she never saw any white person in company when they (the conspirators) talked of burning the town but her master, her mistress, and Peggy. It is true, she did so; and indeed it was very ill done: but, should that one false step preponderate to invalidate her whole evidence? Much might be said to aggravate this offence, much also in extenuation of it. We cannot expect evidence concerning these deeds of darkness, from witnesses of unblemished characters, free of all exception. Say she was sworn to the conspiracy; though it did not appear that she was so; and if it was true, it were something strange, one would think, that not a criminal under execution, or otherwise, who confessed their own guilt and impeached others, should have declared it; but on the contrary, confirmed her testimony against themselves in the torments of flames, attesting, that "she had spoke the truth, and could name many more," i.e. that her account of the conspiracy and conspirators, given at their trial was true; which is the utmost attestation that can be to the credibility of any person, as to the matter treated of. And if they had known she was engaged in the conspiracy, from the resentment they must have borne to her as a principal evidence in their conviction, it might have been expected, it would naturally have bolted out from them; nor did Sarah Hughson, the daughter, so much as insinuate it, whose spleen was very inveterate towards her, as the cause of their detection: but perhaps Hughson's daughter was more artfully instructed; for if it came out that Burton was sworn in a party, that might add strength to her testimony, and fix the guilt more strongly upon the parties she accused, by an implied confession of the most material part of her evidence; and if she were not sworn of the confederacy, it might seem strange to some that the conspirators trusted her so much with their secrets.

There are allowances to be made, with regard to the special circumstances this girl was under in this case, and some passions and qualities which seemed natural to her: she came over young into this country, an indented servant, a year or two before her first master, after some service, assigned over her indenture to John Hughson for the remainder of her term, the midsummer before this iniquity broke out, when she was between fifteen and sixteen years of age: the girl thus becoming under the power of Hughson, a stranger in the country, and not a friend to advise with; her situation was surely somewhat deplorable; for, being in the hands and under the influence of so hopeful a family, and held to secrecy by her apprehensions of the danger she was beset with from these assassins, she might think her condition helpless, and that she could only wish for deliverance: she was of a warm hasty spirit, had a remarkable glibness of tongue, and uttered more words than people of her supposed education usually do; such a temper, one might think, could ill brook the ceremony of attending and serving upon slaves, and such a band of black and white ruffians; which, it seems, was the service enjoined her, neither could they think themselves safe with her, unless they could seduce her to their wicked purposes, which they might have hopes they should compass at last; and though at first they might think she was not to be trusted at all adventures; yet it so happened, that by degrees, it seems, the conspirators (as depending upon a master's influence over one in her circumstances, added to the terrors of their threatenings to murder her if she made discovery) flattered themselves they had her sure, and at length became so familiarized and unreserved towards her, that they heeded not saying or doing any thing before her; and thus she might be let into their secrets, upon a persuasion that she durst not tell.

The girl, doubtless, must be under terrible apprehensions when her life was thus endangered, both from blacks and whites, if she made discovery; this must have been matter of great restraint to her, and, in her hurry and confusion of thought, might occasion her to utter that through inadvertency, which, upon calm reflection, she became conscious was wrong, though at the time, it might be an involuntary suppression only of part of the truth, arising from an overhastiness in answering, and want of due reflection: which, therefore perhaps, after making all candid and ingenuous allowance, will not be rigorously construed a wilful and deliberate falsehood.

But it so happened that for some time before this grand jury was discharged, there arose great clamour against Mary Burton; for so many negroes being daily taken into custody (though not solely through her evidence, but rather principally upon discovery made by the confessions of their black associates already in custody, and their testimony corroborated with hers) some people began to be afraid of losing their slaves; for, as matters were then likely to turn out, there was no guessing where or when there would be an end of impeachments; every one had reason to fear that their own negro would be sent for next; and indeed all things duly considered, it was most probable there was but few of them that were not in the secret; and the girl had declared, that there were many negroes concerned, whose persons she could or might probably remember, but many whose names she knew not; so that it should seem, at length some masters of these slaves, as well as the conspirators, endeavoured to bring the witnesses, and the notion of a plot, into discredit, if perchance it might put a stop, not only to further prosecution, but further inquiry and discovery also: and these attempts, luckily for some, had such an effect, that several whites, as well as negroes, escaped justice; who, had the same evidence appeared against them a few weeks before, would scarce have been thought objects of mercy; nor, from what we may have observed, would Mary Burton's evidence have stood single against them.

However, when the first grand jury drew near their discharge *[on August 31],* they were importunate with Burton, to discover all the persons she knew to be engaged in this villanious design; for about this time she had suggested to some, that there were white people of more than ordinary rank above the vulgar, that were concerned, whom if she told of they would not believe her. This having been intimated to the grand jury, they were very pressing with her to discover all she knew, whoever they were; but the girl stood mute; nor could the grand jury prevail with her to name any, not with threatenings of imprisonment; at length, being tired with her obstinacy, they delivered her over to two of the judges, requesting them to endeavour to sift the matter out; but they could not prevail with her to be explicit. She complained (as it seems she had before done to the grand jury) that she had been very ill used; that her life had been threatened by conspirators of both complexion, and frequently insulted by people of the town for bringing their negroes in question, and that people did not believe what she said, so what signified speaking? or to this purpose she expressed herself. She intimated withal, that there were some people *in ruffles* (a phrase as was understood to mean persons of better fashion than ordinary) that were concerned. At last, having been threatened to be imprisoned in the dungeon, she named several persons which she said she had seen at Hughson's amongst the conspirators, talking of the conspiracy, who were engaged in it; amongst whom she mentioned several of known credit, fortunes and reputations, and of religious principles superior to a suspicion of being concerned in such detestable practices; at which the judges were very much astonished;

others again were imperfectly described by her, whose reputed religious profession might square with such wicked designs, concerning whom the girl had long before given broad hints, but said she did not know their names, or what part of the city they lived in; but it came out at last, that one of them was a doctor (a professed papist, as common fame had it) whom she had seen several times afterwards in the streets, and who upon sight of her, always turned another way, to avoid meeting her: however it was, this person had the discretion to remove himself out of this province soon after; and it is said, into foreign dominions; and it were much to be wished, that such others, as were justly liable to impeachment, would act with the same prudence and follow his example, for the sake of their own safety, as well as the peace and security of ourselves. But upon the whole, there was reason to conclude, that this girl had at length been tampered withal; might it not be suggested to her, that the reward offered by proclamation for the discovery, she was already sure of, for she was entitled to it; and might she not be tempted to make further advantage of the affair? upon this supposition, the conspirators could not have devised a more effectual means (if they could but prevail with her) to put a stop to further inquiry, to procure the names of persons to be called in question at last, concerning this scene of villainy, whose fortunes and characters set them above suspicion: they very well knew (for papists or priests as Ury intimated, as "too wise and too cunning") if they could but prevail in this, they would thereby not only put a stop to further discovery, but likewise have some pretence, according to their usual custom, to clamour loudly, there was no plot at all: it was a mere dream! and to serve this turn, they had luckily with them some owners of slaves, who happened to humour this artifice, though upon a different view.

It was fit this matter should be stated in its proper light; that on the one hand the evidence of this witness (but for whom next under the interposition of divine providence, this city would in all probability have been laid waste in ashes, so far as deserving of credit) and on the other hand, that where she may be justly suspected to have executed the bounds of truth, there a step may be made, to consider, and conjecture, how it might have come to pass, that she told some things incredible at the winding up of this affair; and weigh impartially also, the whole current of the other evidence, remarking how it appears to confirm and establish her testimony, so far as it has been judged proper and fitting to publish it.

Conclusion

That a plot there was, and as to the parties and bloody purpose of it, we presume there can scarce be a doubt amongst us at this time; the ruins of his majesty's house in the fort, are the daily evidence and moments of it, still before our eyes: if the other frights and terrors this city was alarmed with, to their great consternation, are, as to some amongst us, so soon slipped into oblivion; yet surely others will think we ought once a year at least, to pay our tribute of praise and thanksgiving to the Divine Being, that through his merciful providence and infinite goodness, caused this inhuman horrible enterprize to be detected, and so many of the wicked instruments of it to be brought to justice, whereby a check has been put to the execrable malice, and bloody purposes of our foreign and domestic enemies, though we have not been able entirely to unravel the mystery of this iniquity; for it was a dark design, and the veil is in some measure still upon it!

PART THREE

Related Documents

1

NEW YORK WEEKLY JOURNAL

A full and particular Account of the Negro Plot in Antigua, *as reported by the Committee appointed by the Government there to enquire into the same*

March 7, 1736

In 1736, many of the white residents of one of Britain's Caribbean sugar colonies, Antigua, feared that they had uncovered a slave uprising. As a plantation society, eighteenth-century Antigua had a very large black majority population (almost 90 percent): 24,000 blacks to 3,000 whites. Any plan for a revolt never came to fruition. The investigation by the courts took about six months. In the end, eighty-eight slaves were executed and thirty-six banished. As in New York, no new slave code followed the trials.

There were several similarities to the New York plot. The ringleaders were the servants of local elites, and much of the plotting was thought to have taken place in taverns. Like New York's, this investigation had an urban focus: Most of those executed lived in the towns, rather than on the rural plantations, of the island. On the other hand, there is no evidence of any white involvement in the plot. In this first article of a five-part series on the suspected slave uprising that was printed in a New York newspaper, the committee that investigated the plot described the ringleaders (Court and Tomboy) and the methods by which they convinced others to join them.

Antigua

To His Excellency in Council.

In Obedience to an Order of Your Excellency and Council made the 9th Day of this instant *December,* We attend You with a Report of Our Proceedings upon the weighty Affair of the Late Conspiracy of Our Slaves, intrusted to us by Your Excellency, with the Consent of the Council and Assembly: The Substance of what appeared to us therein, is,

That the Slaves had formed and resolved to execute a Plot, whereby all the white Inhabitants of this Island were to be murdered, and a new Form of Government to be established by the Slaves among themselves, and they entirely to possess the Island. The Slaves chiefly concerned in this Conspiracy were those born upon the *Gold Coast,* in *Africa,* whom we stile *Coromantees,* and those born in one or another of the Sugar Colonies, whom we call *Creoles.* At the Head of the former was *Court,* alias *Taskey,* a *Coromantee* Negro Man Slave, belonging to *Thomas Kerby,* Esq.; and at the Head of the latter was *Tomboy,* a *Creole,* born in *Antigua,* a Master Carpenter, belonging to Mr. *Thom. Henson;* The Persons and Characters of those two Chiefs were so well known to Your Excellency and to this Island in general, that little need be said of either: However, we shall beg so much of Your Time as just to mention that (as we are told) *Court* was of a considerable Family in his own Country; but not as was commonly thought, of Royal Blood; and yet it was fully proved, that he had for many Years, covertly assumed among his Country Men here the Stile of KING, and had been by them addressed and treated as such: He appeared to us artful and ambitious, very proud, and of few Words; was brought hither as a Slave about Ten years of Age, and was executed at about Forty five. His Indulgences from his Master, were great and uncommon, which gave him the Opportunity of acquiring more Money than it's hardly ever known Slaves are Master of; which he perverted in engaging his poorer Country Men in his evil Designs. At the

New York Weekly Journal, March 7, 1736.

Time of his Execution, he endeavoured to put on a Port[1] suitable to his asserted Dignity of King. *Tomboy* was also very kindly used by his Master; being admitted for his own Advantage, to take Negro Apprentices, and to make all the Profits he could of his own and their Labour, paying his Master only a monthly Sum, far short of his usual Earnings; so that he too was generally master of Money, and did not fail applying it on all Occasions to propagating his vile Purposes among the *Creoles;* and being a Fellow of robust strong Body and resolute Temper, he had great Influence over them, and had a Genius adapted to Caballing.[2]

To these two Chiefs were joined other Principals, *viz., Hercules,* belonging to Mr. *John Christophers; Jack* and *Scipio,* belonging to Mr. *Philip Derby; Ned,* belonging to Col. *Jacob Morgan; Fortune,* belonging to Mrs. *Johanna Lodge;* and *Toney,* belonging to Col. *Samuel Martin;* these were all *Creoles* (except *Fortune,* of who 'tis doubted, whether he was a *Creole* or brought hither sucking at the Breast) and had all with their Chief *Tomboy,* been lately Baptized; and several of them could read and write. But the most Active Incendiaries under Tomboy, were *Freeman's Secundi,* and Sir *William Codrington*'s *Jacko,* both *Creoles* of *French* Parentage, and initiated into Christianity according to the Romish Persuasion. Of these Chiefs and Principals, we can assuredly say, that they had Hearts and Minds capable of conceiving, Heads fit for contriving, and Hands and courage for executing the deepest and most bloody Crimes, even that unparallel'd Hellish Plot formed by them, against his Majesty's Government of this Island, and our Lives and Fortunes; and yet they could none of them justly complain of the Hardships of Slavery; their Lives being as easy as those of our white Tradesmen and Overseers, and their Manner of Living much more plentiful than that of our common Whites, who were lookt upon by some of them for their Poverty and Distress, with Contempt: Their Employments were handicraft Trades, Overseeing, or as House-Servants.

To fix certainly the Person and precisely the Time, by whom and when, this Design was first set on foot, is not to be done: It being something, tho' not very doubtful, whether *Court* or *Tomboy* first moved it; tho' generally imputed to the former, and it is most difficult to find out any Period of Time from the Evidence given by Slaves, who

[1] *put on a Port:* Assume a character.
[2] *Caballing:* The forming of secret and harmful intrigues.

are not acquainted with our Manner, nor indeed have any certain Manner of computing it: But we have, by all the Evidence, reason to believe, *Court* was the first Author; and have Proof that it was undoubtedly in Agitation, about November 1735; at which time *Martin's Jemmy,* by an Artifice of *Tomboy*'s being made drunk at *Treblin*'s, was brought in to take an Oath or Engagement, as one of the Conspirators; for *Court* being sensible how impossible it was to effect his Designs by the Coromantee's only, found himself under a Necessity of engaging the *Creoles,* who are the most numerous, sensible, and able Body of our Slaves; and to that end, after a long Coldness between him and *Tomboy,* courted *Tomboy*'s friendship, and obtained it, and found him every way ready for, and equal to his Purpose.

The chief Measure used by the two Heads, to corrupt our Slaves, were Entertainments of Dancing, Gaming and Feasting, and some of them very chargeable ones; always coloured with some innocent Pretence, as commemorating some deceased Friend, by throwing Water on his Grave, or christening a House, or the like, according to the Negro Customs: Whether they were debauched with Liquor, their Minds imbittered against their Masters and against their Condition of Slavery, by strong Invectives thrown out against both; and Freedom with the Possession of their Master's Estates were to be Rewards of their Perfidy and Treachery; and they never failed to bind their new Proselites to Fidelity and Secrecy, and to bring all Assistance in their Power, as they had done each other, by Oaths taken after their Country Customs, mentioned hereafter more at large. A new Government was to be established, when the Inhabitants were intirely extirpated; *Court* was amused and flattered by all with being *KING* of the Island, but the *Creoles* had resolved unknown to him and his *Coromantees,* to settle a Common-Wealth, and to make slaves of the Coromantees & Negroes of all other nations, and to destroy *Court,* and all such who should refuse to submit to such terms the *Creoles* should please to impose upon them.

2

PUBLIC RECORD OFFICE

The Confessions of Wan an Indian Slave belonging to Peter Low and of York a Negroe belonging to Peter Marschalk

June 18, 1741, and June 20, 1741

Most of the events and confessions of the 1741 trials have been preserved only through Horsmanden's Journal. *Unfortunately, the Supreme Court records for the 1740s have disappeared. Besides a very brief record of the legal events (the dates of arrests, indictments, and so forth), there is little external evidence against which to test the biases of Horsmanden's account. On June 20, 1741, however, New York's lieutenant governor enclosed copies of a few of the confessions that had been made in the previous few days when he wrote to the Cabinet member who oversaw the colonies, the Duke of Newcastle. These have remained undisturbed in Britain's national archive, the Public Record Office.*

Two of these confessions have been reproduced here. Compare them carefully with the versions in Horsmanden's Journal. *One of the confessions is very similar to the one in the* Journal; *the other has significantly more detail than the* Journal. *Consider why and how Horsmanden's version is different. Does it make any difference for our assessment of the reliability of the* Journal? *It may be helpful to take into account the description that the judge gives in his introduction of how confessions were recorded.*

[In this first confession, a slave named Wan (Juan) gives his account of sharing a drink with a free black, who is also named Wan.]

18TH JUNE 1741[1]

THE CONFESSION OF WAN AN INDIAN SLAVE BELONGING TO PETER LOW

Says that last Summer two Days after Whitsontide[2] he was taking a Walk with a Free negroe named Wan (who is Gone to Cuba in Captain Cosby's Company) who asked him whether he would drink a Mug of Beer with him he say'd Yes and thereupon they went to Huson's and Drank it—as they were going away Hughson say'd stay I have something to say to you and then told him it was against the Law for him to Sell Liquor to Negroes and that he (the Prisoner Wan) was half Drunk already and would tell of it and would have them Swear the free Negroe went out and say'd what does the Fellow mean—Hughson then took Wan aside and told him of the Generall Conspiracy and persuaded him to Come in and say'd it would be good for him and then took a Book and Swore him The Tenor[3] of the Oath was that he wished the Thunder and Lightning might Strike him Dead and the Devil fetch him If he told of it. The prisoner was to set his Master's house on Fire and Murther[4] his Master Huson said all the Negroes must Come in that after he was Sworn Hughson put his name down on a list, and told him he must Stand to it. When the Time Comes That Mr Casporson's Negroe saw him Swear that he was sworn in a Small back Room fronting the yard were[5] there was a Comptor[6] There were a great many more Negroes in the other Room who might posibly see him but who they were he does not know, He says Bastian Vaarick's Negroe there a playing papa's[7] with many others. Huson told him the first fire was to be in the Fly That the Fort was to be burnt and that each Negroe was to set fire to his Master's House and to

[1]This confession is listed under June 19 in the *Journal.*
[2]*Whitsontide:* Whitsuntide, or Pentecost, the seventh Sunday after Easter.
[3]*Tenor:* General sense, overall meaning.
[4]*Murther:* Murder.
[5]*were:* Where.
[6]*Comptor:* A counter, or a desk, for keeping money or accounts.
[7]*playing papa's:* Presumably some sort of dice or card game.

Colonial Office Papers, series 5, 1094, page 111. June 18, 1741. Public Record Office, London.

Murther their Masters, were to have what white Women they pleas'd and that each Negroe was to take his Master's Gun that when the City was on Fire all the Negroes were to meet on the Plain before the Fort. Wan says he never was at Huson's but[8] that Time that he did not See the Spanish Negroes there nor ever spoke to them about it since, except Bosche's Francis and Gomez's Coffee who have asked him two or three times whether it was not time to begin And that he saw them behind Van Rants Storehouse.

Taken 20 June, 1741

THE CONFESSION OF YORK A NEGROE
BELONGING TO PETER MARSCHALK

Acknowledges that what the Witnesses said on his Tryal Yesterday being the 19 Day of June 1741 was true. That he went on Sunday Morning early above two Years agoe to Huson's House with Kipps's Samuel (who has been dead 2 Years) and bought a Quart of Rum and went with it to Mr Bayards out of Town That Comforts Jack about Christmass last informed him first of the Plot. Jack met York by his gate and told him of the Plot and appointed him to meet at Huson's that he went to Husons and that he was there the Sunday the Feast was as mentioned by the Witnesses at Court, that he has been twice at Huson's and once at Comforts that he was to be a Captain, was Sworn, that many Negroes were present and all Swore and Consented; agrees to the Circumstances told of the Plot in Generall. Spanish Negroes were there the prisoners with him at the Bar and many other Negroes also were there at Husons. That Huson and his Wife and Daughter Swore first when those who were at the upper End of the Table near Huson swore upon a Book and the others at a Distance without a Book by Thunder etc. He York agreed to Set his Master's house on Fire but say'd he would not do it till he saw somebody Else begin and then he would he was to kill his Mistress. Went to Husons on a Sunday just after afternoon Church out and believes that meeting was about 6 weeks before the Fort burnt, London (his fellow Servant) Was

[8]*but:* Except.

Colonial Office Papers, series 5, 1094, page 112. June 20, 1741. Public Record Office, London.

to be a private Man under him Comforts Jack's meeting was two Week's after this At Comfort's House, He and Kipp's Harry were in the Shop, above twenty there, Jack went backwards and forwards from the Shop to the Kitchin Huson proposed to them to get as many other Negroes in as they Could he did not go into the Kitchen but Heard a great many were there Huson told them at his House that the Spaniard knew better than York Negroes how to fight and they were all to Stand by one another and assist the French and Spaniards they were to Stop for them some time and if they did not Come they were to do all themselves every one in the Shop had knives and they were Sharpning of them and they were to cut the White Men's heads off.

3

LIEUTENANT-GOVERNOR GEORGE CLARKE

Letter to the Lords of Trade

June 20, 1741

Two to three times each month, the royal representative in New York wrote to the men who oversaw the British colonies in North America, a royal commission entitled the Lords of Trade. In several previous letters to officials in London, Lieutenant-Governor Clarke recorded his shifting opinions about the events in New York. In his first letter, he had described the burning of the fort as an accident; in the second, he had suspected that slaves, urged and organized by John Hughson, had committed the arson. In this letter, written soon after the trials of the Spanish prisoners and the execution of the Hughsons, but before the official arrest of John Ury, Clarke considers the possibility that he is observing a Catholic plot unfold. He also comments on the difficulty he is having raising troops to fight in the Caribbean when white residents feared both a slave uprising and an invasion from the Catholic French to the north.

E. B. O'Callaghan, ed., *Documents Relative to the Colonial History of the State of New York* (Albany: Weed, Parsons and Company, Printers, 1853–87), 6:197–98.

LIEUTENANT-GOVERNOR CLARKE TO THE LORDS OF TRADE.

NEW YORK JUNE THE 20. 1741.
My Lords

Before the Assembly rose I had the honor to receive a letter from his Grace the Duke of Newcastle signifying his Majesty's Commands to me to raise what recruits or new levies the General of the forces on the Expedition should write for . . . I expect likewise to meet with great difficulties in raising men at the time, for the confusion which the conspiracy some white people and the Negroes entred in to burn this town and to destroy the inhabitants has begat a general opinion that no man ought to leave his habitation to go out of the Province and the apprehension of a French warr as this is a frontier Province will make every one, who has any thing at stake industrious to discourage men from inlisting themselves for this expedition lest a rupture with France should soon happen, these are my apprehensions, however I will use my utmost application to raise recruits when the General writes for them, for as I did last year raise a greater proportion of Troops than any of our Neighbouring Colonies, as will I believe evidently appear by examining the lists of white people in the Colonies, I shall be very sorry to fall short now. . . .

(The fatal fire that consumed the buildings in the fort and great part of my substance, for my loss is not less than two thousand pounds, did not happen by accident as I at first apprehended, but was kindled by design in the execution of a horrid Conspiracy to burn it and the whole town and to Massacre the people, as appears evidently not only by the Confession of the Negro who set fire to it in some part of the same gutter where the Plumber was to work but also by the testimony of several witnesses, how many Conspirators there we do not yet know every day produces new discoveries and I apprehend that in the town, if the truth were known, there are not many innocent Negromen, and it is thought that some Negroes of the Country are accomplices and were to act their part there, and to this belief I am led by the villany committed in New Jersey sometime after the fort was burnt, for at a Village called Newark seven Barnes were burnt in one night, for which two Negroes were tried and executed; In this Town there have been already executed for this Conspiracy seventeen vizt[1] Three Whites (Huson the contriver and main spring of the whole design, his wife and another white woman who lived in Huson's house,

[1]*vizt: Videlicet,* namely.

and had a bastard by one of the Negro Conspirators) and fourteen Negroes Huson is hung in chains, for the rest that or may be executed, I desired the Judges to single out only a few of the most notorious for execution, and that I would pardon the rest, on condition that the pardon be void if they be found in the Province after a certain day, whereby their masters will transport them out of hand, I do myself the honor to send your Lordships the minutes taken at the tryal of Quack who burned the fort, and of another Negro, who was tryed with him, and their confession at the stake, with some other examinations, whereby your Lordships will see their designs, it was ridiculous to suppose that they could keep possession of the Town, if they had destroyed the White people, yet the mischief they would have done in pursuit of their intention would never the less have been great.

My loss sits very heavy upon me, His Majesties bounty and goodness, I am sensible[2] are vastly great, but yet I know not how to hope for relief, unless thro the protection of his Grace the Duke of Newcastle, upon your Lordships favourable recommendation which I beg leave to ask.

Whether or how far the hand of popery has been in this hellish conspiracy I cannot yet discover, but there is room to suspect it, by what two of the Negroes have confest, Vizt that soon after they were spoke to, and had consented to be parties to it, they had some checks of conscience which they said, would not suffer them to burn houses and kill the White people; whereupon those who drew them into the conspiracy told them, there was no sin or wickedness in it, and that if they would go to Huson's house, they should find a man who would satisfy them but they say they would not nor did go; Margaret Kerry was supposed to be a papist, and it is suspected that Huson and his wife were brought over to it: there was in Town some time ago a man who is said to be a Romish Priest, who used to be at Huson's, but has disappeared ever since the discovery of the conspiracy and is not now to be found, upon this occasion I do myself the honor to send your Lordships a paragraph of General Oglethorps letter to me. . . .

I am with the highest respect and honor

My Lords

Your Lordships

most humble and

most obedient Servant

Rt Honble the Lords of Trade. GEO: CLARKE

[2]*sensible:* Aware.

4

Letter to Cadwallader Colden

Summer 1741

In the middle of John Ury's trial, Cadwallader Colden, a member of the governor's council and a politician, received an anonymous letter sent from Massachusetts. The letter writer compared the slave executions in New York to a series of infamous trials in Massachusetts just fifty years earlier: the Salem witchcraft trials. In the winter of 1692, several young women accused other members of the community, primarily other women, of practicing witchcraft. The courts pressured the accused to confess, who often in turn incriminated others. By the following fall, 156 people had been officially accused of witchcraft and jailed. Twenty people were eventually put to death by the court's orders. Ministers and other officials became increasingly concerned about the use of "spectral (or spectre) evidence," the visions of the devil or his agents that the accusers claimed to feel or see speaking to the accused witches. By the fall of that year, skeptics had convinced the governor to disallow the use of such invisible evidence. As one minister famously insisted, "It were better that ten suspected witches shall escape, than that one innocent person should be condemned." At the same time, the accusers had begun to charge wealthy and elite women of witchcraft, even accusing the governor's wife. Massachusetts officials quickly distanced themselves from the trials once they had ended in the winter of 1693. By 1702, the General Court had declared the trials unlawful, and by 1711, the colony had passed a bill that cleared the names of all those originally accused of witchcraft and that offered some restitution for their heirs. The writer of the letter reproduced here drew several parallels between the New York trials and those in Salem, arguing that the plot in New York would eventually turn out to be just as specious as the one in Salem, and would also end when elites were accused. Consider carefully the author's claim: What other evidence did the prosecution present other than confessions? Do you agree with the author that confessions are as inherently unreliable as he or she suggests? Note also the humanitarian basis of the writer's argument.

Letter from [anonymous] to Cadwallader Colden, Boston (n.d.), in *Letters and Papers of Cadwallader Colden,* New-York Historical Society, *Publications,* 67 (1934): 270–72.

PROVINCE OF THE MASSACHUSETTS BAY 1741 (JULY 23?)

Sir,

I am a stranger to you & to New York, & so must beg pardon for the mistakes I may be guilty of in the subsequent attempt; The Design whereof is to endeavour the putting an end to the bloody Tragedy that has been, & I suppose still is acting amongst you in regard to the poor Negros & the Whites too. I observe in one of the Boston News letters dated July 13th that 5 Negros were executed in one day at the Gallows, a favour indeed, for one next day was burnt at the stake, where he impeached several others & amongst them some whites. Which with the former horrible executions among you upon this occasion puts me in mind of our New England Witchcraft in the year 1692 Which if I dont mistake New York justly reproached us for, & mockt at our Credulity about; but may it not now be justly retorted, *mutato nomine de te fabula narratur.*[1] What grounds you proceed upon I must acknowledge my self not sufficiently informed of; but finding that these 5 who were put to Death in July denied any Guilt, It makes me suspect that your present case, & ours heretofore are much the same, and that Negro and Spectre evidence[2] will turn out alike. We had near 50 Confessors, who accused multitudes of others, alledging Time & Place, & Various other circumstances to render their Confessions credible, that they had their meetings, form'd confederacies, sign'd the Devils book &c. But I am humbly of Opinion that such Confessions unless some certain Overt Act appear to confirm the same are not worth a Straw; for many times they are obtain'd by foul means, by force or torment, by Surprise, by flattery, by Distraction, by Discontent with their circumstances, through envy that they may bring others into the same condemnation, or in hopes of a longer time to live, or to dy an easier death &c. For any body would chuse rather to be hanged than to be burnt. It is true I have heard something of your Forts being burnt, but that might be by Lightning from Heaven, by Accedent, by some malicious person or persons of our own colour. What other Feats have been performed to petrify your hearts against the poor blacks & some of your neighbours the whites, I cant tell; But 2 things seem impossible to me almost *in rerum natura,*[3] That whites should join with the Blacks, or that the Blacks (among whom there are no doubt some rational persons) should attempt the Destruction

[1]"Change the name, and the story is about you." Horace, *Satires* 1.1.69–70.
[2]*Spectre evidence:* See the headnote to this letter.
[3]*in rerum natura:* "In nature," "in the world."

of a City when it is impossible they should escape the just & direfull Vengeance of the Countries round about, which would immediately & unavoidably pour in upon them & destroy them

Possibly there have been some murmuring amongst the Negroes & a mad fellow or 2 has threatened & design'd Revenge, for the Cruelty & inhumanity they have met with, which is too rife in the English Plantations (& not long since occasioned such another tremendous & unreasonable Tragedy at Antego)[4] And if that be all it is a pity there have been such severe animadversions.[5] And if nothing will put an end hereto till some of higher degree & better circumstances & Characters are accused (which finished our Salem Witchcraft) the sooner the better, lest all the poor People of the Government perish in the merciless flames of an Imaginary Plot.

In the mean time excuse me & dont be offended, if out of Friendship to my poor Countrymen & compassion to the Negros (who are flesh & blood as well as we & ought to be treated with Humanity) I intreat you not to go on to Massacre & destroy your own Estates by making Bonfires of the Negros & perhaps thereby loading yourselves with greater Guilt than theirs. For we have too much reason to fear that the Divine Vengeance does & will pursue us for our ill treatment of the bodies & souls of our poor slaves and therefore

Let Justice be don to your own people, whatever Treatment the People of Massachusets may meet with when you set in Judicature about their affairs. All which is humbly submitted by a Well wisher to all humane Beings & one that ever desires to be of the mercifull side &c.

[4]*Antego:* Antigua. See the Introduction and Document 1.
[5]*animadversions:* Judicial punishments.

5

DANIEL HORSMANDEN

Letter to Cadwallader Colden

August 7, 1741

In the period between John Ury's sentencing and his execution, Daniel Horsmanden took a small vacation from his labors on the court. During this time, he wrote a letter to his friend Cadwallader Colden, a member of the governor's council and a politician. In this letter, Horsmanden ruminated on the process of the trials, on the discovery of popery, the credibility of Mary Burton, and even his own personal relationship to the trials. Compare these private musings, written at the time of the trials, with his Conclusion, written three years later.

AUGUST THE 7TH 1741

Dear Sir

After a long cessation of Correspondence I take the Liberty of resuming the pen, partly with design of Apologizing & also not without view of provoking you to renew the Combat, which we may be engag'd in with honour without Loss of Blood. Ever Since the fire at the Fort which was on the 18th March I've been engag'd in perpetual hurry, insomuch that I've been forced to dedicate part of my resting time to the publick Service in presenting an Enquiry into the rise & occasion of Our Late Disorders in the City of New York, but I think the Labour bestowed has not been in Vain; for tho' the Mystery of Iniquity has been unfolding by very Small & Slow Degrees, it has at length been discovered that popery was at the Bottom, & the Old proverb has herein also been verified That there is Scarce a plot but a priest is at the Bottom of it, or as the like pert[1] priest (Ury) said upon his Defense at his Trial (tho Sarcastically) "according to the vogue of the World where there is a plot, the first & last Link are usually fas-

[1]*pert:* Bold, saucy.
[2]*girdle:* Belt.

Daniel Horsmanden to Cadwallader Colden, August 7, 1741, New-York Historical Society, *Collections,* 51 (1918): 224–28.

tened to the priests—"girdle;"[2] but he must excuse us in his case, if the last Link be fastened to his Neck, for he is Convicted as one of the Principal Conspirators, & is Condemned to be hanged on next Saturday Sev'night.

He appear to have been a principal promoter & encourager of this most horrible & Detestable piece of Villany a Scheme which must have been brooded in a Conclave of Devils, & hatcht in the Cabinet of Hell; so bloody & Destructive a Conspiracy was this, that had not the mercifull hand of providence interposed & Confounded their Devices, in one & the Same night the Inhabitants would have been butcher'd in their houses, by their own Slaves, & the City laid in ashes; & this was to be perpetrated under the Obligation of an infamous Oath administered to the Conspirators, (Most Negroes, & Some Soldiers & other Whites, the more's the Shame,) by John Hughson, now in Chains, & this Ury the priest, by whose craft they were perverted, and in expectation of a (fools) paradise, Baptized into the most holy Roman Catholick Faith, & under Colour of Absolution & pardon of Sins, past present & to come; & while they were going to Sacrifice to the Devil were made to believe by destroying of Hereticks they would do God good Service. Tantum Religio Potuit Luadere [*Suadere*] malorum![3]

And tho' we have been So Successful in prying into this Scene of Darkness & horror As to bring to Light near 90 Negroes & I think about a Dozen Whites Engaged to be actors in this black Tragedy, of the former whereof 30 odd have been executed, & this priest makes the 4th White, And tho' the Town were well pleas'd with the first fruits of Our Labours and inflicting the deserved punishment on the Offenders. Yet when it comes home to their own houses, & is like to affect their own propertys in Negroes and Cosinship[4] in others; then they are alarm'd & they cry out the Witness must needs be perjured; & so we come under a Necessity of making a Sort of Stand, for the present, & it is almost incredible to Say, that great pains has been taken by Some amoung us, to bring a discredit upon Mary Burton the Original Witness, whom providence one would think had designed for the happy Instrument of all this Discovery & whose Testimony has been confirmed by Several Negroes in Flames who obstinately denyed their guilt til they came to the Stake to be burnt. So Soon have her Services been forgotten! & a stop affected to be put to her doing any further!

As to the characters of other witnesses who have been accomplices

[3]"Such great evil could superstition prompt!" Lucretius, *De Rerum Natura,* I. 101.
[4]*Cosinship:* Relationship (perhaps; this word appears nowhere else in English).

in this wickedness designed against us, what can be expected to be said for them they are Such as the Wisdom of the Law allows to be Legal & Good Evidences & that from the Necessity of the thing. For how can a Discovery of Such works of Darkness be expected but from some of the Confederates themselves; & if the witnesses are kept apart & Examined apart as most of them have been in both Instances upon most if not all of the Trials, & their respective Testimonys Tally & agree, what better Evidence can be desired or expected?

And tho' Mary Burton has from the beginning been an unwilling witness thro' the Terror of having her life threatened both by Blacks, & Whites, & tho' she has declared from the beginning, That should She tell all she knew that people would not believe her; And tho' she has been prevailed upon after being threatened to be imprisoned upon her Standing mute & Obstinately refusing to name any names tho' She confess'd She knew more; Yet, when She did name them we could not but be Shockt, the persons mentioned being beyond Suspition; & the Consequence followed, that great Clamor has thence been raised against her & now, by Some, She must be esteemed a person of no Credit: I do think her Case is attended with Singular hardships, & at the same time, the thing She Says, cannot but Stagger ones beliefs in Some measures; but I must observe, that this is not the First time her Examinations have had that Effect upon me, but Several times, from my first taking her in hand, yet til now, every thing that has come from her, has in the Event been confirmed; but here must be a Suspension of Credit for a while, & time only can clear the matter up: I must own I'm glad I've got an Opportunity of a little Relaxation from this intricate pursuit, tho' at the same time from the length of my Letter you may take occasion to imagine I'm not quite tired of it, but if my design of this imperfect narrative by way of Amusement may be thought to answer that Intention, it will at the Same time in some measure Appologize for Former Defects & also vindicate my Sincerity. . . .

I am

Dear Sir

Your most Affectionate Friend & humble Servant

Daniel Horsmanden

A Chronology of the New York Conspiracy Trials of 1741 and Related Events (1624–1763)

1624 Dutch settle Manhattan (part of New Netherland)

1626 First slaves brought to Manhattan

1664 Dutch surrender New Netherland to England

1702–1713 Queen Anne's War: England against France and Spain

1712 Slave uprising in New York, in which nine whites die and twenty-five slaves are executed

1734 Slave uprising suspected in New Jersey

1736 Antigua Rebellion in which eight-eight slaves were executed

1739–1748 War of Jenkins' Ear and King George's War: Britain against Spain; France enters war in 1744

1739 *January:* In New Jersey, a slave murders a child and sets fire to a barn; burnt at the stake

1739 *September:* Stono Rebellion in South Carolina: roughly twenty whites killed

1739 *November:* Admiral Vernon takes Porto Bello in Panama from the Spanish

1741: *Conspiracy Trials*
February 28: Robbery at the Hoggs
March 1: John Gwin committed to jail
March 4: Mary Burton deposes regarding the robbery
March 18: First fire, at Fort George
March 20: Prince committed
March 25–April 6: Nine more fires
April 10: Hughsons committed
April 11: First award for information offered by the Council
April 21: First grand jury impaneled
April 22: Burton's first deposition regarding the conspiracy

May 8: John Gwin and Prince sentenced
May 11: John Gwin and Prince executed
May 22: Sawney's first deposition
May 30: Quack and Cuffee burned at the stake
June 12: Hughsons and Kerry hanged
June 13: Spanish prisoners arraigned
June 19: Governor's proclamation promising a pardon to those who confess or inform
June 24: First mention of John Ury
June 29: Trial of John Ury
August 29: Ury executed

1748 King George's War ends

1756–1763 French and Indian War, at the end of which the French and Spanish threat to British North America is removed

Questions for Consideration

1. What is the best evidence that there was a conspiracy in New York City in 1741? What sort of conspiracy was it? Was it a wholesale revolution by slaves and poor whites to overturn the social structure of New York and find freedom and equality for themselves? Was it a smaller-scale rebellion fueled by smoldering resentments? Were the fires free-standing acts of terrorism, or part of a larger plan? If they were part of a larger plan, was it a plot to commit rebellion, or to commit thefts?
2. What is the best evidence that there was no conspiracy in New York City in 1741? If there was no conspiracy, what is the best explanation for the trials and executions? Of the many fears that beset New York judges and juries, which seem to be the most compelling reason for the trials: fears of slave insurrections, of foreign invasion, of Catholics, of disorder, of attacks on property, of interracial mixing?
3. What is the role of masculinity and femininity in the trials? What difference does social class, ethnicity, race, or freedom make in how women and men are regarded, behave, and relate to each other? Conversely, what do the trials reveal about men and women in society at large?
4. Some historians have considered this text a carefully constructed argument written by a man with an axe to grind. How useful is a text with such a clear bias? In what ways can the bias help us better understand eighteenth-century New York, and in what ways does it obscure the colonial city? As part of this question, consider the omissions that Horsmanden alludes to in his record (such as the defendants' questions to witnesses and the related documents that corroborate or question his version of events). What might this text have looked like if it had been written by someone else, perhaps Burton, Kerry, one of the Hughsons, Gwin, or Prince?
5. In an article about Vesey's Rebellion, a suspected slave revolt in Charleston, South Carolina, in 1822, historian Michael P. Johnson has written that the real plot was formed by the white court, who intentionally conspired to execute black men in order to maint

power in a slave society.[1] Johnson's argument rests on his vigorous critique of the "official report" of the 1822 court, a document not unlike Horsmanden's *Journal* in that it was produced by the prosecution, after the fact, in order to bolster the court's reputation. When historians base their acceptance of an attempted slave conspiracy on such a document, Johnson argues, they too become "unwitting co-conspirators with the court." Is Johnson's thesis applicable also for the New York trials of 1741? Why or why not?

6. How and why do different people confess in these trials? What do their confessions tell us about the power dynamics of the trials? We know that one contemporary observer compared these trials to those of Salem fifty years earlier. Is this a valid comparison of the context of the confessions? It may be helpful also to think about the retracted confessions. What are the patterns of confession that led to further accusations?
7. How consistent is Burton's testimony throughout the trials? How do the changes in her testimony affect our interpretation of her trustworthiness?
8. How convincing is John Ury's defense? Did he adequately answer the charges against him?
9. Throughout the trials, Horsmanden draws connections between race and behavior. What can be learned from these editorial asides about Horsmanden's understanding of race and his racial attitudes? What can this text reveal about the racial attitudes of witnesses and defendants?
10. The trial transcripts and editorial comments of the 1741 slave conspiracy trials are rich in details about everyday life in eighteenth-century New York, about New Yorkers' attitudes and assumptions, and about their fears and hopes. What does the *New York Conspiracy* tell us about:
    a. Elite white male New Yorkers' attitudes toward slaves?
    b. Working white New Yorkers' attitudes toward slaves?
    c. Elite white male New Yorkers' beliefs about race?
    d. Working white New Yorkers' beliefs about race?
    e. Enslaved men's attitudes toward white New Yorkers?
    f. Sexual activity in colonial New York?
    g. Drinking in colonial New York?

[1]Michael P. Johnson, "Denmark Vesey and His Co-Conspirators," *William and Mary Quarterly,* 3rd ser., 58 (October 2001): 917–76.

h. Attitudes toward strangers in colonial New York?
i. Women in colonial New York?
j. War in colonial New York?
k. Being a slave in colonial New York?
l. Being a servant in colonial New York?

Selected Bibliography

COLONIAL NEW YORK

Archdeacon, Thomas J. *New York City 1664–1710: Conquest and Change.* Ithaca: Cornell University Press, 1976.

Bonomi, Patricia U. *A Factious People: Politics and Society in Colonial New York.* New York: Columbia University Press, 1971.

Bonomi, Patricia U. *The Lord Cornbury Scandal: The Politics of Reputation in British America.* Chapel Hill and London: University of North Carolina Press for the Institute of Early American History and Culture, 1998.

Burrows, Edwin G., and Mike Wallace. *Gotham: A History of New York City to 1898.* New York and Oxford: Oxford University Press, 1999.

Goebel, Julius, and T. Raymond Naughton. *Law Enforcement in Colonial New York: A Study in Criminal Procedure (1664–1776).* New York: The Commonwealth Fund, 1944; reprint, 1970.

Goodfriend, Joyce. *Before the Melting Pot: Society and Culture in Colonial New York City, 1664–1730.* Princeton and Oxford: Princeton University Press, 1991.

Greenberg, Douglas. *Crime and Law Enforcement in the Colony of New York, 1691–1776.* Ithaca and London: Cornell University Press, 1974.

Greene, Jack P. "Pluralism in New York." In *Interpreting Early America: Historiographical Essays,* edited by Jack P. Greene. Charlottesville: University Press of Virginia, 1996.

Gunderson, Joan R., and Gwen V. Gampel. "Married Women's Legal Status in Eighteenth-Century New York and Virginia." *William and Mary Quarterly,* 3rd ser., 39 (January 1982): 114–34.

Kammen, Michael. *Colonial New York: A History.* New York and Oxford: Oxford University Press, 1975.

Katz, Stanley N. *Newcastle's New York: Anglo-American Politics, 1732–1753.* Cambridge: Belknap Press of Harvard University Press, 1968.

Klein, Milton. *The Politics of Diversity: Essays in the History of Colonial New York.* Port Washington, N.Y., and London: Kennikat Press, 1974.

Lustig, Mary Lou. *Privilege and Prerogative: New York's Provincial Elite, 1710–1776.* Madison, N.J.: Associated University Presses, 1995.

Lydon, James G. "New York and the Slave Trade, 1700–1774." *William and Mary Quarterly,* 3rd ser., 35 (April 1978): 375–94.

Matson, Cathy D. *Merchants and Empire: Trading in Colonial New York.* Baltimore: Johns Hopkins University Press, 1998.

McManus, Edgar J. *A History of Negro Slavery in New York.* Syracuse: Syracuse University Press, 1966.

McManus, Mary Paula. "Daniel Horsmanden: An Eighteenth-Century New Yorker." Ph.D. diss., Fordham University, 1960.

Narrett, David. *Inheritance and Family Life in Colonial New York City.* Ithaca: Cornell University Press, 1992.

Nash, Gary B. *The Urban Crucible: Social Change, Political Consciousness, and the Origins of the American Revolution.* Cambridge, Mass., and London: Harvard University Press, 1979.

Rothschild, Nan. *New York City Neighborhoods: The Eighteenth Century.* San Diego: Academic Press, 1990.

Stokes, I. N. Phelps, comp. *The Iconography of Manhattan Island, 1498–1909.* 1915. Reprint, New York: Arno Press, 1967.

COLONIAL SLAVERY

Berlin, Ira. *Many Thousands Gone: The First Two Centuries of Slavery in North America.* Cambridge, Mass., and London: Harvard University Press, 1998.

Blackburn, Robin. *The Making of New World Slavery: From the Baroque to the Modern, 1492–1800.* London and New York: Verso, 1997.

Bolster, W. Jeffrey. *Black Jacks: African American Seamen in the Age of Sail.* Cambridge: Harvard University Press, 1997.

Davis, Thomas J. "These Enemies of Their Own Household." *Journal of the Afro-American Historical and Genealogical Society,* 5 (1984): 133–49.

Hansen, Joyce, and Gary McGowan. *Breaking Ground, Breaking Silence: The Story of New York's African Burial Ground.* New York: Henry Holt, 1998.

Higginbotham, A. Leon. *In the Matter of Color: Race and the American Legal Process: The Colonial Period.* New York and Oxford: Oxford University Press, 1978.

Hodges, Graham Russell. *Root and Branch: African Americans in New York and East Jersey, 1613–1863.* Chapel Hill and London: University of North Carolina Press, 1999.

Hodges, Graham Russell, and Alan Edward Brown, eds. *"Pretends to Be Free": Runaway Slave Advertisements from Colonial and Revolutionary New York and New Jersey.* New York: Garland, 1994.

Jordan, Winthrop D. *White over Black: American Attitudes toward the Negro, 1550–1812.* Chapel Hill: University of North Carolina Press for the Institute of Early American History and Culture, 1968.

Landers, Jane. *Black Society in Spanish Florida.* Urbana: University of Illinois Press, 1999.

Morgan, Edmund S. *American Slavery, American Freedom: The Ordeal of Colonial Virginia.* New York: Norton, 1975.

Morgan, Philip D. "The Black Experience in the British Empire, 1680–1810." In *The Oxford History of the British Empire: The Eighteenth Century,* edited by P. J. Marshall. Oxford and New York: Oxford University Press, 1998. 465–86.

Prude, Jonathan. "To Look Upon the 'Lower Sort': Runaway Ads and the Appearance of Unfree Laborers in America." *Journal of American History,* 78 (1991): 124–60.

Smith, Billy G., and Richard Wojtowicz, eds. *Blacks Who Stole Themselves: Advertisements for Runaways in the Pennsylvania Gazette, 1728–1790.* Philadelphia: University of Pennsylvania Press, 1989.

Thornton, John. *Africa and Africans in the Making of the Atlantic World, 1400–1680.* New York: Cambridge University Press, 1992.

White, Shane. *Somewhat More Independent: The End of Slavery in New York City, 1770–1810.* Athens, Ga., and London: University of Georgia Press, 1991.

SLAVE REVOLTS

Aptheker, Herbert. *American Negro Slave Revolts.* New York: Columbia University Press, 1943.

Davis, T. J. *A Rumor of Revolt: The "Great Negro Plot" in Colonial New York.* New York: The Free Press, 1985.

Foote, Thelma Willis. "Black Life in Colonial Manhattan, 1664–1796." Ph.D. diss., Harvard University, 1991.

Gaspar, David Barry. *Bondmen & Rebels: A Study of Master-Slave Relations in Antigua, with Implications for Colonial British America.* Baltimore and London: Johns Hopkins University Press, 1985.

Gross, Robert A. "*Forum:* The Making of a Slave Conspiracy, Part 2," *William and Mary Quarterly,* 3rd ser., 59 (January 2002): 135–202.

Hoffer, Peter Charles. *The Great New York Conspiracy of 1741: Slavery, Crime, and Colonial Law.* Lawrence: University Press of Kansas, 2003.

Johnson, Michael P. "Denmark Vesey and His Co-Conspirators." *William and Mary Quarterly,* 3rd ser., 58 (October 2001): 917–76.

Launitz-Shurer, Leopold S., Jr. "Slave Resistance in Colonial New York: An Interpretation of Daniel Horsmanden's New York Conspiracy." *Phylon,* 16 (1979): 137–53.

Linebaugh, Peter, and Marcus Rediker. *The Many-Headed Hydra: Sailors, Slaves, Commoners, and the Hidden History of the Revolutionary Atlantic.* Boston: Beacon Press, 2000.

Scott, Kenneth. "The Slave Insurrection in New York in 1712." *New-York Historical Society Quarterly,* 45 (1961): 43–74.

Szasz, Ferenc M. "The New York Slave Revolt of 1741: A Re-Examination." *New York History,* 48 (1967): 215–30.

EIGHTEENTH-CENTURY EMPIRES AND IMPERIAL CULTURES

Breen, T. H. "The Meaning of the Things." In *Consumption and the World of Goods,* edited by John Brewer and Roy Porter. New York: Routledge, 1994. 249–60.

Bushman, Richard L. *The Refinement of America: Persons, Houses, Cities.* New York: Random House, Vintage Books, 1992.

Carson, Cary. "The Consumer Revolution in Colonial British America: Why Demand?" In *Of Consuming Interests: The Style of Life in the Eighteenth Century,* edited by Cary Carson, Ronald Hoffman, and Peter J. Albert. Charlottesville and London: University Press of Virginia for the United States Capital Historical Society, 1994.

Castells, Manuel, and Alejandro Portes. "World Underneath: The Origins, Dynamics, and Effects of the Informal Economy." In *The Informal Economy: Studies in Advanced and Less Developed Countries,* edited by Alejandro Portes, Manuel Castells, and Lauren A. Benton. Baltimore and London: Johns Hopkins University Press, 1989.

Colley, Linda. *Britons: Forging the Nation, 1707–1837.* New Haven: Yale University Press, 1992.

Conroy, David W. *In Public Houses: Drink and the Revolution of Authority in Colonial Massachusetts.* Chapel Hill and London: University of North Carolina Press for the Institute of Early American History and Culture, 1995.

Hough, Charles Merrill. *Reports of Cases in the Vice Admiralty of the Province of New York and in the Court of Admiralty of the State of New York, 1715–1788.* New Haven: Yale University Press, 1925.

Lydon, James. *Pirates, Privateers, and Profits.* Upper Saddle River, N.J.: Gregg Press, 1970.

Marshall, P. J., ed. *The Oxford History of the British Empire II: The Eighteenth Century.* Oxford and New York: Oxford University Press, 1998.

Salinger, Sharon V. *Taverns and Drinking in Early America.* Baltimore and London: Johns Hopkins University Press, 2002.

Steele, Ian K. *The English Atlantic, 1645–1740: An Exploration of Communication and Community.* New York: Oxford University Press, 1986.

Thompson, Peter. *Rum Punch and Revolution: Taverngoing and Public Life in Eighteenth-Century Philadelphia.* Philadelphia: University of Pennsylvania Press, 1999.

PRINTED PRIMARY SOURCES

Horsmanden, Daniel. *The New York Conspiracy.* Reprinted by Thomas J. Davis. Boston: Beacon, 1971.

———. *The New-York Conspiracy or a History of the Negro Plot, With the* Journal of the Proceedings *Against the Conspirators at New-York in the Years 1741-42.* New York: Southwick & Pelsue, 1810. Reprint, New York: Negro Universities Press, 1969.

O'Callaghan, E. B., ed. *The Documentary History of the State of New York.* 4 vols. Albany: Weed, Parsons, and Co., Printers, 1849.

———, ed. *Documents Relative to the Colonial History of the State of New York: procured in Holland, England, and France by John Romeyn Brodhead, Agent,* Vol. I–XIII. Albany: Weed, Parsons, and Co., Printers, 1853–1881.

Index